S0-AZT-394

# BARDISMS

ALSO BY BARRY EDELSTEIN

*Thinking Shakespeare*

# BARDISMS

## Shakespeare for All Occasions

WONDERFUL WORDS FROM THE BARD ON LIFE'S BIG MOMENTS (AND SOME SMALL ONES, TOO) PLUS TIPS ON HOW TO USE THEM IN A TOAST, SPEECH, OR LETTER

Barry Edelstein

COLLINS
*An Imprint of* HarperCollins*Publishers*

HarperCollins books may be purchased for educational, business, or sales promotional use. For information please write: Special Markets Department, HarperCollins Publishers, 10 East 53rd Street, New York, NY 10022.

FIRST EDITION

*Designed by Emily Cavett Taff*

Library of Congress Cataloging-in-Publication Data

Edelstein, Barry.

Bardisms : Shakespeare for all occasions : wonderful words from the bard on life's big moments (and some small ones, too), plus tips on how to use them in a toast, speech, or letter / Barry Edelstein—1st ed.

p. cm.

Includes index.

ISBN 978-0-06-149351-5

1. Shakespeare, William, 1564–1616—Quotations. I. Shakespeare, William, 1564–1616. Selections. 2009. II. Title.

PR2892.E28 2009

822.3'3—dc22

2009002042

09 10 11 12 13 WBC/RRD 10 9 8 7 6 5 4 3 2 1

for Tillirose

*You gods, look down*
*And from your sacred vials pour your graces*
*Upon my daughter's head!*

# "...And the Contents o' th' Story..."

*"We Will Have Such a Prologue . . ."*
Introduction xi

*"My Instructions May Be Your Guide"*
Seven Steps to Shipshape Shakespeare xxiii

THE SEVEN AGES OF MAN xli

*Chapter 1*
AT FIRST THE INFANT
**Shakespeare for the Occasions of Birth and Family Life**

*Shakespeare on the Experience of Childbirth* 3

*Shakespeare on Newborns* 7
*Shakespeare on Daughters* 12
*Shakespeare on Sons* 18
*Shakespeare on Mothers* 23
*Shakespeare on Fathers* 26
*Shakespeare on Siblings* 30

*Chapter 2*
**THEN THE SCHOOLBOY**
**Shakespeare for the Occasions of Childhood**

*Shakespeare on Children* 40
*Shakespeare on School* 43
*Shakespeare on the Commencement Address* 51
*Shakespeare on Sports and Exercise* 57
*Shakespeare on Holidays* 63

*Chapter 3*
**AND THEN THE LOVER**
**Shakespeare for the Occasions of *L'amour***

*Shakespeare on Love* 76
*Shakespeare to Say "I Love You"* 81
*Shakespeare on Lovemaking* 92
*Shakespeare on Getting Engaged* 98
*Shakespeare on Weddings* 100
*Shakespeare on Wedding Vows* 109
*Shakespeare on Relationship Troubles* 116

Chapter 4

## THEN A SOLDIER
## Shakespeare for the Occasions of Professional Life

*Shakespeare on Soldiers* 125
*Shakespeare on Reputation* 129
*Shakespeare on Violent Confrontation* 134
*Shakespeare on Winning and Losing* 139
*Shakespeare on Motivating the Troops* 143
*Shakespeare on Work* 147

Chapter 5

## AND THEN THE JUSTICE
## Shakespeare for the Occasions of Life's Middle Years

*Shakespeare on Middle Age* 157
*Shakespeare on Justice* 160
*Shakespeare on Witty People and Bores* 166
*Shakespeare on Thanks* 172
*Shakespeare on Apologies and Forgiveness* 175
*Shakespeare on Parties* 179

Chapter 6

## THE LEAN AND SLIPPERED PANTALOON
## Shakespeare for the Occasions of Old Age

*Shakespeare on Old Age* 191
*Shakespeare on Grandparenthood* 195
*Shakespeare on Tributes* 197

*Shakespeare on Health and Medicine* 202
*Shakespeare on News* 210
*Shakespeare on Weather* 213

Chapter 7

**MERE OBLIVION**
**Shakespeare for the Occasions of the End of Life**

*Shakespeare on Death* 226
*Shakespeare on the Loss of Loved Ones* 235
*Shakespeare on Memorials and Elegies* 241
*Shakespeare on God, Spirituality, and Faith* 251

*"I Have a Kind Soul That Would Give You Thanks"*
Acknowledgments 257

*". . . Index to the Story We Late Talked of"*
Subject Index 259
Index 263

*"If We Do Meet Again, Why We Shall Smile"*
Keep in Touch 275

*"Is It a World to Hide Virtues In?"*
About the Author 277

# "We Will Have Such a Prologue . . ."

## INTRODUCTION

*O let my books be then the eloquence . . .*
—Sonnet 23.9

Some years ago I was called upon to speak in public at a number of big life moments that took place over the course of a short span of months. Two of my best friends got married, and I toasted them. I got married, and I spoke at engagement parties, in the ceremony itself, and in a toast to my bride at the reception. I stepped down from a long-held post, and I saluted my staff and supporters. I roasted a colleague at a swank party for a watershed birthday, and I eulogized a dear family friend at a quiet memorial service.

Casting about for inspiration as I prepared my remarks for each event, I turned immediately to a volume that's been at the heart of my professional career for nearly two decades. That tome is Western literature's greatest repository of wit, wisdom, solace, spiritual nourishment, poetic uplift, psychological insight, emotional passion, poetic virtuosity, and just plain beautiful writing: *The Complete Works of William Shakespeare.*

The Bard didn't let me down. Through my work directing, writing about, and teaching him, I knew his canon pretty well cold. But I was dazzled to find the incredible number of passages in his plays and poems that seemed tailor-made for celebrations, personal milestones, and just about every one of life's big moments. Shakespeare, I was relieved and delighted to discover, is pitch-perfect for all occasions.

Soon I'd collected Shakespeare quotations for my various needs.

For my best friend and his bride, whose love for one another struck me as uncommonly deep, I talked about this line from *As You Like It*: "My love hath an unknown bottom, like the Bay of Portugal." (I explained that in Shakespeare's day, the Bay of Portugal was thought to be the deepest body of water on Earth, so any love that's like it must be pretty darned deep.)

At a religious ceremony the weekend before my wedding, during which the story of Noah was read from the Bible, I commented on the amazing fact that there's a line in Shakespeare that actually talks about both weddings and also old Noah himself (it's in *As You Like It* as well, when Jaques the cynic encounters a gathering of three betrothed pairs and says: "There is, sure, another flood toward, and these couples are coming to the ark").

At my colleague's fiftieth birthday party, I reassured him with this line from Sonnet 104: "To me, fair friend, you never can be old."

And at my family friend's funeral, I shared this beautiful passage from the little-known play *Cymbeline*:

> Fear no more the heat o' the sun,
> Nor the furious winter's rages;
> Thou thy worldly task hast done,
> Home art gone, and ta'en thy wages:
> Golden lads and girls all must,
> As chimney-sweepers, come to dust.

In the years since that run of toasts and tributes, I've quoted Shakespeare on even more varied occasions, sometimes when speaking in public, but just as often when sending a note or even when simply musing to myself:

On the occasion of my parents' fiftieth wedding anniversary: "The benediction of these covering heavens / Fall on their heads like dew, for they are worthy / To inlay heaven with stars!"

On the occasion of a magnificent sunrise over Joshua Tree National Park: "But look, the morn in russet mantle clad / Walks o'er the dew of yon high eastward hill."

On the occasion of hearing a grandmother tell her grandson not to eat so fast: "With eager feeding, food doth choke the feeder."

And on the occasion of my godson's *bris*: "This was the most unkindest cut of all."

Before long, people who had heard me wax Shakespearean on some occasion or other began to call or e-mail me for advice.

> *Hey Barry, I've also got to give a toast at a friend's wedding. Is there a good Shakespeare quote you can send my way?*
>
> *Yikes! I have to make a presentation in front of the whole company at a product launch next week. Got any Shakespeare for me?*
>
> *Baz, I went out with a really great girl last night and I totally fell for her. I want to send her an e-mail asking her out on another date. Can you shoot me some good Shakesey that'll really blow her away?*

I had a great time answering every request.

Shakespeare for the Occasion of a Wedding? Try Sonnet 116, the nuptial classic: "Let me not to the marriage of true minds / Admit impediments."

Shakespeare for the Occasion of a Pep Talk? Lots of great choices. Check out "There is a tide in the affairs of men / Which taken at the flood leads on to fortune," from *Julius Caesar*, or "We few, we happy few, we band of brothers," from *Henry V.*

Shakespeare for the Occasion of Seeking a Second Date? Here's a good one from *The Tempest*: "I would not wish / Any companion in the world but you."

Fielding countless such requests, and dispatching hundreds of lines of Shakespeare to family, friends, and acquaintances from all over who were in the midst of life events of every kind, it occurred to me that what I was doing was something that Shakespeare himself would have recognized. There's a moment in *Hamlet* when the eponymous prince, thunderstruck at the discovery that his seemingly charming and gregarious uncle is in fact a fratricidal maniac, decides to write down that piece of information for future reference: "My tables," he cries, referring to his tablebook, a kind of Elizabethan notepad,

> My tables—meet it is I set it down
> That one may smile and smile and be a villain.
> At least I'm sure it may be so in Denmark.

Modern audiences chuckle at the odd sight of a man who's just met his father's ghost taking the time to jot down the general life lesson he's learned in the process. But audiences in the Renaissance wouldn't have found the behavior the least bit peculiar. They, like Hamlet, routinely took note of epigrams and aphorisms, memorable turns of phrase, and other useful bits and bobs of knowledge encountered in their reading or their lives. They collected these linguistic cuttings, organized into categories, in scrapbooks called Commonplace Books, a "commonplace" being any adage, axiom, or maxim that seemed to express some pearl of wisdom about some universal human condition or situation. The English Renaissance, a period when the classical profundities of the sage ancients were revered as the highest possible cultural values, was the heyday of these books. They were regarded as so essential to living a properly intellectual life that the technique of keeping a good Commonplace Book was taught in school, and they were so beloved that they became a literary subgenre, and eminent scholars and gentlemen often published theirs to benefit the wider reading public.

Many Commonplace Books from the period survive. They share a conspicuous and striking feature: the author most frequently quoted—seventy-nine times in one particular book—is none other than William Shakespeare. Even in his own day, the Bard was recognized as the leading author of language that renders pithily all the immense size and scope and feeling and sweep of the human experience. When the stakes are as high as they ever get, the emotions as turbulent, and the psychic strain as immense—when we learn that our uncle murdered our father, say—no normal utterance, no mere quotidian language, can express our state. Such times demand something of an entirely different magnitude: the immensity and scale of Shakespeare. His is a sensibility at the human frontier; his, an imagination that holds fast the wildest intangibles; his, a language capable of expressing in finite terms those outsized, amorphous, jumbled storms that shake and roil a human heart under duress. And his, a literary technique and writerly skill that can condense all this into a few lines.

Call them *Bardisms.* Shakespeare's bite-sized quotes for the outsized human occasion.

*Bardisms: Shakespeare for All Occasions* is my contribution to the Commonplace Book tradition. Inspired by all those friends to whom I've sent Shakespeare quotes over the years, its aim is to enhance public discourse and enrich private reflection with a compilation in one place of Shakespeare's many grand thoughts on life's special moments.

A few words about how *Bardisms: Shakespeare for All Occasions* is organized, and how it might be useful.

This book's purpose is not only to gather and present Shakespeare's choicest observations on myriad human affairs, but also to provide concrete tools for using them in remarks both written and delivered aloud. Its simple pointers, drawn from my many years' experience as a teacher and director of Shakespeare's plays, are easy enough for anyone to apply and are explained in terms basic enough for anyone to understand. These tips help unlock the mysteries of Shakespeare's text, lifting the veil of obscurity from his words and making his writing feel as fresh and vital as this morning's newspaper. *Bardisms* will foster a sense of ownership of Shakespeare's words and a new appreciation for the wide variety of his writing, turning it into a natural frame of reference not only for countless special life moments but also for the stuff of the everyday. The book is meant to inspire confidence that you can quote this celebrated and wonderful writer without sounding phony, dilettantish, or the least bit cockamamie.

*Bardisms* is designed for ease of use. After this introduction comes "Seven Steps to Shipshape Shakespeare," a survey of the basic techniques that professional theater artists use to achieve immediate clarity with Shakespeare's text, and which the average reader can apply to the same end. Next is the heart of the book: Shakespearean passages about dozens of life occasions, explicated. The book sticks to the practical Shakespeare, a writer who talks about the regular things that make up daily life. It eschews, for the most part, the ruminative Shakespeare, the poetical thinker about broad or abstract concepts. Thus you'll find Shakespeare for the Occasion of a Funeral, words applicable to a real-life situation, but not Shakespeare for the Fate of the Eternal Soul, philosophical meditations on an ineffable human concern. (That stuff will come in this book's sequel!)

Quotations are presented in rough chronological life order, as organized by the categories in one of the most famous of all Shakespearean speeches: the "Seven Ages of Man," from *As You Like It*. Thus, Chapter One, "At First, the Infant," includes Shakespeare on the occasions of birth and the subject of family. Chapter Two, "Then the Schoolboy," presents Shakespeare for life occasions related to youth, education, recreation, and holidays. Chapter Three, "And Then the Lover," comprises material on love, courtship, marriage, and weddings. Chapter Four, "Then a Soldier," considers Shakespeare for martial occasions, as well as those of our professional years, such as work, confrontations, reputations, winning, and losing. Chapter Five, "And Then the Justice," includes occasions on which the Justice described in the "Seven Ages" would be full of opinions: middle age, wit, boredom, gratitude, apologies, and parties. Chapter Six, "The Lean and Slippered Pantaloon," mines Shakespeare's thoughts on the issues of old age: retirement, health and medicine, grandparenthood, and so forth. Finally, Chapter Seven, "Mere Oblivion," focuses on how Shakespeare views the occasions of life's final phase, including death, funerals, memorials, and the loss of loved ones. Each chapter opens with a close reading of the apposite lines from the "Seven Ages of Man," along with some observations on what they can add to our appreciation of the phase of life they survey.

The Shakespearean excerpts in the book vary in length from a few words to a few dozen lines, and the selections draw upon almost all of Shakespeare's plays and poems, providing a broad overview of the range of genres, styles, and modes in which he wrote, the more to appreciate his works and his genius. Each excerpted passage is accompanied by a commentary made up of some combination of three discrete sections. The first, "In Other Words," translates Shakespeare into accessible and easy-to-understand modern English. Next, "How to Say It" or "How to Use It" offers a bulleted list of tips that show how to apply the techniques from the "Seven Steps to Shipshape Shakespeare" to the specific text in question. This section sometimes also recommends ways to frame a given excerpt with brief introductory remarks, and in many cases suggests how to use it elegantly in written communication. When a given Shakespeare quote includes language specific to the dramatic situation in the play from which it's taken—proper names, gendered language, and so on—"How to Say It" suggests minor textual adaptations that can widen the excerpt's range of applicability.

The third section following each entry is called "Some Details," and it explores provocative historical or literary insights into the text under review. These cover a wide swath, from some technical aspect of Shakespeare's writing present in the quoted lines to contextual information about the play in which the passage appears, an examination of illuminating particulars from Shakespeare's life and times, or a discussion of what eminent readers have thought about questions raised by the lines. In short, this part of the commentary delves into the sublime and the ridiculous in Shakespeare: material that can be useful, surprising, amusing, or just plain silly. The information in "Some Details" can help add nuance and dimension to your use of Shakespeare for the occasions of your life, but even if you're not planning to quote him at your niece's confirmation or your neighbor's housewarming, "Some Details" shows how endlessly fascinating he is and how much fun delving into the Bard and his works really can be.

Two indexes make both the Shakespearean excerpts and the commentary easy to search for subjects and occasions of interest.

All the Bard in this book is taken from *The Norton Shakespeare*, Stephen Greenblatt, editor, which I regard as the best single-volume edition of the plays and poems now in print. Citations give the speaker's name, the play's name, and the relevant act, scene, and line numbers in the format *act.scene.line*. (For example, "Messenger, *Much Ado About Nothing*, 1.1.40" means the quoted text appears at Act 1, Scene 1, line 40 of *Much Ado*, and is spoken by the Messenger.) *The Norton Shakespeare* is based in large part on *The Oxford Shakespeare*, a cutting-edge and quite controversial 1986 edition of the *Complete Works*. Despite its overall excellence, the *Oxford* is marred by a sometimes unbridled revisionist spirit, and it makes some idiosyncratic choices—changes in characters' names, changes in titles of plays, omissions of cherished passages—all buttressed by careful and sound scholarship, but all regarded as wildly iconoclastic in the very conservative world of Shakespeare studies. The *Norton* editors took note of the backlash against the *Oxford*'s aggressive idiosyncrasies and retreated from the most excessive examples. But *The Norton Shakespeare* still retains some readings that would disorient the non-specialist public, and so when I've quoted a Bardism that the *Norton* renders in some unfamiliar way, I've taken the liberty of silently reverting to a less alienating form.

One of the things about Bardisms that make them so much fun to quote is that they can sometimes seem to turn Shakespeare into an expert on things that weren't even invented during his lifetime. That is, because a Bardism lifts Shakespeare's lines out of their proper surroundings in the rest of Shakespeare's plays or poetry, a Bardism can make Shakespeare say things he never said. An example: I determined when my daughter was born that she'd start hearing Shakespeare from the moment she got home from the hospital.* In her first weeks, a lot of my bonding time with her came at the changing table, so I started looking for a Bardism on the subject. I discovered that the word *diaper* appears exactly once in Shakespeare, in the rarely performed prologue to *The Taming of the Shrew*. There, the word is used in its Elizabethan sense, as a synonym for "napkin" (some servants discuss what they'll provide for their lord when he sits down to dinner, and they note that he'll need a basin in which to wash his hands, and a diaper with which to dry them). I knew I wouldn't find *Pampers* in the canon, so I did some lateral thinking and searched for Bardisms on the general subject of *change*. At last I found this line, spoken by Iago in Act 1, Scene 3 of *Othello*: "She must have change, she must!"

In its native dramatic context, this line has nothing to do with diapers, of course. It is Iago's slimy *She's Gotta Have It* insinuation that Othello's wife, Desdemona, cannot help but betray her husband by sleeping with Cassio, then Roderigo, then every other man in town. After all, Iago argues, Desdemona's from Venice, a city known for the expertise of its prostitutes and the near-nymphomaniacal lusts of its young women. So she must have new sexual partners. She *must*.

Standing over my sweet, innocent babe at 3:00 A.M., elbow deep in diaper ointment and wipes, was I somehow insulting her virtue by

---

* That's what happens when your dad is a Shakespeare director. My wife likes to joke that when she grows up, our angel's favorite Shakespeare quote will be from Celia in *As You Like It*, and she'll go around school asking all of her friends, "Wilt thou change fathers? I will give thee mine" (1.5.85; *change* means "exchange," "swap").

quoting the nefarious Iago? Obviously not. One of the ways Shakespeare manages to speak to all occasions is by virtue of having survived long enough to address them. In every new generation and every new cultural circumstance, he slips the surly bonds of dramatic context and morphs into new shapes he never could have imagined. And as we'll see many times in this book, these transformations can be a lot of fun. In this sense, while the original context of a speech from Shakespeare is always interesting, that speech's applicability to the present circumstances is what truly counts. It's what turns a Shakespearean quotation into a Bardism.

During the few months' stint of serial Shakespeare citation I described at the beginning of this introduction, I discovered something new about this writer I'd by then come to regard as an old friend. I already knew the extent to which he had enriched my life; my work on his plays as an artist and teacher has shown me around the United States, much of Europe, and parts of Asia, and the places he's taken me in my imagination have been even more extraordinary. And I already knew his work's unique way of revealing new details, nearly infinite resonances, each time I went away from it and then came back. But what I learned about the Bard's knack for saying just the right thing on all occasions is that all occasions are enhanced by his words. What's special about his poetry is that as it forges new links between experience as it's lived and experience as it's described, it somehow manages to *deepen* lived experience by describing it as vividly as it does.

I'm not the first person to make this claim of old Will, which is fortunate, because it means there's someone I can turn to for corroboration.

As I write this introduction, the great Shakespearean actor Patrick Stewart is starring on Broadway in a new production of *Macbeth.* In an interview about it with the *New York Times*, he offered a lovely anecdote about how Shakespeare's touch on all occasions makes those occasions sweeter, richer, and more memorable:

> Mr. Stewart described an experience he had recently, as he walked alone before dusk near his rural village in Oxfordshire. "Suddenly I had this urge to speak the role, and there's nobody about," he said. "So I started at the top of the play, with 'So foul and fair a day I have not seen,' and I said the whole role through aloud, just to refresh my memory. It was a long walk.
>
> "But it hit me before I said the lines 'Light thickens, and the crow / Makes wing to the rooky wood'—That's exactly how it was," he continued. "And I thought: This is wonderful. Every night in New York when I come to that part, I'll remember where I was, on this lonely road with bare fields on either side, and there's a mist hanging over the field, and indeed there are crows."

Mists, crows, thick light, and rooky woods—Shakespeare talks about them all, just as he talks about birthdays, funerals, and every other human event in between. He's graced the occasions of my life in so many beautiful ways, and it's my joy to commend him to yours.

# "My Instructions May Be Your Guide"

## SEVEN STEPS TO SHIPSHAPE SHAKESPEARE

These keys to unlocking the Bard's secrets are distilled from the basic principles of Shakespearean acting taught to actors daily in the country's leading drama schools. (And I should know: I teach them there!) They can help lift the veil of obscurity off Shakespeare's alien-seeming language and reveal the familiar and comprehensible English hidden underneath.

Apply some of the following techniques to the excerpts of Shakespeare in this book, or to any others you fancy, and you'll find his language starting to feel as comfortable in your mouth and sound as familiar in your ears as the words you speak and hear in regular conversation. You may also find that your appreciation for all poetry, and not just Shakespeare's, gets an unexpected and altogether happy boost.

Here, then, the Seven Steps to Shipshape Shakespeare.

### STEP 1: *Know What You're Saying*

It's extremely easy to regard the strange vocabulary and alien syntax in Shakespeare as either insuperable obstacles or generalities to be approximated rather than understood. After all, the language is four hundred years old, and English in Shakespeare's day resembled German—the tongue from which it most recently derived—much more than it does today, and shared many byzantine grammatical structures with that still highly complex language. But a great way to get specific with the text, to bring it into your mouth and brain sounding fresh and new four centuries after it was written, is to ensure that you know exactly what you're saying. A great way to do that is to translate Shakespeare into modern, accessible, colloquial English that makes it effortlessly clear in your own mind. Write a paraphrase. Actors preparing a Shakespearean role sit with dictionaries and scholarly editions and work through their lines word by word to make certain they know what everything means. To save you that time-consuming, brain-boiling work, I have included paraphrases with almost every excerpt of Shakespeare in this book, the exceptions being those passages whose language is simple and clear enough that they're self-explanatory. You'll note that my paraphrases have a very colloquial style, a loosey-goosey aspect that lends them a certain energy and flow. This is deliberate. Paraphrases help most when they're simplest. They needn't be pedantically precise, such as "To exist, or to negate existence: this is the central inquiry" (Hamlet's "To be or not to be, that is the question"), nor need they restate the obvious, as in "The day after today, and the day after today, and the day after today" (Macbeth's "Tomorrow and tomorrow and tomorrow"). Instead, they should express each of the basic thoughts in Shakespeare's text in terms that are immediately comprehensible to a modern ear. To achieve this, they might need to spell out certain concepts that Shakespeare leaves veiled, or even to rearrange things ever so slightly. Thus, for Hamlet: "What I'm wondering is whether I should go on living or not"; for Macbeth: "Time moves along relentlessly, inexorably, slowly." Sometimes they'll sound a little goofy, like "Watch out for March fifteenth!" (that's "Beware the ides of March" from *Julius Caesar*), and often they'll render soaring poetry in terms that are eye-rollingly flat, as does "The glory of the divine presence can be seen even in things as ordinary as a dying bird" (that's Hamlet's "There's a special providence in the fall of a sparrow," and it really loses something in translation). A good paraphrase will clarify abstruse terms, burn away the fog that can obscure simple thoughts, and reveal arguments in language that's maximally easy to wrap one's head around.

### STEP 2: *Antithesis: The Juxtaposition of Opposites Is Everywhere in Shakespeare*

Americans well know these famous phrases:

> Ask not what your country can do for you, ask what you can do for your country.
>
> The world will little note, nor long remember, what we say here, but it can never forget what they did here.

Anyone speaking the first passage aloud will naturally emphasize the words that oppose each other, as JFK did at his inauguration, because those words convey the very meaning of the thought. Stressing any other words would result in nonsense: "Ask not WHAT your country CAN do FOR you, ask what you can DO for YOUR country." Ridiculous. The very idea being expressed depends upon—is built upon—the contrast between two opposites: What *your country* can do for *you* versus what *you* can do for *your country.* Similarly, no English speaker in his right mind would quote Lincoln talking about the difference between "WHAT we say HERE" and "what THEY did HERE." Preposterous. The only way to make this extraordinary sentence comprehensible is to stress the contrasts between the ideas *not remember* and *never forget*, and between *what we say* and *what they did*. At Gettysburg, opposition communicates meaning.

Rhetoricians call the juxtaposition of strongly contrasting ideas within a balanced grammatical structure *antithesis*. Shakespeare is addicted to it:

> *To be* or *not to be*, that is the question.
>
> Two loves I have, of *comfort* and *despair.*
>
> The fault, dear Brutus, is not in *our stars,*
> But in *ourselves,* that we are underlings.
>
> Now is the *winter* of our discontent
> Made glorious *summer* by this son of York.
>
> That which hath made *them* **drunk** hath made *me* **bold.**
>
> I come *to bury* Caesar, not *to praise* him.
> The **evil** that men do lives after them,
> The **good** is oft interrèd with their bones.
> In *peace,* there's nothing so becomes a man
> As modest stillness and humility,
> But when the blast of *war* blows in our ears,
> Then imitate the action of the tiger.*

Antithesis is so widespread in Shakespeare that you can flip open your *Complete Works* to any page, point your finger to any line, and find within three or four lines of it something that sounds a lot like the

* Citations: Hamlet, *Hamlet*, 3.1.58; Sonnet 144.1; Cassius, *Julius Caesar*, 1.2.140–41; Gloucester, *Richard III*, 1.1.1–2; Lady Macbeth, *Macbeth*, 2.2.1; Mark Antony, *Julius Caesar*, 3.2.80–82; King Henry, *Henry V*, 3.1.3–6.

excerpts above. Every antithesis requires its speaker to emphasize the juxtaposed ideas. Stress any words other than those directly opposed to each other, and you'll make a hash of what's being said.

To help you identify the words you need to lean upon in order to get the most out of Shakespeare's antitheses, I will list them in my comments where necessary.

### STEP 3: *The Changing Height of Language: Shakespeare's Language Swings Back and Forth from Highly Poetical to Very Simple*

The best way to understand what a shift from heightened to simple language does is to observe one in action. Consider the first line of Act 1, Scene 4 of *Hamlet*, spoken by the play's title character. It's late on a winter night, and he's out on the castle ramparts with his friend Horatio and the soldier Marcellus, awaiting the reappearance of his father's ghost. He says:

> The air bites shrewdly. It is very cold.

The second of these two sentences requires no paraphrase. *It is very cold* is not heightened or elevated, nor for that matter "Shakespearean," in any way at all. It's just a simple declarative statement, something any of us might say on any February evening. The first sentence is something else entirely. It imagines the air as a living being of some sort, complete with a mouth and teeth. This biting air is tactical, strategic: it bites in a shrewd manner, that is, cannily, subtly, with an ulterior motive. The adverb *shrewdly* acquires its meaning from the shrew, a tiny rodent with a long snout that allows it to insinuate itself into even tightly closed places. A literal translation of Hamlet's first sentence, then, might read, "The air is a shrew biting my skin." This vividly metaphorical expression of coldness could be rendered in an even simpler paraphrase: "It's very cold." Put that paraphrase next to the second sentence, and you'll find that Hamlet is saying, essentially, "It's very cold. It's very cold."

Why does Hamlet say "It's cold" twice? The answer is about the changing height of his language. Hamlet, educated at Germany's Wittenberg University, is comfortable with heightened language and complex thought. Perhaps he says the first sentence to Horatio, also a distinguished WU alumnus ("*Knock*wurst, *Brat*wurst, go, Vit, **go**!"), but says the second, simpler half to the lumpen soldier Marcellus. Perhaps he says the first sentence to Marcellus, who doesn't get it, forcing Hamlet to clarify with the second sentence. Perhaps Hamlet says the first sentence aloud to everyone, and then turns aside and says the second sentence to himself. Or vice versa.

We can't know what Shakespeare had in mind when he wrote these words. All we can do is interpret them and use our best efforts to bring them to life in a truthful way. In this sense, there's never any correct or incorrect way to say the lines. None of the four interpretations I posited above is right, nor is any wrong. They're just ideas for actor and director to try in rehearsal. The key point about all of them is that they arise from a close reading of the text that reveals that one half of the line is heightened, and the other is not. Anyone trying to communicate its underlying ideas must first recognize the change that happens halfway through it, think about *why* that change is there, and then say the line in a manner that uses its change of height to make both parts of it sharp, lifelike, and clear.

### STEP 4: *Verbs: Special Heightening Agents*

Verbs are specially charged by definition, because they are words whose syntactical job—to cause action—requires of them a greater energy than that called for from the other parts of speech. Hamlet says that the reason the fear of death is so powerful is that it "*puzzles* the will" and "*makes* us rather *bear* those ills we *have* / Than *fly* to others that we *know not* of." The italics are mine, of course, and they indicate the verbs (or verb phrases), which happen to be the words that any speaker of English will naturally stress as they try to make Hamlet's ideas clear. Try to say these phrases sans emphasis on the verbs, and all you'll have is mush.

One of the most effective ways to bring Shakespeare alive in your mouth or in your mind is to underline the verbs as you work through the text. Their communicative vigor is so copious, potent, and expressive that they will actually haul you right through a speech's thoughts from start to finish . . . if you let them. Always, always hit the verbs. And use them in whatever form they appear: participial or gerundial verbs used as adjectives or other parts of speech ("the pangs of *disprized* love"; "there's nothing either good or bad but *thinking* makes it so") carry great energy and are indispensable.

I will flag useful verbs, verb forms, and verb phrases throughout this book.

## STEP 5: *Scansion and Meter: The Time Signature Behind the Lines*

The majority of Shakespeare's work, and the majority of the excerpts quoted in this book, is written in *verse*. As distinct from its antithesis, *prose* (of which there's plenty in Shakespeare, some of which we'll see as well), verse is language that's composed in individual lines that conform to a given rhythm. That rhythm is created by the individual syllables in the words of the line, some of which receive stress and some of which don't. The art and science of counting the stressed and unstressed syllables in a line and then affixing to them a label that helps readers navigate the poem is called *scansion*, and it serves to identify the poem's *meter*, or time signature.

The most important meter for anyone working on Shakespeare is the famous *iambic pentameter*. That's a fancy label for a verse line whose count (*meter*) is five (*penta*, as in *pentagon*) so-called *feet*, or sets of syllables, which are *iambs*. An iamb is a foot comprising two syllables, the first of which is unstressed and the second stressed. It sounds like this: *dee-DUM*. New York is iambic: *new YORK*. So are Detroit (*de-TROIT*) and hello (*hel-LO*) and goodbye (*good-BYE*) and shalom (*sha-LOM*). Standard scansion notation marks the first syllable with a caret and the second with an accent mark: **ň ń**.

Put five iambs next to one another, and they look, and sound, like this:

**ň ń   ň ń   ň ń   ň ń   ň ń**

*dee-DUM dee-DUM dee-DUM dee-DUM dee-DUM*

Any verse that conforms to that ten-syllable, fivefold, unstressed-STRESSED pattern is labeled *iambic pentameter* or its non-technical synonym, *blank verse*.

Friends, Romans, countrymen, lend me your ears
(friends ROM-ans COUNT-ry-MEN lend ME your EARS)

Now is the winter of our discontent
(now IS the WIN-ter OF our DIS-con-TENT)

There is a tide in the affairs of men
(there IS a TIDE in THE af-FAIRS of MEN)

To be or not to be, that is the question
(to BE or NOT to BE that IS the QUES-[tion])

Tomorrow and tomorrow and tomorrow
(to-MOR-row AND to-MOR-row AND to-MOR-[row])

All Shakespeare, and all iambic pentameter.

Trained Shakespearean actors bang through the stressed and unstressed syllables in their scripts like so many Tito Puentes drumming away at a very literate set of timbales:

the FAULT dear BRU-tus IS not IN our STARS
*ba-BANG ba-BOOM ba-BING ba-BLAM ba-BUMP*

but IN our-SELVES that WE are UN-der-LINGS
*dee-DUM dee-DUM dee-DUM dee-DUM dee-DUM*

This percussive analysis reveals all sorts of fascinating things about the rhythm of Shakespeare's lines:

- It can tell you that a certain word you thought was unimportant actually falls in a position where the scansion gives it stress. "In" in the two lines above is an interesting case. Most of us would ignore that little word, but Cassius deliberately stresses it both times he uses it. Bang out the meter on your tabletop, and you'll hear that interesting detail.

- It can tell you that a certain word is pronounced differently in Shakespeare than we're used to hearing it. That special pronunciation might require you to emphasize a given syllable in a surprising way, as in this antithesis-crammed line from *Much Ado About Nothing*: "Thou pure impiety and impious purity!" *Impious*, the opposite of pious, which we pronounce *im-PYE-us*, is pronounced *IM-pyus* in this line as it is every time it's used in Shakespeare, and here *purity* is pronounced with two syllables, not three: *PURE-tee*. Thou PURE im-PYE-uh-TEE and IM-pyus PURE-tee. Without hammering through the scansion, we'd never say the words correctly.

- It can point to inflections in prefixes or suffixes to words, like that famous stressed *-ed* at the ends of words that's such a prominent part of Shakespeare's characteristic sound. Octavius Caesar opens Act 5 of *Julius Caesar* with this Bardism, Shakespeare on the Occasion of Good News:

  Now, Antony, our hopes are answered.

- If you pronounce *answered* with two syllables, as a modern English speaker instinctively would, the line will only have nine syllables, not the ten that iambic pentameter demands. Only by stressing the *-ed* ending will the meter be complete, and only then will Shakespeare's hopes be answerèd.

Throughout this book I will mark inflected *-ed* endings with an accent grave (*-èd*), and I will point out other places where the scansion demands an unusual pronunciation.

I will also point out where it's best to *disregard* what the scansion suggests when it leads to a reading that's overly pedantic, technical-sounding, weird, and alienating. Would any English-speaker's instincts produce this reading?

friends ROM-ans COUNT-ry-MEN lend ME your EARS

Unlikely. Although technically correct, this is instinctively wrong. It sounds bizarre, herky-jerky, shouty. Let the scansion go, and you'll find that the line will probably come out more like this:

FRIENDS, ROM-ans, COUNT-ry-men, LEND ME your EARS

Spoken according to natural instinct, the line turns out to be iambic pentameter in name only. Its natural rhythm is far more nuanced and interesting. Shakespeare regards iambic pentameter as more of a guide than a prescription; a map, not a destination. He's like a jazz musician, establishing a baseline rhythm, then improvising around it, syncopating it into something much more loose and free. Actors are trained to understand this, and to recognize that for every line of verse, there's the scansion that the meter suggests and the scansion that natural instinct suggests; that is, there's the *metric stress* and the *natural stress*. The best actors know that scansion can provide important, often surprising, information about the words in the lines, but that this information is only useful insofar as it helps clarify what the line is trying to say. Think of scansion and meter as tools that refine your instincts, but don't replace them.

### **STEP 6:** *Phrasing with the Verse Line: Cover the Speech with a Piece of Paper and Read It One Line at a Time*

Take a look at how this Bardism, Shakespeare on the Evil Maniac in a Horror Movie, is arranged:

> 'Tis now the very witching time of night,
> When churchyards yawn and hell itself breathes out
> Contagion to this world. Now could I drink hot blood,
> And do such bitter business as the day
> Would quake to look on. Soft! Now to my mother.
>
> —HAMLET, *Hamlet*, 3.3.358–362

In other words, "It's now dead midnight, when graves gape open and hell breathes disease into the world. Now I could guzzle hot blood, and do the kind of terrible things that daylight itself would shudder to behold.—Take it easy!—Now I'll visit my mom."

Notice what happens at the end of each line in the excerpt. Lines 1 and 3 are marked with commas, and line 5 ends with a period. That punctuation falls where it does because the thoughts expressed in lines 1, 3, and 5 all end at the ends of the lines. That is, there is a change or development in the direction of Hamlet's thinking between *night* and *when*, and between *blood* and *and*, and the commas denote the end of one phase of that thinking and the beginning of the next. And Hamlet completes a thought about his mom with *mother*, so the period marks that stop. Lines 1, 3, and 5 are therefore called *end-stopped* lines, because the ideas on them stop where the verse line ends.

Lines 2 and 4, however, have no punctuation at all. They don't need any, because the thoughts they express continue unbroken from the end of one line onto the start of the next. Line 2 is about how *hell itself breathes out contagion*, but that thought is too long to fit on one line of iambic pentameter, so Shakespeare spreads it over two lines, dividing it between *out* and *contagion*. Similarly, line 4 is concerned with business *the day would quake to look on*. Again, this unbroken thought, too long for line 4 to contain, spills onto line 5. Lines 2 and 4 are not end-stopped; the thoughts they express don't stop at the ends of the lines. Their thoughts run onto the next line, and so we call them *run-on* lines.*

How should one phrase this language? Lines 1, 3, and 5 take care of themselves. The fact that they're end-stopped will automatically make any Hamlet break his phrasing at the ends of the lines, precisely where the commas and period indicate a break, breath, or slight suspension of momentum. Lines 2 and 4 are trickier. Should you phrase them according to the punctuation? That would sound like this:

---

* You may have heard this idea called by a technical term: *enjambment*, from the French for "on legs." Enjambed lines and run-on lines are the same thing.

> When churchyards yawn and hell itself breathes out contagion to this world.
>
> And do such bitter business as the day would quake to look on.

These readings are clear enough, but they transform poetic verse carefully composed in iambic pentameter into a kind of modern prose devoid of any kind of rhythmic signature. Bitter business indeed.

Suppose instead we separate the lines again and think of their ends as *moments of thought*. What if we imagine Hamlet thinking in the moment and choosing words to express his thoughts, asking himself exactly what it is that hell itself breathes into the world, and just what the day would do when it sees the bitter business he's going to conduct? Watch what happens to the odd endings of lines 2 and 4 if we force Hamlet to ask himself those questions:

> When churchyards yawn and hell itself breathes out . . . *(what?)* . . .
> Contagion to this world.
>
> And do such bitter business as the day . . . *(what?)* . . .
> Would quake to look on.

Hamlet could say that hell itself breathes out any of a million things into this world, and that the day would do any of a thousand things when it sees his bitter business. But the exact words he chooses are *contagion* and *quake*. The line endings give him opportunities to find specific ideas and express them in specific words.

Run-on lines are very special in Shakespeare, as in all verse. They provide the actor an opportunity to make his mind and his character's one and the same. They tell the actor to ask "What next?" and then to search for precisely the right word that expresses in every last nuance what it is he's trying to say. Ask *(what?)* at the end of every single line, or have a friend shout it out for you, and as you answer the question you'll begin to write the language for yourself.

> 'Tis now the very witching time of night, *(whaddaya mean?)*
> When churchyards yawn and hell itself breathes out *(what?)*
> Contagion to this world. Now could I drink hot blood, *(what else?)*
> And do such bitter business as the day *(what about it?)*
> Would quake to look on. Soft! Now to my mother.

A technique I call the "Paper Trick" is an easy and effective way to quickly get you phrasing verse one line at a time. Simply take a blank piece of paper and cover the speech you're working on, revealing only its very first line. Say that line, and when you reach its end—and only when you reach its end—slide the paper down to reveal the next line—and only the next line. Say that line, slide the paper down again, say the next line, then slide and speak, slide and speak, slide, speak, until you reach the end of the speech. I promise that the speech will become significantly clearer and easier to say on the very first pass through it. With practice, this one-line-at-a-time phrasing will become as instinctual to you as normal speech.

Two caveats. First, beware of regarding the line ending as a pause. It isn't. It's a moment of thought, a momentary scan of your mental hard drive, or, as the eminent British Shakespeare director Sir Peter Hall calls it, an "energy point." It *moves you forward* onto the next idea, just as a springboard moves you forward from the pool's edge into the water. The line ending isn't about stopping, it's about continuing ahead. Listen to yourself and make sure you're not sounding like a metronome—ten beats, pause, ten beats, pause, ten beats, pause. Know that if the technique of phrasing with the verse line sounds awkward to your ears or makes you feel uncomfortable, you can ignore it and read the lines as though they were prose.

You might disappoint the English professors among your listeners, but the Shakespeare police won't come and throw you in theater jail.

Second, don't interpret phrasing with the verse line as a command to ignore punctuation altogether. Especially within lines, the punctuation provides invaluable information about sense, rhythm, phrasing, and even tone. Strike a balance between following it and hewing to the rigorous construction of the verse, and you're home free.

## STEP 7: *Monosyllables and Polysyllables: Note the Words with Only One Syllable and the Ones with a Lot of Them*

One of Shakespeare's specialties is to work dazzling rhythmic magic by alternating between passages in which the words have only one syllable and passages comprising words with many syllables.

Monosyllables generally require an actor to slow down and really invest in an idea one word at a time. It's no coincidence that many of Shakespeare's most famous phrases are monosyllabic: "Hath not a Jew eyes?" "To be or not to be." "To thine own self be true." "Out damned spot, out I say." "It was Greek to me." "The ides of March." Even the not-so-famous phrase we saw above, "Now could I drink hot blood." In each case, each individual word is important and demands emphasis, and the overall thought demands a deliberate, if not to say stately, pace, which makes it endure in our minds.

Polysyllables, on the other hand, have a sprightliness and speed. In the "hot blood" passage above, the eight words *very witching, churchyards, itself, contagion, bitter business,* and *mother,* all polysyllabic, take on a distinctive quality simply because they are sprinkled amidst thirty-six thudding monosyllables. These words demand their own particular pace and feeling.

I'll point out the places where a series of monosyllables is particularly noteworthy, or where a sudden switch to polysyllables makes a word or idea jaunty, memorable, and fun.

So there you have it: the Seven Steps to Shipshape Shakespeare.

There are many more techniques to discuss—how important words tend to fall in certain places in the lines; how vowels and consonants come together to make a very idiosyncratic Shakespearean music—and I will touch on some of them throughout this book.

But for starters, try these seven. Try a handful; try only one. Each will help demystify some small corner of Shakespeare's legend. Each will bring Shakespeare's language closer to you, and you closer to Shakespeare's language. Through these techniques, Shakespeare will become to you, as he is to me now two decades into my work on him, a friend to whom you can turn on all occasions.

# Bardisms

# The Seven Ages of Man

All the world's a stage,
And all the men and women merely players:
They have their exits and their entrances;
And one man in his time plays many parts,
His acts being seven ages. At first the infant,
Mewling and puking in the nurse's arms.
And then the whining school-boy, with his satchel,
And shining morning face, creeping like snail
Unwillingly to school. And then the lover,
Sighing like furnace, with a woeful ballad
Made to his mistress's eyebrow. Then a soldier,
Full of strange oaths, and bearded like the pard,
Jealous in honor, sudden and quick in quarrel,
Seeking the bubble reputation
Even in the cannon's mouth. And then the justice,
In fair round belly with good capon lined,
With eyes severe, and beard of formal cut,
Full of wise saws and modern instances;
And so he plays his part. The sixth age shifts
Into the lean and slippered pantaloon,
With spectacles on nose and pouch on side,

His youthful hose well saved, a world too wide
For his shrunk shank; and his big manly voice,
Turning again toward childish treble, pipes
And whistles in his sound. Last scene of all,
That ends this strange eventful history,
Is second childishness and mere oblivion,
Sans teeth, sans eyes, sans taste, sans everything.

—Jaques, *As You Like It*, 2.7.135–165

CHAPTER I

# At First the Infant

## SHAKESPEARE FOR THE OCCASIONS OF BIRTH AND FAMILY LIFE

*At first the infant,*
*Mewling and puking in the nurse's arms.*

It begins with caterwauling and vomit.

Such is the stark and altogether unceremonious verdict rendered upon life by William Shakespeare, the eternal, inimitable, and ineffable Bard of Stratford-upon-Avon.

So much of the mystery and mythology surrounding Shakespeare has to do with the beauty and wisdom of his insights into human nature, and the noble sensibility behind their poetic expression. Yes, yes, that sparrow's fall does indeed have a certain special providence about it, and, to be sure, the defining quality of mercy is precisely that way it cascades gently down, like rain from heaven. But a baby? Alas, what descends from a baby are substances resistant to euphemizing metaphor, and defiant to characterization by such felicities as "God-like uniqueness" and "heavenly rain." No, no. From a baby drop drool, spit-up, pee-pee, and poop. Not even the epochal mimetic gifts of Shakespeare could poeticize those.

This is why his description of the First Age of Man, infancy, is so marvelous. Instead of some lines-long rhapsody about skin soft as down, or dove-like cooing, or beatific smiles, Shakespeare offers only two gerundial verbs, two little words, of brain-addling noise and stinking bodily fluids: *mewling* and *puking*. There's nothing grand about them, nothing noble. The Sweet Swan of Avon is nowhere to be found. Rather, we're visited by a tired, even slightly irritated father, trying to go about his day while Junior cries and makes. It's an image striking in its realism, honesty, and truthfulness, and in all its blunt indecorousness, it sounds a lot like infancy as we know it to be.

I think of this Shakespeare, the one who trades in vomit and caterwauling, as the doppelgänger of that other, more familiar Shakespeare, he of the whatever-named but still sweet-smelling rose, and the summer's day to which I'm not sure I shall compare thee. And if the latter Shakespeare writes poetry, then the former writes a kind of anti-poetry, a poetry of what's usually non-poetic, composed in an unmistakably "Shakespearean" language whose beauty, such as it may be, is its ordinariness, Shakespearized.

Such a language is audible in the odd prosody of *mewling* and *puking*. It takes a great writer to serve perfect *mewl* when the mental thesauri of mere mortals would run dry after *shriek*, *screech*, *wail*, and, in a reach, *waaah*. Making *mewl* the first syllable in a verse line is also a neat trick. It breaks the expected rhythm of iambic pentameter, which would place an unstressed syllable in that position, and places a stressed one there instead. This syncopation not only jars our ears in the same manner as a baby's cry but also sets us up for the one-two punch landed when the pattern repeats milliseconds later in *puking*, also accented on its first syllable. In its resolutely non-iambic refusal to go with the flow, this language suggests that there's no way this particular baby will be calmed. Then, there's the assonance of the "liquid U" in both words (the sound that letter makes as a long vowel: *you*), a pretty piece of poesy that suggests at once the cloying nasality of a baby's drone, as well as that apt exclamatory response to all things gross-out, *ewwwwwww*. *Mewling* and *puking* may speak well about cacophonous midnight meltdowns and hot regurgitation, but they well bespeak a writerly gift for marshaling an offbeat and idiosyncratic imagination to the English language at its most muscular, expressive, and bracing.

This gift is on display in all the Shakespeare excerpted below. Shakespeare on infancy may not wield the emotional heft of Shakespeare on love or pack the philosophical wallop of Shakespeare on death, but it lacks none of the linguistic virtuosity, uncanny verisimilitude, or heart-stopping incisiveness of any of the excerpts we'll find in the latter Six Ages of Man when we hear Shakespeare on the occasions of grown-up life.

## SHAKESPEARE ON THE EXPERIENCE OF CHILDBIRTH

*The pleasing punishment that women bear.*

—Aegeon, *The Comedy of Errors*, 1.1.46

Though never depicted onstage, births deliver quite a few bouncing babies offstage in Shakespeare's plays. Since he had three children of his own, he no doubt knew something about the birthing process, and it's interesting to note which aspects of it stick in his mind. This selection of Bardisms covers a range of childbirth experiences.

## WHY NEWBORNS CRY

Here's Shakespeare's explanation of what's behind that piercing bawl that's every human being's first utterance.

> We came crying hither;
> Thou know'st, the first time that we smell the air,
> We wail and cry.
> . . .
> When we are born, we cry that we are come
> To this great stage of fools.
>
> —King Lear, *King Lear*, 4.6.172–77

***How to use it:***

- I found these lines of great comfort to my inconsolable little one, or, perhaps more accurately, of great comfort to myself in rationalization of my failure to console her.
- If you don't have a baby of your own, keep this handy as a nicely erudite editorial comment on the nearest squalling bundle of joy. (Just think how much cruising-altitude tension could be eliminated were flight attendants instructed always to quote this Bardism, Shakespeare for the Screaming Kid in the Bulkhead Seat.)

***Some details:***

This excerpt is from the famous "Dover Cliff" scene in *King Lear.* Gloucester, the king's old friend and counselor, blind, in pain, and despairing over his son's treachery, has come to Dover to commit suicide by jumping off its famous white cliffs. Lear, too, is desperate, driven mad by the cruelty of his daughters Goneril and Regan, and he's been wandering the countryside, railing at the world's manifold injustices. He encounters his sad friend and philosophizes with extraordinary insight and considerable cynicism about life and death.

Lear's interpretation of why babies cry is certainly a dark one, and strikingly modern in its bleakness and nihilism. It seems almost to belong to the worldview of the twentieth-century master Samuel Beckett ("we are born astride a grave"), and indeed, some productions of *King Lear* render the knolls atop Dover Cliff as a landscape as grim as that in Beckett's seminal work *Waiting for Godot*. Yet the image of life as a "stage of fools" is in its own way a comic one. (Certainly whenever I whispered these lines to my crying baby daughter, they struck me as sounding more comforting than ominous.) The best productions of *King Lear* capture this double-sidedness, this proximity of the funny and the awful, and create from the image of two broken old men pondering the dilemmas of infancy a kind of horrid laughter.

## ADOPTION

Shakespeare's view of childbirth isn't limited to the biological. He also explores adoption, a process by which a child already born to one mother is "born" to a second.

> I say I am your mother,
> And put you in the catalogue of those
> That were enwombèd mine. 'Tis often seen
> Adoption strives with nature, and choice breeds
> A native slip to us from foreign seeds.
> You ne'er oppress'd me with a mother's groan,
> Yet I express to you a mother's care.
>
> —Countess, *All's Well That Ends Well*, 1.3.126–32

***In other words:***

I'm telling you: I'm your mother. And I count you among the list of my biological children. We see plenty of cases where adoption parallels the natural process, such as when we graft a twig from an unusual plant onto another one, making two distinct species into one. You never made me groan with pain in childbirth, yet I still feel for you all a mother's love.

***How to say it:***

- This is a passage in which antithesis does a lot of work. Be sure to stress the oppositions between *adoption* and *nature*, *native slip* and *foreign seeds*, *mother's groan* and *mother's care*, and *oppress'd me* and *express to you*.
- The verbs in the passage are also quite expressive and should be highlighted: *am*, *enwombèd*, *strives*, *breeds*, *oppress'd*, and *express*.
- I once heard an adoptive mother say these lines on her daughter's wedding day. It was quite moving.

***Some details:***

The image in line 5, about *native slip* and *foreign seeds*, is worth a closer look. Scientific inquiry took off during the English Renaissance, and in particular, understanding in the area of natural sciences leapt forward. The notion that man could "strive with nature" to nature's betterment remained a new and controversial idea, but in botany, at least, it was demonstrated repeatedly and vividly through the creation of many new hybrid species of flowers and other plants. Shakespeare turns again and again to images of gardening, planting, and cultivation in his works, but hybridization seems to interest him especially. (His most thorough examination of the subject is in *The Winter's Tale*, where Perdita and Polixenes conduct a long debate on the morality of the process, and that of tinkering with nature at all.) He sees plant grafting as somehow magical, a perplexing riddle, in which something can be man-made, yet still have about it all the authenticity and power of nature at its purest. Paradoxes of this sort riveted Shakespeare, and in this regard, he is very much a man of his time: countless other Renaissance writers and thinkers wrestled with the disorienting ramifications of the period's new scientific discoveries. Yet the incisiveness of Shakespeare's imagination—his remarkable ability to translate specific scientific knowledge into sublime poetic insight—marks him very much a man apart. To view a mother's love for her adopted child as a kind of botanical procedure is something that only this writer would, or could, do.

## SHAKESPEARE ON NEWBORNS

> *I think I shall never have the blessing of God till I have issue o' my body, for they say bairns are blessings.*
>
> —Clown, *All's Well That Ends Well,* 1.3.21

After pregnancy and delivery comes that fateful trip home when Mom and Dad find themselves alone for the first time with their little bundle of joy. Their hungry, screaming, pooping, sleepless little bundle of joy. Between reassuring phone calls from family and friends—"Don't worry, by three months it'll be *much* easier"—these lines of Shakespeare can help you cope with some of the craziness that comes with a newborn, and help deepen your love for your angel.

## BABY LOOKS LIKE MOM AND DAD

Sonnet 3 is one of the series of seventeen "you should have a baby" poems that open Shakespeare's famous collection of verse. It contains his most memorable description of a child's resemblance to his or her mother:

> Thou art thy mother's glass, and she in thee
> Calls back the lovely April of her prime.

(A "glass" is a mirror, and Mama's "lovely April" her springtime days of youthful beauty.)

Shakespeare didn't write about a baby's resemblance to Papa until nearly twenty years later:

> [*indicating a baby*] Behold, my lords,
> Although the print be little, the whole matter
> And copy of the father: eye, nose, lip,
> The trick of's frown, his forehead, nay, the valley,
> The pretty dimples of his chin and cheek, his smiles,
> The very mould and frame of hand, nail, finger.
>
> —PAULINA, *The Winter's Tale*, 2.3.98–103

***In other words:***

Look, everyone: it may be a small copy, but it reproduces the father in every detail. Eyes, nose, lips, his very distinctive frown, his forehead—no, seriously—even the little indented groove between his nose and upper lip,* the cleft on his chin, the distinctive dimples on

---

* Exactly what *the valley* refers to is unclear. Probably the feature described in my paraphrase (officially called the *philtrum*), it may alternatively mean the cleft in the chin (although that's mentioned in the next line), or perhaps the hollow area beneath the lower lip, or even the ridges in the forehead caused by *the trick of's frown*.

his cheeks, his smile, and the exact pattern and structure of his hands, nails, and fingers.

***How to use it:***

- I love reading this short passage with my daughter in my arms, although I'm happy that it's not entirely true (especially the nose part) and that she resembles her beautiful mother far more than she does me!
- Although the baby in the play is a girl, nothing in the speech prevents it being said of a boy. And if, as in my daughter's case, it's the mom who is more clearly reflected in the wee one's features, simply substituting *mother* for *father* in line 3, *her* for each *his* in the speech, and *of her* for *of's* in line 4, will make it work fine.

## LULLABY

One way to help a baby sleep is to sing a lullaby. Shakespeare writes a very pretty one in *A Midsummer Night's Dream*. It's sung by the fairies for their queen Titania as she retires for the night.

You spotted snakes with double tongue,
    Thorny hedgehogs, be not seen;
Newts and blindworms, do no wrong;
    Come not near our Fairy Queen.

*Chorus:*
    Philomel with melody,
    Sing in our sweet lullaby;
Lulla, lulla, lullaby; lulla, lulla, lullaby.
        Never harm
        Nor spell nor charm
    Come our lovely lady nigh.

So good night, with lullaby.

Weaving spiders, come not here;
Hence, you long-legged spinners, hence;
Beetles black, approach not near;
Worm nor snail do no offense.

*Repeat chorus.*

—FAIRIES, *A Midsummer Night's Dream*, 2.2.9–23

***In other words:***

Don't show your faces, all you multicolored, forked-tongued snakes, and you spiky hedgehogs. Don't make trouble, you poisonous lizards and tiny-eyed reptiles. Don't come near our fairy queen.

*Chorus*: You nightingale, sing and make our sweet lullaby. Lulla, lulla, lullaby. May no ill will, nor no evil spell nor magic charm, ever come near our lady. So lullaby and good night.

Don't get near us, you poisonous web weavers, you long-legged silk makers. Just get away from here! Don't come around, you black beetles. Don't make mischief, you worms and snails.

*Repeat chorus.*

***How to say it:***

- The music to which Shakespeare set this lullaby doesn't survive from the play's first performance in 1594. Modern productions must commission new tunes for it, and for the handful of other songs in the play. Even without music, however, the soft beauty of the lines is easy to hear. Harley Granville-Barker, one of the great Shakespearean directors of the early twentieth century, described how the language of this and the other songs in the play literally conjures the fairy world to life: "The lilt, no less than the meaning [of the song], helps to express them [i.e., the fairies] to us as beings other than mortals, treading the air."

- To tread the air yourself, be sure to take note of the rhyme scheme in the song (*tongue-seen-wrong-queen*, *hear-hence-near-offense*, etc.) and the strong rhythmic pulse of every stanza, and if you don't want to make up a tune of your own, use these in a kind of chant or legato bedtime rap, and with them create the smoothly soporific tone every lullaby requires.

- Whether you sing or speak the lines, try to convince your listener that you're really talking to all those nasty creepy-crawlies in the song and commanding them to stay away. The more the creatures sound like a catalogue of Halloween goblins, the better the chorus works to create a bedtime atmosphere of safety and sweetness.

- If you're singing to a boy, substitute *baby* for *lady* in the chorus. *Fairy Queen* is slightly trickier to rewrite, because whatever replaces it must rhyme with *seen*. You're in luck if your son is named Dean, Gene, or, in a stretch, Ian, but if he's not, then I'd go with *little bean*.

***Some details:***

The fairy world of *A Midsummer Night's Dream* has inspired more creativity in directors and stage designers than perhaps anything else in Shakespeare. Be the fairies portrayed as gossamer-winged, Pre-Raphaelite cherubs with flowing white gowns and shoulder-length curls; pale-skinned, black-eyed Victorian urchins in sailor suits and velvet dresses; or some abstract collection of imps informed by cultural influences as diverse as the Brothers Grimm, Japanese Kabuki, or post-punk 1990s London—all of which I've seen, and many others besides—their appearance does much to define the tone of the play and its world. It also determines whether the emphasis of this lullaby is on the universe of scary, poisonous creatures who threaten nightly to attack Titania in her sleep (in one production I saw, a fairy in mid-verse found a spider crawling along the ground and, in an Elizabethan version of *Fear Factor*, ate it), or whether the point of the song is that Titania will rest safe and sound despite whatever potential dangers lurk around her (this is the more usual approach, all featherbedding, diaphanous linens, and harp glissandos).

## SHAKESPEARE ON DAUGHTERS

*I have done nothing but in care of thee,*
*Of thee, my dear one, thee, my daughter.*
—Prospero, *The Tempest*, 1.2.16–17

In Shakespeare's period as today, readers were tempted to parse works of fiction for traces of their authors' biographies and personal beliefs. And just as today our own Philip Roth has filled novel after novel with screeds against readers who assume a priori that his characters speak his own personal views and that his life and his art necessarily coincide, so the authors of the English Renaissance vociferously denied that their works contained details from their own lives, or that their characters bore any resemblance to real-world figures a clever reader could identify. Still, none other than Shakespeare's friend and rival Ben Jonson, the Philip Roth of his day, tacitly acknowledged that no matter how vigorously he may deny it, an author's personal life simply must suffuse his works. In a moving poem written in memory of his son Benjamin junior, who died in childhood, Jonson calls the boy his "best piece of poetry." Life and art may not be the same thing, Jonson seems to say, but at times the line between them shrinks very, very thin.

We cannot know if Shakespeare read Jonson's poem, although we can suppose he shared the sentiment, because his own son Hamnet died a few years before Jonson's. Hamnet Shakespeare. Swap out the *n* in his name for an *l*, and it's hard not to see English drama's most famous character, who dies prematurely while trying to live up to his father's expectations of him, as in some way a manifestation, if not an outright reincarnation, of the playwright's only son. It's almost impossible to read all of Shakespeare and not come away with a sense that the deepest of the man's private obsessions, emotional wounds, pet peeves, and secret dreams are on display in his pages. He hated crowds, he preferred the country to the city, he found France beautiful even though the French drove him crazy, he didn't smoke, he didn't like drunks. He grieved his son's memory. He adored his mother but found his father frustratingly aloof.

Nowhere do Shakespeare's personal manias creep into his works more clearly than in his depictions of fathers and their daughters. If Hamlet is a projection of his son, then Juliet, and Goneril, and Regan, and Cordelia, and Perdita, and Marina, and Miranda, and Rosalind, and Portia, and on and on, might be projections of his daughters, Susanna, born only six months after Shakespeare's marriage to Anne Hathaway, and Judith, Hamnet's twin. The joys and frustrations of fathering a girl are so vividly particularized in Shakespeare that it's tempting to imagine him writing these father-daughter relationships as a kind of therapy.

Tempting, however, is different from advisable. As a reader who would yearn for the *Complete Works of Roth* as well as a *Complete Shakespeare* if ever I were abandoned on a desert island, I hastily admit that biographical speculation of the sort I've indulged in here is extremely hazardous, and as an imaginative artist myself, I recognize that one needn't have lived every possible experience in order to depict some of them believably in fiction. But as you browse this selection of Shakespeare for Daughters, as well as Shakespeare for Sons, for Fathers, and for that matter, for Mothers, ask yourself this: no matter how supreme his imagination may have been, could Shakespeare have captured these relationships so truthfully without reflecting at least a little on his own experience of them?

## A BLESSING FOR A DAUGHTER

This brief Bardism dedicates this book to my precious daughter. That says about all I need to about how lovely I find it, and the occasion for which I find it apt. (I had planned for it to be the first words my daughter heard when she was born, but the experience of being in the delivery room and watching her entrance into this world crashed my mental hard drive so completely that all I could manage were a few gurgles, yelps, and sighs.)

**You gods, look down,**
**And from your sacred vials pour your graces**
**Upon my daughter's head.**

—Hermione, *The Winter's Tale*, 5.3.122–24

***Some details:***

Shakespeare knew his Bible. This passage reverses one in the Book of Revelation, where heaven is asked to pour down not graces but anger: "And I heard a great voice out of the temple, saying to the seven angels, / Go your ways, and pour out the vials of the wrath of God upon the earth." The Bard was apparently moved by this scripture, because elsewhere in his plays contemporaneous with *The Winter's Tale* he also imagines the gods who hover above now and then dropping something wonderful down to us mortals who live below. These lines from *The Tempest* are one example: "Look down, ye gods, / And on this couple drop a blessèd crown."

But poetry wasn't the only way Shakespeare made godliness float down onto humanity. Sometimes he'd just have one of the gods drop in for a visit. Theater historians tell us that a small roof hung over the outdoor stage of the Globe Theatre, making a kind of ceiling above the actors' heads. On it was painted a representation of the heavens, complete with stars, planets, and other astrological symbols (Hamlet calls it "this majestical roof fretted with golden fire"). This ceiling featured a hidden hatch through which actors, singers, or pieces of scenery could descend, suspended on a rig of pulleys and ropes. Hymen, god of marriage, appears from this hatch at the end of *As You Like It*, and in the late plays this equipment gets a real workout: Jupiter appears in *Cymbeline*, Juno and Ceres in *The Tempest*, and Diana in *Pericles*. Critics call these sequences *theophanies*, which means, literally, "appearances of God."

All of this is to say that at *The Winter's Tale*'s Globe premiere back in 1610, when Hermione looked up and asked the gods to pour their holy water on her daughter, audiences could have been excused for expecting a literal deluge. And whenever I quote Hermione's words over my little angel's head, I too await the opening of the sky and the descent of grace.

## THIS BABY GIRL WILL GROW UP TO BE AMAZING

In Shakespeare's play about him, King Henry VIII asks Archbishop Thomas Cranmer to stand as godfather to his daughter Elizabeth. Cranmer agrees, and offers an extraordinary public tribute to the little princess with a long speech about how fabulous she will be when she grows up. It's the definitive piece of Shakespeare for Daughters.

This royal infant—heaven still move about her—
Though in her cradle, yet now promises
Upon this land a thousand thousand blessings
Which time shall bring to ripeness. She shall be—
But few now living can behold that goodness—
A pattern to all princes living with her,
And all that shall succeed. Saba was never
More covetous of wisdom and fair virtue
Than this pure soul shall be. All princely graces
That mould up such a mighty piece as this is,
With all the virtues that attend the good,
Shall still be doubled on her. Truth shall nurse her,
Holy and heavenly thoughts still counsel her.
She shall be loved and feared. Her own shall bless her;
Her foes shake like a field of beaten corn,
And hang their heads with sorrow. Good grows with her.
In her days every man shall eat in safety
Under his own vine what he plants, and sing
The merry songs of peace to all his neighbors.
God shall be truly known, and those about her
From her shall read the perfect ways of honor.

—Cranmer, *Henry VIII*, 5.4.17–37

***In other words:***

This royal baby—may heaven always revolve around her!—although she's still in her crib, already promises a million blessings, which will in the fullness of time come to fruition. She will one day be—although few people alive today will see it—an inspiration to all the leaders of her generation, and all that will come after. Not even Beersheba desired wisdom and goodness more than this pure soul will, and Beersheba journeyed all the way to visit King Solomon in order to gain wisdom from him. All the graces customarily associated with a princely person (which this baby is) and all the virtues customarily associated with a good person (which this baby is) will always be multiplied in her. Truth will breast-feed her. Holy and heavenly thoughts will advise her. She'll be adored and respected. Those who know her will bless her. Those opposed to her will tremble like grain in the wind, and hang their heads in sadness. Goodness will prosper as she prospers. During her lifetime, every man will be safe in his own home, will enjoy the fruits of his own labor, and will sing happy songs of peace to all his neighbors. True religion will prevail, and everyone around her will learn from her how to be honorable in all things.

***How to say it:***

- The long speech is one of the best demonstrations of how the Paper Trick, described in "Seven Steps to Shipshape Shakespeare" above, can really unlock a dense passage of Shakespeare. As you'll recall, in order to use it, you simply take a blank piece of paper and cover all but the first line of the speech. Take a breath, say that line (*This royal infant—heaven still move about her—*), and when you reach its end, slide your paper down to reveal the next line. Take a breath, then say that line (*Though in her cradle, yet now promises*). Then move your paper down, breathe, and say the next line. Continue like this until you reach the end of the speech, and you'll find that the speech unfolds from your mouth like a flower blossoming in spring. Repeat the Paper Trick a few times, then try the speech once without it, trying to make it flow as naturally as you can. Notice how the line-by-line structure of the verse remains in your mind even when you're not concentrating on this formal aspect of the speech. That's how Shakespeare writes. You can never go wrong if you phrase his verse speeches one line at a time.

- Because the speech is long, and because some of the thoughts in it are either quite complicated or not entirely the sentiments a friend might want to wish his friend's child, you should feel free to make cuts wherever you'd like. For example, life expectancy in our time being rather longer than it was in Shakespeare's, I'd drop line 5. I'd also cut line 15 and the first clause of line 16—do I really want to predict that a baby will have enemies before she's even left her swaddling clothes? I'd probably also lose the first half of line 20 (*God shall be truly known*), not because I don't wish a religious life on a lovely baby girl, but because this line is really about the disputed politics of religion in Shakespeare's day, and it doesn't speak quite as directly to our own.

## SHAKESPEARE ON SONS

*O wonderful son, that can so astonish a mother!*
—HAMLET, *Hamlet*, 3.2.300

Shakespearean parents of daughters love their girls but try desperately to control them out of a deep fear that things might go horribly wrong if the girls' fates are left to themselves, especially where husbands are concerned. Shakespearean parents of sons love their boys no less, but they don't even try to influence their life choices, because they know that no matter what they suggest, want, or do, their stubborn boys will simply reject it out of hand. Put more simply, in Shakespeare, daughters are delightful, enchanting, and entirely lovable—until they discover boys. Then the gates of hell open wide, and there's never a peaceful moment again. Likewise, sons in Shakespeare are sources of pride and warmth, joy and love—until they reach a crossroads of their own. But it's not girls that are their undoing, it's their own pigheadedness, insistence on independence, and implacable, infuriating willfulness. These will wreck a parent's peace of mind as totally as any bad behavior a wayward daughter can muster.

And yet, of all the varieties of familial love one encounters in the *Complete Works of Shakespeare*, the love of parents for sons, and especially firstborn sons, may be the most intense and incandescent. To be sure, Shakespearean moms can be less than perfect, loving their sons not wisely but too well, and the Bard's dads can be imposing, distant figures who intimidate and belittle their boys. But despite their flaws, they love. And love, and love even more. Here are but two expressions of this abundant affection, both of which move me whenever I use them.

## IT'S GOOD TO HAVE SONS

When a dear friend called to tell me his pregnant wife's ultrasound revealed she was carrying twin boys, I rifled through my *Complete Works* to find something that might take the edge off the happy panic I heard in his voice. I found a wonderful Bardism to commend to anyone blessed with a baby boy.

> **Why, 'tis a happy thing / To be the father unto many sons.**
>
> —King Edward iv, *Henry VI, Part III*, 3.2.104–5

## I ADORE MY SON

This is one of my favorite Shakespeare passages, because it seems to me so truthful and mature an expression of a father's love for his son.

Free of sugarcoating, it captures the way in which parenthood is magical, despite being full of moments as frustrating and hair-raising as any in life.

LEONTES My brother,
Are you so fond of your young prince as we
Do seem to be of ours?
POLIXENES If at home, sir,
He's all my exercise, my mirth, my matter;
Now my sworn friend, and then mine enemy;
My parasite, my soldier, statesman, all.
He makes a July's day short as December,
And with his varying childness cures in me
Thoughts that would thick my blood.

—*The Winter's Tale*, 1.2.164–72

***In other words:***

LEONTES My dear friend, do you adore your young son as much as I appear to love mine?

POLIXENES When I'm at home, he's everything I do, every moment of my time. He's my every delight, he's all I think about. One minute he's my best friend, the next, he hates my guts. He's a hanger-on, he's a fighter, he's a negotiator—he's all things. He makes a long summer day feel as short as the winter solstice, and his boyish ways, in their constant changes, snap me out of dark moods and depression.

***How to say it:***

- I sent this excerpt to a friend after a wonderful conversation in which he told me how much he'd lately been enjoying time spent with his little boy.

- Don't worry too much about Leontes' lines that cue Polixenes' wonderful speech. I've included them here only for context. Polixenes' speech stands on its own, and can even begin with line 4, *He's all my exercise*, or, if you like, *Tommy's all my exercise*, or whatever Junior's name may be.

- Polixenes' speech (his name is pronounced *puh-LICKS-uh-neez*) has some interesting features. *If at home* is simply there because at this point in the play he's been away from his beloved boy for nine long months and he misses him. Feel free to drop this phrase in the interest of clarity. The antitheses between *friend* and *enemy* and *July* and *December* are important. The two occurrences of *all*, in lines 4 and 6, can be quite powerful: Polixenes' son takes up his *every* moment (line 4), and is absolutely *everything* to him (line 6).

- You can make this speech describe your daughter by changing each *he* to *she* and, perhaps, cutting line 6—about the parasite, soldier, and statesman—because to Shakespeare these were exclusively masculine character types.

***Some details:***

Lines 7 and 9 merit closer inspection. When Polixenes mentions *a July's day*, he simply assumes that his listeners know he's referring to how *long* such a day is (as opposed to how *hot* or *bright* or any of the other things summer days are). Good parallel construction would require him to contrast a long July's day to, say, *a day as short as one in December.* He doesn't say anything like that, but instead collapses this latter image into the name of the month itself. Yet we understand full well what he means. This kind of poetic density, in which meanings are implied rather than spelled out, and in which language is imprecise on its surface yet exquisitely concrete in the thoughts behind it, is characteristic of late Shakespeare, and of *The Winter's Tale* in particular. It's Shakespearean writing at its most sophisticated.

Also typical of late Shakespeare is his ability to convey a person's entire life through one short phrase. Polixenes says that the best thing about his son's mercurial boyishness is that it eliminates *thoughts that would thick* [his] *blood*. In this provocative phrase we get a glimpse of a whole person, with moods, heartbreaks, dark moments, a past that's led to all these, and a life that extends beyond the boundaries of this moment, this scene's dramatic circumstances, and even this play itself. But what makes the phrase noteworthy is how unnecessary it is. The story of the play doesn't require it; Polixenes needn't have a history of struggles with depression in order for *The Winter's Tale* to make sense, and all that's really required of the character is that he do things that move the plot forward. Still, details such as this one make the whole play more believable, more lifelike, and more real. It's just good writing, and it's also gold for an actor: What kind of thoughts are thickening Polixenes' blood? What's preoccupying him? Is he worried about his cholesterol, perhaps, or something more metaphysical? For our purposes, such queries are irrelevant—when I sent the passage to my buddy, I wasn't suggesting that he was in need of antidepressants—but they do help us understand why Shakespeare is for all occasions: because his characters seem to be real people with real lives, to reflect life as we know it to be lived, and, through their extraordinary turns of phrase, to give voice to our own experiences in all their varieties and complexities.

## SHAKESPEARE ON MOTHERS

*Nature makes them partial.*
—Polonius, *Hamlet*, 3.3.33

Given the strength of the bond between mother and child, it's remarkable how little Shakespeare actually wrote about it. He dramatizes mother-son (and, to a much lesser extent, mother-daughter) relationships in a number of plays, but he doesn't exactly anatomize them. His preference is less to talk in the abstract about how mothers and their children relate than simply to show them in action and let these relationships speak for themselves.

Sometimes he chooses not to address the subject at all. Many of the mothers in the plays are conspicuous by their absence: Prince Hal's mother, the mother of Lear's three daughters, the mother of Shylock's beloved daughter Jessica, the mothers of Miranda, Rosalind, Desdemona, Portia, Ophelia, Viola—we hear a resounding silence from these women, who are dead before the curtain rises on the plays in which their children feature. And interestingly, in the case of the character who is arguably the most complex, vividly drawn, and loquacious mother in the plays, Coriolanus' mother, Volumnia, the most emotional moment her son shares with her has in it no language at all, as this simple stage direction from the play demands: "He holds her by the hand, silent."

What accounts for this strange lacuna in Shakespeare's output? What do these absent mothers mean? Four hundred years' worth of critics have had a field day essaying these questions. The political: Shakespeare is a misogynist, so he marginalizes mothers in his works. The practical: In his period, women on stage are played by men in drag, and there is a limited number of talented female impersonators in London's acting pool, so Shakespeare wisely keeps the number of mothers he needs to a minimum. The poetical: He enhances the metaphorical power of his characters by endowing them with an acute version of a very resonant existential problem, the search for a mother's love. The psychological: He has an Oedipal attraction to his own mother, and his shame over it causes him to erase the mothers in his plays. The psychological, version B: He has abandonment issues with his own mother, so he can't help but portray motherless children in his plays. (Poor Mary Arden! Forever subject to character assassination by armchair shrinks, simply for having given birth to the Greatest Writer of All Time.)

We'll never know the reasons why Shakespeare so scants mothers and motherhood in his works. But whenever I apply the Bardisms below to the mom-related occasions of my life, I sometimes hear King Henry V's admonition to his outnumbered troops: "The fewer men, the greater share of honor." That is, the fact that Shakespeare says relatively little about mothers per se simply makes me appreciate those things he does say even more. See if you agree as you survey these bits of Shakespeare for Occasions of the Maternal.

## I LOVE MY MOM

Here are two short Bardisms for children who love their mothers. The first works great spoken directly to Mom; the second is best suited to a toast, either from a son to his mother or about a particularly loving fellow who sees the phrase "mama's boy" as a sincere compliment.

The first:

> **My heart / Leaps to be gone into my mother's bosom.**
>
> —MARINA, *Pericles*, 22.66–67

Second:

> There's no man in the world / More bound to's mother.
>
> —VOLUMNIA, *Coriolanus*, 5.3.159–60

***How to use them:***

- The first line is great for any son or daughter eager to hug Mom after an absence, or just because.
- Volumnia says the second line to her son while trying to make him do something he doesn't want to do. Reminding him how bound he is to her, she guilt-trips him into obeying her. Therefore, some mothers may well wish to emulate Volumnia and use this Bardism to bend their wayward child to their desires. But the line can also be of use on any occasion when a parent wishes to praise a wonderful child, when a child describes his or her devotion to Mom or Dad, or when a third party admires a friend's filial devotion.
- Transgender the line if necessary with these changes: "There's no woman in the world / More bound to her mother," or "There's no man in the world / More bound to his father."

## MOTHERS WILL STOP AT NOTHING TO PROTECT THEIR CHILDREN

Throughout this book we'll see the Bard turn to the natural world in search of metaphors that might shed light on human predicaments. Bees, flowers, fish, trees, weather formations, and especially animals are endless sources of inspiration to him. Like the sermonizing pastor who mines some nugget of holy writ and explicates its moral content as instruction to his parishioners, Shakespeare observes nature in action, then abstracts some detail from what he sees and develops it into a poetic image for human edification. Here, in *Macbeth*, Shakespeare looks at the protective parental instincts of the animals, particularly the matriarchs of the ornithological realm:

The poor wren,
The most diminutive of birds, will fight,
Her young ones in her nest, against the owl.

—Lady Macduff, *Macbeth*, 4.2.9–11

***In other words:***

When her babies are in her nest, even the lowly wren, the tiniest bird of all, will fight hard against predators many times her size.

***How to use it:***

- As a testament to the courage and mettle of mothers, this line is hard to beat. In the playground, at parent-teacher night at school, at the pediatrician's office, or on the checkout line at Babies"R"Us, quote it whenever you see a mom advocating hard on behalf of her little one.

## SHAKESPEARE ON FATHERS

*To you your father should be as a god.*

—Theseus, *A Midsummer Night's Dream*, 1.1.47

The relative shortage of mothers in Shakespeare stands in marked contrast with what can only be called a superabundance of fathers in the plays. Dads and their concerns are one of Shakespeare's major subjects. The plays feature good dads and bad ones, aloof dads and meddlesome ones, timid dads and self-assured ones, successful dads and failures, controlling dads and ones who are laissez-faire, wealthy patriarchs and impoverished dependents, dads who are anxious, tempestuous, and altogether neurotic, and dads who are as chill as a medicine cabinet full of Prozac. And as varied as are the paternal personalities on display, just as diverse are the emotions they arouse in their progeny.

For all their variety, however, there's a remarkable consistency to what Shakespeare's fathers want, namely, the best for their children, but with this caveat: that their paternal benevolence be both proffered and accepted on their own terms. Fathers of sons want their boys to be respectable and respectful, upright and worthy. If they step out of line and fail to live up to their fathers' expectations, these boys'll hear about it, and if they do make something of themselves, they'd better be quick to attribute their achievements to the inspiration provided them by Papa. Fathers of daughters want their girls to be virginal until marriage, and when they do walk down the aisle, it must be only into the arms of the man hand-picked for them as the most suitable. If they want to marry some other fellow, they'll feel a hot and relentless wrath, and they'll find no end of obstacles placed in their way. (So central is this marriage veto to the father-daughter relationship in Shakespeare that were it taken away, the plots of nearly half of his plays would collapse.)

The young men and women on the receiving end of the fatherly upbraidings in the plays respond in kind, and things grow quickly turbulent. Yet those children who manage to please their fathers both hear from them and say to them some of the most tender, stirring, and unexpected love poetry in the plays.

## I LOVE YA, POP

The mother of all father speeches in Shakespeare comes near the beginning of *King Lear*, when the monarch asks his three daughters to tell him how much they love him. Goneril, up first, lays it on thick:

> Sir, I love you more than words can wield the matter;
> Dearer than eye-sight, space, and liberty;
> Beyond what can be valued, rich or rare;
> No less than life, with grace, health, beauty, honor;
> As much as child e'er loved, or father found;
> A love that makes breath poor, and speech unable;
> Beyond all manner of so much I love you.
>
> —Goneril, *King Lear*, 1.1.53–59

***In other words:***

Dad, I love you more than words can say. I love you more than my eyesight, more than freedom, more than free will. I love you more than any object, however expensive or unusual. I love you no less than I love life itself—life that's full of grace, good health, beauty, and honor. I love you as much as any child ever loved or any father ever felt. My love can't be given voice, can't be put into words. There's no metaphor I can conjure that can express my love, which is beyond expression of any kind.

***How to say it:***

- This speech relies on one of Shakespeare's favorite pieces of dramaturgical sleight-of-hand. Goneril says there's no language that can possibly express her love, and then proceeds to talk quite eloquently about it for several lines. Whenever actors encounter this articulate inarticulacy in Shakespeare, they know that the playwright is giving them a very specific directorial note: you must discover this language as you go along. That is, you must take your time and really find each new line, each new idea, as you get to it. The Paper Trick helps you do that. Just cover all but the first line of the speech, and say only that line. Then move the paper down, revealing the next line only, and say it, and so on. You will find the words forming in your mind a phrase at a time, just as Goneril does.

- Alliteration, or the repetition of consonant sounds, is an important aspect of this speech. The paired consonants in *words / wield*, *eye-sight / space*, *rich / rare*, *less / life*, and *father / found* give Goneril's speech a wonderful deliberateness and formality, as well as a distinctly poetic sound.

- Antitheses and verbs do much good work here: *child loved* versus *father found*; *love*, *wield*, *be valued*, *loved*, *found*, *makes*, and *love*.

- The simple fact that Goneril says *love* or some variation on it four times in only seven lines is also worth noting. You don't need a Ph.D. in Shakespeare to know that Goneril doesn't mean a word of this speech and that Lear's failure to apprehend her hypocrisy leads to cataclysm. Some might say, therefore, that to quote these lines as an expression of sincere love for one's father is disingenuous at best and an invitation to some seriously bad karma at worst. This notwithstanding, I disagree that the speech should be avoided, and I once attended a wedding where I saw someone address this issue with glorious aplomb. The bride said these lines to her father—quite beautifully—in thanks for making her big day so sumptuous and grand, and then she added something like this: "In Shakespeare, those words are lies, excessive and empty. But to me, they're as true, simple, and heartfelt as any I've ever said." The spontaneous "*Awwwwwww*" that arose from the wedding guests testified to the effectiveness of this strategy. I know my friend won't object if I recommend it.

Not every Shakespearean expression of love for a father is spoken by a lying sociopath like Goneril. Some are true-hearted and straightforward, and all the more touching for being so. Here's a Bardic boast that any child proud of his or her father can make with absolute sincerity.

> The spirit of my father grows strong in me.
>
> —Orlando, *As You Like It*, 1.1.59

***How to use it:***

- The father whose spirit energizes Orlando is, alas, no longer alive. This line is therefore particularly well suited to those moments in life when paternal values imparted long ago suddenly seem relevant and finally make sense, and when your conduct in a difficult situation really puts into practice lessons from your dad that you never even knew you'd learned.
- But it needn't be solely for occasions focusing on a deceased father; an athletic dad who coaches his son's Little League team, say, might spend his days hoping to hear his little boy utter this line as he steps into the batter's box before swatting a line drive.

## SHAKESPEARE ON SIBLINGS

> *We few, we happy few, we band of brothers.*
>
> —King Henry, *Henry V*, 4.3.60

John and Mary Shakespeare had eight children. Joan and Margaret, their first- and second-born, died in infancy. William was number three, followed by Gilbert, another Joan, Anne, Richard, and Edmund. When Will died in 1616 at age fifty-two, only his sister Joan was still alive. She lived another thirty years, to age seventy-seven, which was an unusually long time in this period of short life expectancies.

Little is known about these brothers and sisters of the great man. Like the first Joan and her sister Margaret, Anne also died young, not in infancy but at age eight. Gilbert spent a few of his early adult years in London but returned to his native Stratford and became a successful businessman there. The only evidence of Richard is a record of his funeral, at age thirty-nine, in a Stratford parish register. The second Joan is remembered primarily because both her son and grandson achieved some fame as actors in London, in her brother William's plays. (Joan's grandson, Charles Hart, was the great Falstaff of the Restoration period.)

Only in the case of Edmund, the youngest Shakespeare sibling, sixteen years William's junior, does enough evidence survive to allow us to speculate about what kind of brother the Bard might have been. Like Joan's descendants, Edmund also built a reputation as an actor in London, and also, like them, in William's plays. His nascent career was cut short by an outbreak of the plague in 1607, when he was twenty-seven, and it's from reports of his funeral that we can glean how William felt about him.

Held at St. Saviour's, Southwark, the parish church of the Globe Theatre, Edmund's funeral was a tremendously lavish affair. Unusually, it was conducted in the morning, most likely so that Edmund's fellow actors could pay their respects before having to go to work in the playhouses that afternoon. The church's largest bell tolled for him, also unusually, since smaller church bells customarily knelled deaths. Apparently the large bell rang out so loud and for so long that it was heard throughout the City of London, on the opposite side of the Thames. Edmund was interred in the church itself rather than outside in the churchyard, an honor that increased the cost of the funeral more than fivefold. A journeyman actor would not normally be memorialized by such a series of elaborate tributes, so the only explanation that makes sense of all the extravagant circumstances of Edmund's burial is the fact of his last name. Because in 1607 William Shakespeare was at the height of his fame, power, and wealth, it seems reasonable to suppose that he arranged and paid for his brother's funeral. And if this is so, then the lengths to which he went to honor his young sibling suggest that he was a man to whom brotherly love was a very meaningful concept.

Once again we must ask if this smidgen of biographical evidence can shed some light on the fraternal relationships in Shakespeare's works. And once again we must answer yes if we believe that aspects of a writer's fictional creations somehow project his own unconscious into the world, but no if we regard him as a working professional cranking out product, his literary imagination completely compartmentalized from his private emotional life. Judge for yourself: below are some of Shakespeare's writings on the subject of brothers and sisters, and, whether or not they reflect his own feelings, they certainly describe the bond between siblings as one that's powerful, and, for the most part, positive.

## SISTERS ARE CLOSE PALS

One way Shakespeare employs the sibling relationship in his plays is by using it to describe close friendships. If an army is compared to a *band of brothers*, for example, then we infer that it comprises a group of men who share a deep affection and mutual regard for one another. We also learn the converse: that brothers are as tight as any besieged comrades in arms. The metaphor of brotherhood describes the army, and the army expands the resonance of the metaphor of brotherhood.

The female equivalent is a description of what is arguably the closest friendship between girls in the plays. In *As You Like It* the courtier LeBeau tells Orlando that the cousins Rosalind and Celia are a pair "whose loves / Are dearer than the natural bond of sisters." Like the metaphorical connection between soldiers and brothers, this image tells us something about two friends, and also something about the sororal bond: that it must be very deep if it's as deep as this friendship, whose special closeness Celia details in this superb Bardism, Shakespeare for Sisters:

> We still have slept together,
> Rose at an instant, learned, played, eat together,
> And wheresoe'er we went, like Juno's swans
> Still we went coupled and inseparable.
>
> —Celia, *As You Like It*, 1.3.67–70

***In other words:***

We've always slept together, and awakened at the same moment. We've studied, had fun, and eaten together. And wherever we went, we were joined at the hip, like the swans that draw the chariot of Juno, queen of the gods.*

***How to use it:***

- Because to Celia and Rosalind friendship is sisterhood, and sisterhood is friendship, this speech can be used to describe a relationship of either type. A simple introduction—"My relationship with Ashleigh is as close as a beautiful one in a Shakespeare play

---

* A tiny Shakespearean boo-boo here: in mythology it's actually Venus, goddess of love, and not Juno, who is associated with swans. If you prefer your Shakespeare perfect, then blame the error on Celia, who, in an emotional moment, perhaps confuses the goddesses. If you can countenance a Shakespeare who's human, then just imagine he was writing in a hurry or that he forgot to Google *Juno's swans* before penning this line.

called *As You Like It*"—is all the setup you'll require. LeBeau's line can also be pressed into service to describe your favorite sisterly bond. Just start the line with *their* instead of *whose.*

- *Eat* at the end of line 2 is pronounced *et* (rhymes with *bet*), because it's the past tense of the verb *to eat.* Modern Americans would say *ate*, or because of the helper verb *have* in this sentence, *eaten*. But *et* (spelled, confusingly, *eat*) is still in wide use in England, as anyone acquainted with a Britisher will know: "Oy, mate, would you like to 'ave some dinner?" "Cheers, no. I already *et.*"

## BROTHERS ARE CLOSE PALS

Two Bardisms from two very different plays articulate Shakespeare's understanding of brotherly affection. They capture that sense that brothers are intimate teammates, agents for the same secret organization, and co-conspirators on a mission only they are privy to and which can be achieved only through their joint efforts.

> From this hour
> The heart of brothers govern in our loves
> And sway our great designs.
>
> —Antony, *Antony and Cleopatra*, 2.2.154–56

> We came into the world like brother and brother,
> And now let's go hand in hand, not one before another.
>
> —Dromio of Ephesus, *The Comedy of Errors*, 5.1.426–27

***How to use them:***

- Both of these speeches can be used to wish auspiciousness to your brothers, or closest friends, as they embark on any undertaking that you feel must be characterized by a mutual respect and love in order to succeed. The opening of a business or the start of a vacation are two occasions that come to mind. The lines can also help patch up a falling-out between brothers or close friends. Dromio's speech in particular is a heartwarming expression of fraternal equality and warmth.

- Dromio is one-half of a set of identical twins, so his first line is a literal reference to the moment of his and his brother's simultaneous birth.

- Antony is reaching out in friendship toward his rival, Octavius Caesar. His speech is a bit more comprehensible if you imagine a comma at the end of its first line, and the word *may* at the start of its second: "From this hour, may the heart of brothers . . . " That is, Antony is expressing his hope that brotherly hearts—hearts that are loving and intimately bound together—will influence, or *sway*, the feelings between himself and Caesar, and will help them achieve great things together.

- In both Bardisms, replace *brothers* and *brother* with *sisters* and *sister* to get the all-girl versions.

CHAPTER 2

# Then the Schoolboy

## SHAKESPEARE FOR THE OCCASIONS OF CHILDHOOD

*And then the whining schoolboy, with his satchel,*
*And shining morning face, creeping like snail*
*Unwillingly to school.*

A few years have passed and the infant has grown up a bit. His mewling has modulated into less cacophonous but still hardly agreeable whining. His face is now puke-free, freshly scrubbed at the start of each day, and so clean that it shines. No longer in his nurse's arms—and you can bet she's relieved and catching her breath—he's on his own for at least that part of the day it takes him to walk to his destination. It's his daily project to see just how protracted he can make the journey, because what awaits him when he arrives is a bastion of heinousness as forbidding as any torture chamber ever devised in the annals of depravity and tyranny: *school*!

We can all remember taking that long, unwilling walk in the morning, and that's why Jaques' Second Age of Man always summons a smile of recognition. Yet every time I read these lines, even as memories cascade of my own slow, satchel-laden 8:00 A.M. stroll down Hopper Avenue toward Roosevelt Elementary, I'm fascinated that this is the image Shakespeare would choose as the defining emblem of childhood. What about all the fun of those years, the horsing around with friends and siblings, the play and laughter with parents, the thrill of discovery of countless new sights, sounds, sensations, and concepts? Shakespeare overlooks all that—call it the *Highlights* magazine stuff—and focuses instead on an image of complaint, misery, and reluctance. The Second Age of Man is the Age of Goofus, not Gallant.

And so a pattern begins to emerge. The baby pukes and screams, the boy whines and creeps. Next, the lover will write idiotic poetry and sigh himself into hyperventilation, then the soldier intemperately will risk life and limb for something as ephemeral as honor, and the Justice will bore everyone silly with his pontifications and pronunciamentos, and on, and on. Life for Jaques, it seems, hasn't much to do with fun or discovery or even growth or progress. No, life for Jaques—for Shakespeare, for this moment in his writing, anyway—is a series of misadventures, pomposities, and follies. Each misstep is a station on a one-way trip to oblivion, toothlessness, blandness, and blindness.

But Shakespeare isn't Schopenhauer. The Bard isn't Beckett. Shakespeare—well, Jaques; well, both—finds a way to discuss despair with a rather beguiling humor. Jaques' images are unmistakably sharp-edged, but they're presented with a twinkle in the eye, coated in candy. That's the familiar Shakespearean manner. Confront terrible truths, say the hard things, but dip them in sprinkles to make it all go down smoother. The legendary impresario Joseph Papp once described Shakespeare to me as very like an Irish coffee. It's dark, bitter, strong, and spiked with a splash of spirit that gives it a kick, but before you get to any of that, you must first drink your way through a layer of sweet cream. The cream in Shakespeare's Irish coffee is his magical way with words, his transformation via language of something that unsettles into something that entices, charms, and wins. I love Papp's simile because it reminds me that even at his bleakest, Shakespeare remembers beauty, and even at his most scathing, he remembers to laugh.

The whining schoolboy is a perfect illustration of Shakespeare's habit of mixing light and dark. The magnetic force that repels boys from school appears elsewhere in the canon, as when Romeo recalls, "Love goes toward love as schoolboys from their books, / But love from love, toward school with heavy looks," or when Lord Hastings, having dismissed the soldiers he'd planned to deploy in battle against King Henry IV, observes the speed with which they flee the field in all directions and says that, "like a school broke up, / Each hurries toward his home." While these are vivid images delivered by two gifted speakers, neither evinces the detailed texture and rhetorical dazzle of the just-washed schoolboy of Jaques' fancy. Note, for example, how the chipper phrase *schoolboy with his satchel* introduces alliterative *s* sounds that continue into *face*, *snail*, and *school*. Listen to the slight condescension jingling beneath the *shining morning face*, and notice how much information it compresses into three words: They conjure an entire scene of a little boy squirming under washcloth, Ivory soap, and Brylcreem when he'd rather stay in his bedroom fortress playing with his toys and frogs and imaginary pals.

The image is as euphonious as it is artful: it turns the noun *morning* into an adjective modifying *face*, whose *-ing* resonates nicely alongside the participial adjective *shining* even as it carries that suffix forward from the earlier *puking* and *mewling* into the later *creeping* and *unwillingly*. Look at how the placement of *unwillingly* at the beginning of a new verse line gives special prominence to the adverb, by kicking off the line with the unexpectedly accented syllable *un*, and then by throttling back the boy's walk to sub-snail speed: he's not only creeping, he's creeping *unwillingly*. And marvel at how effective *school* is when it appears at the very end of these lines, as opposed to its earlier placement in Romeo's and Hastings' iterations of the image. As the word thuds out, the stabbing *sk* sound that starts it scotches any lingering hope we might have had that the shine on the boy's face was one of happiness. We understand that his arrival at homeroom, long in coming, will be but the beginning of a drudgingly long day of ruler-on-the-knuckles misery and repetitive times-table tedium.

But even though to Jaques, the only way to get an education is to endure the awfulness of Miss Baxter's corporal punishment and droning lectures on verb conjugation, Shakespeare acknowledges elsewhere in the canon that there are other pedagogical methods. He knows that snail-slow walks to school are one kind of childhood fresh-air activity, but he's happy to explore and dramatize many others. One speech in *As You Like It* may record the Second Age of Man as a time of misery, but plenty of passages in the remaining three dozen Shakespeare plays show childhood's manifold brighter aspects.

Below, then, Bardisms on all the Occasions of the Schoolboy's Life: fun and dull, for kids willing and not, to creep and also to race toward.

## SHAKESPEARE ON CHILDREN

*'Tis not good that children should know any wickedness.*
—Mistress Quickly, *The Merry Wives of Windsor*, 2.2.115

Children appear onstage in many Shakespeare plays. In the comedies, their dramatic function is usually to serve as earnest foils for some pompous windbag who needs to be taken down a notch. Falstaff's page is the prime example. In the tragedies and histories, they are used as symbols of virtuous innocence whose ruination by some tyrannical megalomaniac is the turning point in that character's fortunes. The many murders committed by Macbeth and Richard III, for instance, don't seem truly inexcusable until children are their victims; the former's massacre of the Macduff brood and the latter's execution of the two little princes at the tower are the events that carry each man across the Rubicon from criminal into evil despot. In the late plays, children are seen as icons of redemption, salvation, and the possibility that the future might just find a way to avoid the mistakes of the past. Perdita in *The Winter's Tale* and the baby Elizabeth born at the end of *Henry VIII* are examples of this dramatic function.

Whatever its dramaturgical purpose, Shakespeare composed material for and about children that displays all the insight, sensitivity, and eloquence we are accustomed to seeing from him on every subject under the sun.

### THAT'S A WELL-BEHAVED KID

Falstaff's relationship with his wiseacre boy companion is one of endless sniping—W. C. Fields' "Get away from me kid, ya bother me!"

routine is widely thought to be patterned after the fat knight, a role Fields longed to essay but, alas, never did. Yet despite his rancor, we know that deep down Sir John loves the kid. He's not Shakespeare's only old man to have in his heart a soft spot for a tyke. In the opening scene of *The Winter's Tale*, a sage courtier speaks sweetly of Prince Mamillius, King Leontes' little boy.

> It is a gallant child; one that, indeed, physics the subject, makes old hearts fresh. They that went on crutches ere he was born desire yet their life to see him a man.
>
> —CAMILLO, *The Winter's Tale*, 1.1.32–35

***In other words:***

He's an outstanding boy. He's like good medicine for all the citizens of the country. He makes old people feel young. Folks who were at death's door before he was born hope to live a bit longer just so that they can see what he'll be like when he grows up.

***How to use it:***

- This is a perfect bit of Shakespeare for a speech from Uncle Joe on confirmation day or Grandpa Moe on Bar Mitzvah morning. It could also serve as general compliment from anyone for any fine young man of whom they're proud.
- Simply substituting the female gender in the second sentence—*she* and *woman* instead of *he* and *man*—will suit this comment to any wonderful young lady of your acquaintance.
- Emphasizing two antitheses will help clarify this excerpt when it's spoken aloud: *old* versus *fresh*; and *ere he was born* versus *see him a man*.
- The verbs *is*, *physics*, and *makes* in the first sentence do much to communicate the rather complex sense of the thought.

## THAT KID'S GOT BEHAVIOR ISSUES

In the event that your ten-year-old isn't quite as inspiring as young Mamillius, don't worry, Shakespeare's got you covered, too. Grandma's priceless vase in smithereens at the foot of the mantel? Crayon on the living room wall? Play-Doh in your underwear drawer? Try this Bardism:

> Out, you mad-headed ape!
> A weasel hath not such a deal of spleen
> As you are tossed with.
>
> —Lady Percy, *Henry IV, Part I*, 2.3.69–71

***Some details:***

In context, Lady Percy is talking not to a wild toddler but to her husband, Hotspur, who's characteristically acting like one. Her speech is a lot of fun, filled as it is with vivid and unexpected language. The distance between it and a simple paraphrase of what it says shows just how colorful and energetic Shakespeare's English can be.

The basic sense is: "Enough, you crazy monkey! You're more ornery than a weasel." These ten words may communicate the same ideas as Shakespeare's eighteen, but they're nowhere near as terrific. Just consider how much texture and nuance Lady Percy manages to convey with her version of my dry prose. *Out* is an interjection similar in meaning to "fie." That is, she's not literally telling Hotspur to leave the room, but she is chastising him (compare the use of the contemporary phrase "Get outta here!" to mean "Stop that!"). *Spleen* means anger or willfulness, because that organ was believed to be the seat of those emotions, an idea that survives in the adjective "splenetic," which describes someone irritable or hotheaded. The verb *tossed* in this context means disturbed or, possibly, shaken. *Weasels* in Shakespeare are always splenetic troublemakers, who weasel their way into places they don't belong, often birds' nests, and—pop!—unleash all sorts of mayhem, usually by sucking the yolks out of eggs sitting there innocent and vulnerable. ("I can suck melancholy from a song," says Jaques rather deliciously in *As You Like It*, "as a weasel sucks eggs.") *Apes*, too, are for Shakespeare angry and frantic animals who generally do damage and cause chaos.

A side benefit of quoting these lines to your rampaging little one—and I've field-tested them with a wayward nephew—is that in addition to venting some of your own spleen, its surprise mentions of apes and weasels will stop the kid in his tracks. Alas, after a few seconds, if my test subject is predictive of the general course of things, he'll give you a quizzical look and go right back to trashing the joint. But this Shakespeare on the Occasion of a Temper Tantrum will provide at least a momentary reprieve.

## SHAKESPEARE ON SCHOOL

> *'Twere good he were schooled.*
>
> —PEDANT, *The Taming of the Shrew*, 4.4.9

A place we creep toward in the morning, run from in the afternoon, and hate being at for the hours in between hardly seems worth commenting on, let alone waxing poetic about, and indeed, Shakespeare doesn't say much about school itself beyond how loathsome it is. To be sure, he puts a couple of teachers in his plays and he even dramatizes a lesson or two, but these usually function as pretexts for some other dramatic action: a romantic hookup, say, or the relaying of a secret message . . . about a romantic hookup, say. School as civic institution and education as a bedrock civic value just don't attract much attention in the plays.

Perhaps Shakespeare didn't feel it necessary to state what must have struck him as obvious about the value of schooling. After all, his own tremendous erudition proves that an education is a useful thing to have. Or, on the other hand, perhaps Shakespeare kept mum because he recognized something essentially disappointing about the institutions of formal education, something we continue to wrestle with in our own society: inevitably, they fall short of the ideals we hold them to. The gap between the public good school is meant to confer and the rough-and-tumble reality of schooling as it's conducted in the day-to-day is enough to break the heart of even the most bright-eyed educational theorist, in our time as in the Renaissance.

The Bard's own life bears out a certain skepticism toward formal education. We know he did not attend university, yet much anecdotal evidence survives about Shakespeare the autodidact: he was an almost constant presence in the bookstores of London. It makes sense. Without what must have been nearly round-the-clock reading, he could have amassed neither the preternatural store of knowledge he displays in his works, nor his apparently exhaustive familiarity with the literature of his day and the centuries before. Clearly, he was an advocate of what we'd today call continuing education. He records his endorsement of self-guided tutelage in *The Taming of the Shrew*, when Bianca tells two would-be tutors,

> I am no breeching scholar in the schools;
> I'll not be tied to hours nor 'pointed times,
> But learn my lessons as I please myself.

(File that Bardism under Shakespeare for the Occasion of Dropping Out of School!)

Shakespeare's skepticism of formal education rarely gets more intense than Bianca's petulant dismissal, but when it does, it veers close to utter despair. There's no more damning indictment of learning than that delivered by Caliban in Act 1 of *The Tempest*, arguably one of Shakespeare's most world-weary and fed-up of plays. A native on the island occupied by the exiled Milanese duke Prospero—who is, not incidentally, an obsessive reader—Caliban resists Prospero's efforts to "civilize" him through education. He denounces his overlord's patronizing attitude in searing terms:

> You taught me language; and my profit on't
> Is, I know how to curse. The red plague rid you
> For learning me your language!

The only reason to learn language is so that you can curse. That's strong stuff. But even if Shakespeare meant it as he wrote it, he surely also knew that Caliban's sentences, with their alliterative *r*'s and *l*'s, sophisticated punning (*red / rid*), and complex rhythmic structure, contradict the very thought they express. They show that while Shakespeare may not have liked school, he managed to find a way to abide schooling, or at least its results. It's a paradoxical stance that's typically Shakespearean.

## STUDY WHAT YOU LOVE

Here's a Bardism for that second-semester sophomore who can't decide what major to declare.

Good master, while we do admire
This virtue and this moral discipline,
Let's be no stoics nor no stocks, I pray,
Or so devote to Aristotle's checks
As Ovid be an outcast quite abjured.
Balk logic with acquaintance that you have,
And practice rhetoric in your common talk.
Music and poesy use to quicken you;
The mathematics and the metaphysics,
Fall to them as you find your stomach serves you.
No profit grows where is no pleasure ta'en.
In brief, sir, study what you most affect.

—Tranio, *The Taming of the Shrew*, 1.1.29–40

***In other words:***

Listen, boss. We all think highly of ethics and morality. But—please—let's not eliminate fun altogether, or turn ourselves into stuffed shirts. Let's not dedicate ourselves to a life of restraint and throw away pleasure altogether. (Let's not get all hung up with that stickler Aristotle about stuff like right and wrong, and throw Ovid's stories about people who get naked right out the window.) Work on your analytical skills by figuring out how to split the check. Use linguistic theory in your everyday chitchat. By all means listen to music and read poetry, but purely for your enjoyment. As for math and philosophy, get involved in that stuff only when you're really in the mood. You can't learn anything if you're miserable. Here's my point: as far as study goes, stick to the subjects you like.

***How to say it:***

- I wish I'd known this passage when I overheard a college roommate on the phone with his parents, explaining to them why he'd decided to drop one of his required pre-med classes in order to take African Drum Ensemble instead. "But Mom, Dad, I'm just following Shakespeare's advice!"

→ These lines of early-career Shakespeare flow easily and reveal their sense without requiring too much decoding. A few comments on the handful of terms that are a bit obscure should help get you past any bumps:

- *Stoics / stocks.* This witty little antithesis puns on the ancient Stoic philosophy, a worldview that advocated austerity and repression, and welcomed suffering. *Stocks* are the awkward penal device that restrained a prisoner's legs between large blocks of wood. To compare a person to the stocks is to suggest that person is heavy, dull, and overly restrictive.

- *Aristotle* is here lumped in with the Stoics because he argued that only the contemplative life was worth living, an assertion that earned him a reputation as an ascetic. His *checks* are his principles of monk-like self-denial.

- *Ovid*, apparently Shakespeare's favorite author, was renowned not only for the *Metamorphoses*, his masterpiece about life, death, and transformation, but also for his erotic poetry, which was probably more widely read. His *Ars Amatoria* (*The Art of Love*) features a lot of nudity, by the way.

- To *balk logic* is to banter about that subject; "trade quibbles" would be a decent paraphrase. *Quicken* means "enliven," and *stomach* here means "appetite."

→ An important feature of this speech is the subtle way in which Tranio portrays all philosophy as a big, humorless drag. He manages to make *Aristotle* and *Ovid* into antithetical thinkers, the second a wild and crazy pornographer, the first all heavy and dark. Your listener may not be aware of these aspects of these classic authors' personas, so you must help them hear these qualities as you say the speech. *Aristotle* is a pill, *Ovid* a delight. *Virtue* and *moral philosophy*, *stoics* and *stocks*, are downers. On the other hand, *acquaintance*, *common talk*, *quicken*, and *stomach* are bright, attractive, warm, and fun. It's a question of how you color the words as you say them. If you *think* "spry," "fun," and "gamesome" as you say *quicken*, the word will come out of your mouth so inflected, and the argument you're making will roar to life.

→ *Good mistress* rather than *good master* aims the speech at a woman.

**LET'S FURTHER THINK ON THIS . . .**

—Claudius, *Hamlet*, 4.7.120

Tranio's mentions of *mathematics* and *metaphysics* remind me of two great scholars in those fields who knew their Shakespeare. The prolific Isaac Asimov, writer of science fiction and interpreter to the layman of science's most arcane mysteries, was a devoted Bardophile. His giant *Asimov's Guide to Shakespeare,* at fifteen hundred pages, almost as long as the collection of work it explicates, returns frequently to one aspect of Shakespeare that Asimov particularly admires: his intellect. Here's a description I love about the power of Shakespeare's brain to shape ours:

> ***Shakespeare has said so many things so supremely well that we are forever finding ourselves thinking in his terms.***

Another scientist, Thomas Edison, also found Shakespeare's mental prowess admirable. This is the light the Wizard of Menlo Park shed on the matter:

> ***Ah Shakespeare! He would have been an inventor, a wonderful inventor, if he had turned his mind to it. He seemed to see the inside of everything.***

## LIFE TEACHES THE MOST EFFECTIVE LESSONS

The School of Hard Knocks is the one educational institution in which Shakespeare believes without reservation. Those of his characters who are not SHK alumni teach there, or are otherwise on staff. The "Hell Gate" Porter from *Macbeth* is the school's mascot ("Here's a knocking indeed!"); its fight song, "We must have knocks, ha! Must we not?" was written by King Richard III; and Regan from *King Lear* is headmistress. Here's her view of how life teaches some tough lessons:

> To willful men,
> The injuries that they themselves procure
> Must be their schoolmasters.
>
> —Regan, *King Lear*, 2.4.297–99

***In other words:***

The only way stubborn people learn anything is from the bad situations they create for themselves.

***How to use it:***

- These are my standard words of wisdom for anyone who's painted himself into a corner. Use it to encourage some willful person you care about to learn from his or her mistakes.

Regan's advice may strike some as a tad harsh. If some occasion in your life calls out for a more sympathetic view of life's way of teaching lessons, try this Bardism from Antonio in *Two Gents*.

> Experience is by industry achieved,
> And perfected by the swift course of time.
>
> —Antonio, *The Two Gentlemen of Verona*, 1.3.22–23

***In other words:***

It takes hard work to get good at anything, and the investment of a lot of time to get perfect at it.

***How to use it:***

- Produce these lines as an impressive substitute for "Practice makes perfect." When that same someone you know has once again painted himself into a corner, Shakespearize him with this gentle reminder that it takes work and time to become an assured painter. He'll appreciate it much more than Regan's observation that it's his own fault his life's so tough.

***Some details:***

Sometimes, in the name of fealty to Shakespeare's intentions, we are obliged to speak his lines in ways that sound crazy today. The Bardism from *Two Gents* quoted here offers an example.

According to Antonio, two things are true of experience: it's *achieved*, and then it's *perfected*. Modern English-speakers will pronounce Antonio's second adjective with the accent on its second syllable: *per-FECT-ed*. But if you scan the line according to iambic pentameter, you'll find that that doesn't work and that the perfect pronunciation is actually *PER-fect-ed*:

˘ ´ ˘ ` ˘ ´ ˘ ´ ˘ ´

**and per | fect ed | by the | swift course | of time**

To be sure, choosing to read and work on Shakespeare in the first place requires a commitment to language that's four hundred years old and often odd-sounding as a result. If you're really interested in saying the words he wrote, sometimes you're going to have to say some strange stuff. But sometimes that strangeness can become a barrier between you and your listeners, and can prove confusing or, worse, downright off-putting. If you quote Antonio to your friend who's painted himself into a corner, and tell him that experience is "PER-fect-ed by the swift course of time," he'll look at you like you're dumber than he is. He'll understand your point much more clearly if you insist that experience is "per-FECT-ed." That rumbling you'll feel beneath your feet will be Shakespeare spinning in his grave, and any English teacher in the vicinity might well angrily splatter you with some of your pal's paint. But to insist on correctness at the expense of comprehensibility is a kind of arrogance. Shakespeare himself surely would mock it as misplaced pedantry. Better to violate the letter of his language in order to put across its spirit. Except in the case of flagrant violations, the Shakespeare SWAT team won't arrest you, and you might even win some new friends to the Bard's cause by helping him bridge a gap of four centuries and speak immediately and directly to our time.

## SHAKESPEARE ON THE COMMENCEMENT ADDRESS

*Have more than thou showest,*
*Speak less than thou knowest,*
*Lend less than thou owest,*
*Ride more than thou goest,*
*Learn more than thou trowest,*
*Set less than thou throwest.**

—Fool, *King Lear*, 1.4.101–6

---

* *In other words:* Don't display your wealth too ostentatiously. Don't talk too much. Don't lend more than you can afford. Don't walk when riding is an option. Don't believe everything you hear. Don't bet all your chips on one roll of the dice.

The commencement address is the life occasion that shows in the Shakespeare quotation derby, losing to the wedding and the funeral, the win and place horses, by a nose. Commencement calls for wisdom, warmth, pith, and humor, delivered by eminences whose scars from the battles of life prove that they've earned the right to dispense advice about success, failure, and everything in between. The best of the graduation-day VIPs know that a good speech serves up its sagacity buffet-style, offering a wide menu of counsel that includes morsels helpful to the whole range of the assembled graduates. They understand that there's no better way to appeal to everyone than by reference to recognized authorities and canonical texts that lend their insights the imprimatur of the tried and true.

Recognized authority. Canonical text. Tried and true. Did someone say "Shakespeare"? A quick Lexis search confirms that lots of graduation speakers say his name indeed, and that Shakespeare looks pretty good in a cap and gown. Lexis further reveals that other frequently cited commencement-day doyens look positively haggard in comparison. Abraham Lincoln, Benjamin Franklin, Albert Einstein, Ronald Reagan, Mahatma Gandhi, the rabbis of the Talmud, Winston Churchill, Mark Twain, Bob Dylan, Yogi Berra, Warren Buffett, and, in at least one documented case, Batman—these formidable thinkers may have some pointers for the average baccalaureate, but on those spring mornings when "Pomp and Circumstance" plays, they are but apprentices at the master's feet.

Two Bardisms are the standards on graduation day: the Fool's advice to Lear, above (stopping just before he counsels the old king not to drink too much and not to patronize prostitutes—not because either piece of advice is bad, but because there may be more appropriate times than commencement to express them!), and the one below.

## HERE'S SOME GOOD ADVICE

Polonius' advice to his son, Laertes, is one of Shakespeare's most famous speeches. Its familiarity sometimes turns it into background noise and makes us take it for granted. But look at it closely and you'll find some quite sound recommendations from someone who's been around the block to someone just getting started on life's journey.

These few precepts in thy memory
See thou character. Give thy thoughts no tongue,
Nor any unproportioned thought his act.
Be thou familiar but by no means vulgar.
Those friends thou hast, and their adoption tried,
Grapple them to thy soul with hoops of steel,
But do not dull thy palm with entertainment
Of each new-hatched unfledged comrade. Beware
Of entrance to a quarrel, but being in,
Bear't that th'opposèd may beware of thee.
Give every man thine ear but few thy voice.
Take each man's censure, but reserve thy judgment.
Costly thy habit as thy purse can buy,
But not expressed in fancy; rich not gaudy;
For the apparel oft proclaims the man,
And they in France of the best rank and station
Are of a most select and generous chief in that.
Neither a borrower nor a lender be,
For loan oft loses both itself and friend,
And borrowing dulls the edge of husbandry.
This above all—to thine own self be true,
And it must follow, as the night the day,
Thou canst not then be false to any man.

—POLONIUS, *Hamlet*, 1.3.58–80

***In other words:***

Make sure you carve this handful of principles into your mind. Don't say everything you're thinking, and never take any action before you've fully thought it through. Be friendly, but don't share intimacies with people you've only just met. The friends you already have, whose friendships are tried and tested—hold on to them as tightly as you can. But don't get calluses from shaking hands with every Tom, Dick, or Harry who comes along. Try not to get into fights, but if you do, handle yourself in such a way that the other guy is scared of you. Listen to everyone, but don't talk to everyone. Hear every opinion, but decide things for yourself. Wear the most expensive clothes you can afford, but make sure they're not over the top. They should be elegant, not ostentatious, because your clothes tell people who you are. (The French upper classes really get this, and understand how to display their rank through their fine garments.) Don't borrow money, and don't lend any. Loans go south and take friendships with them, and relying on credit makes you spend too much. Here's the most important thing: be true to yourself. If you do that, then as sure as night follows day, there's no way you'll ever let anybody down.

***How to say it:***

- At twenty-four lines, this is a long and intimidating speech. A great way to tackle it is to break it down into smaller chunks, and then concentrate on communicating each one of these in detail, rather than feeling an obligation to put across the speech as a whole. You can arrange the speech's subunits (actors call them "beats") in a couple of ways.

    - *By punctuation.* Circle each period in the speech. Then, as you read through, force yourself to speak only one sentence at a time. Ten sentences will feel much easier to manage than twenty-five lines.

- *By concept.* Polonius starts with an instruction to his son to remember what he says. Then he does a line and a half about thoughts, speech, and action. Next is a five-line section about how to handle friendship. Next are two short bits, the first about fighting and the second about opinions. Another five-line chunk discusses how best to dress, then three lines talk about money. Finally, Polonius spends three lines giving his most important piece of advice, about being true to yourself. The structure of the thoughts in the speech, then, might be outlined as follows:

  **Advice for My Son**
  - Intro
  - Thoughts / Speech / Action
  - Friendship (dwell on this)
  - Fighting
  - Opinions
  - Clothes (spend some time here; reference the French)
  - Money
  - True to self (most important of all!)

  Try making your way through the speech as though it were a bulleted list, and let its well-organized structure carry you from one thought to the next.

→ Let antithesis help you as much as you can; it's everywhere in these lines. *Thoughts* versus *tongue*; *unproportioned thought* versus *act*; *familiar* versus *vulgar*; *beware of entrance* versus *beware of thee*; *every man* versus *few*; *ear* versus *voice*; *take censure* versus *reserve judgment*; *rich* versus *gaudy*; *apparel* versus *man*; *borrower* versus *lender*; *loan* versus *borrowing*; *night* versus *day*; *thine own self* versus *any man*; *true* versus *false*.

→ Technically, line 2's *character* is stressed on the second syllable: ka-RACK-ter. Try it, but don't worry if you'd rather let it slide.

- Polonius is often played as a pompous windbag condescending to his son, who, in contemptuous response, spends the whole speech rolling his eyes with boredom and disgust. I don't buy it. First, Shakespeare puts this scene in the play in order to establish the bond of warmth and fondness between Laertes and his father that will help fuel Laertes' revenge when he discovers later that Polonius has been murdered. This dramatic function must fail if the two men make no connection here. Second, the speech's verbs hardly suggest that Polonius is distracted, distant, or careless about his son's welfare. Consider a list: *character, give, be, grapple, dull, beware, bear, give, take, reserve, buy, proclaims, be, loses, dulls, be, follow, be*. There's real vitality here. This isn't some bloviating dad wheeling out a bunch of tired old saws; this is an engaged parent doing everything he can to help his child make the most out of life. Take Polonius seriously, and as you say his words, or write them, or write about them, give yourself the chance to hear and appreciate them even as you generously and with thoughtfulness propose them to your younger charges.
- Feel free to cut the two lines about what great dressers the French are, unless, of course, you're giving the commencement address at the Sorbonne.

## IT'S GREAT TO USE YOUR IMAGINATION

I've never been asked to give a commencement address, but if ever I am, I'll turn to a favorite Bardism that offers some life advice I truly value. (The line itself is a lot shorter than Polonius' speech, too, which I suspect my future listeners will appreciate.)

> Much virtue in "if."
>
> —Touchstone, *As You Like It*, 5.4.92

***Some details:***

This is one of those impossible-to-paraphrase Shakespearean snippets that say in four words what would take most of us a paragraph to communicate. I suppose "It's good to dream" will do as a quick translation into modern English, or perhaps "Fantasy is very important," or "Idealism can be useful," but these don't quite cover everything Touchstone means. John Lennon's song *Imagine* could be construed as a commentary on the line, as could every comic book ever written, movie ever made, or invention ever conjured from the recesses of some visionary's mind. The line is Shakespeare's great call to make the world a better place, to yearn for a better way. "If" makes anything possible: science, politics, love itself. A car that can get eighty miles per gallon of gasoline? "If." Want to marry that sparkly-eyed, raven-haired girl? "If." Middle East peace? "Your 'if' is the only peacemaker," says Touchstone.

"Much virtue in 'if'" is perfect Shakespeare for the Occasion of Commencement, because it's perfect Shakespeare for Inspiration, and ideal Shakespeare for the Occasion of the World Being Your Oyster.

## SHAKESPEARE ON SPORTS AND EXERCISE

> *I'll make sport with thee.*
>
> —Lafeu, *All's Well That Ends Well*, 5.3.319

A proud Shakespeare geek, I don't mind sharing tales of some of my geekiest Shakespeare moments. Most date from my years as a graduate student at Oxford, which is not surprising, not because one's years in grad school are geeky by definition (although they are), nor because I was living Shakespeare 24/7/365 at the time (although I was), but because that great university city's dreaming spires soar through air that flows into town from nearby Warwickshire, Shakespeare's home turf. It's hard not to become intoxicated by the fresh, crisp scent of the Cotswolds as it hits the nostrils. Allowing oneself that little nip of English countryside intoxicant is the first step down the slippery slope of unregenerate Shakespeare geekdom. To wit:

- There was the time while visiting Scotland that I drove from Birnam Wood to Dunsinane. I wanted to affix some branches to the car in fulfillment of the witches' prediction to Macbeth that the forest would march this route, but the friend I was traveling with nixed it.
- There was the time late one night I snuck onto the darkened stage of the Royal Shakespeare Theatre in Stratford, yelled, "O for a muse of fire!" and fled into the wings before anyone could alert security.
- And there was the time I sat on a country hillside and read aloud the wrestling scene from *As You Like It* to the only audience around on a Tuesday afternoon in spring: an indifferent flock of sheep.

I flatter myself that recovering Shakespeare geeks and even non-initiates might have done more or less what I did in the first two situations. The third, perhaps, requires some explanation.

I gave my ovine command performance at a place called Dover's Hill, a bucolic escarpment that overlooks the picture-postcard-perfect Cotswold village of Chipping Camden, about ten miles south of Shakespeare's hometown of Stratford-upon-Avon. The hill's claim to fame is that its namesake, Shakespeare's contemporary Robert Dover, began in the early 1600s to hold an annual festival there designed to counter England's prevailing atmosphere of Puritanical restraint with a few days of fun. The festival featured food, drink, music, and dancing, of course, but the main attraction was a series of sporting competitions Dover called the "Cotswold Olimpicks." Events included cross-country races, horse racing, fencing, jumping, hammer throwing, and one sport that really should make an Olympic comeback: shin kicking. (The best way I can describe it is to point out that the Cotswold Olimpicks are today again an annual celebration on Dover's Hill, and the 2007 Shin Kicking Champion is named—and you can Google it if you don't believe me—"Stupid Steve.")

As entertaining as they were, however, all these events were mere prologue to the games' centerpiece: wrestling. Some say that it's these Cotswold Olimpick bouts that Shakespeare has in mind in the contest between Orlando and Charles the Wrestler in Act 1 of *As You Like It*, and that's why I journeyed there to read the scene.

Wrestling may be the only sport that gets its own Shakespearean scene, but it's by no means the only one mentioned in the canon. Shakespeare talks about tennis, football, equestrianism, fencing, and even some sports he didn't even know he was talking about. Here, then, Shakespeare on the Occasion of the Many Games of the Olimpicks.

## A DAILY CONSTITUTIONAL IS GOOD FOR THE MIND

Shakespeare was way ahead of the cadres of fitness gurus who preach the gospel of daily exercise and its benefits both physical and emotional. Here's the Bard's take:

> **A turn or two I'll walk / To still my beating mind.**
>
> —Prospero, *The Tempest*, 4.1.162–63

***In other words:***

I'll take a little walk to decompress a bit.

## I'M GOING FOR A RUN

Rise early, pull on your Nikes, and, as you hit the road for your morning five miles, listen to this fun Shakespeare song on your iPod:

> Jog on, jog on, the footpath way,
> And merrily hent the stile-a.
> A merry heart goes all the day,
> Your sad tires in a mile-a.
>
> —AUTOLYCUS, *The Winter's Tale*, 4.2.113–16

***In other words:***

Go for a run, go for a run, along the country trail. When you come to a fence, be happy and grab the gate. A happy soul can run all day. A sad sack's exhausted after one mile.

**LET'S FURTHER THINK ON THIS . . .**

Shaquille O'Neal spoke from his heart when the L.A. Lakers won the NBA Championship in 2000, and his heart spoke the words of the Bard. At a rally attended by more than two hundred thousand giddy fans in downtown Los Angeles, he paraphrased *Twelfth Night* as he rendered judgment on what he and his teammates had achieved. "Some men are born great, some achieve greatness, and some have greatness thrust upon them," he told the crowd. Shaq didn't specify which of the three categories his Lakers brought to mind, but he did add a thought

(*Continued*)

that would have sent chills through the starchy and reserved Malvolio, who says the famous line about greatness: "I love ya. Thank you for your support. I love you." A few days earlier, Shaq told reporters that he wanted to be known as "the Big Aristotle," and then quoted the philosopher at a press conference ("Excellence is not a singular act, but a habit"), but at the Championship rally he amended that request. "I want to be 'the Big Shakespeare,'" he told his fans. He earned that moniker that afternoon, so by the power vested in me by Hamlet, Prince of Denmark, I hereby pronounce the name change official.

## WE SWAM LIKE HECK

This vivid description of swimmers making their way through a raging river is worthy of the best play-by-play announcer or the finest narration of some Michael Phelps gold medal triumph. Work all its verbs and verb forms and you'll hear in the very sound of the language itself the gargantuan physical effort it describes. Switch *we* to *he* or *she*, and you've got the perfect Shakespeare to Describe Your Kid's High School Swim Meet.

> The torrent roared, and we did buffet it
> With lusty sinews, throwing it aside,
> And stemming it with hearts of controversy.
>
> —Cassius, *Julius Caesar*, 1.2.109–11

***In other words:***

The water thundered along, and we punched it, our muscles throbbing. We threw it out of our way, and fought it with struggle in our hearts.

## THREE MODERN SPORTS

Here's Shakespeare on the Occasion of a Line Drive to Center Field:

> **A hit, a very palpable hit.**
>
> —Osric, *Hamlet*, 5.2.223

And Shakespeare for the Occasion of Rebuffing an Insult from Brett Favre:

> **You base football player.**
>
> —Kent, *King Lear*, 1.4.74

And when you finally grow sick of waking up stiff and feeling like your spine is as rigid as the steel in the Eiffel Tower, here's Shakespeare for the Occasion of Learning Vinyasa Yoga:

> ANTONIO **I'll teach you how to flow.**
> SEBASTIAN **Do so. To ebb**
> **Hereditary sloth instructs me.**
>
> —*The Tempest*, 2.1.218–19

*Hereditary sloth* means "genetic laziness." Exactly the factor that keeps couch potatoes, Shakespearean or not, away from the yoga studio.

**LET'S FURTHER THINK ON THIS . . .**

Baseball color commentary is replete with memorably stirring lines—"Holy cow!" and "How *'bout* that!" and "That ball's *outta* here!"—but I know of no Al Michaels nor Mel Allen who could beat the late Ned

(*Continued*)

Martin, longtime radio voice of the Boston Red Sox, for sheer literary aplomb. Martin used to quote from *Hamlet* whenever things started to go south for the boys in Fenway. He didn't choose an obvious line, like "Something's rotten in the state of Massachusetts" or "O, what a rogue and peasant slave is this pitcher!" He turned instead to King Claudius, and quoted him verbatim:

**O Gertrude, Gertrude,**
**When sorrows come, they come not single spies,**
**But in battalions.**

Top *that*, Phil Rizzuto!

## SHAKESPEARE ON HOLIDAYS

*Now I am in a holiday humor.*
—Rosalind, *As You Like It*, 4.1.59

Shakespeare celebrates a number of annual holidays in his works. Many are saints' days, the commemorations that organize the Christian calendar around the dates of the deaths of martyrs. St. Crispin's Day, St. David's Day, and St. George's Day receive special mention, and if Sts. David and Crispin can thank Shakespeare for a measure of their posthumous fame, only George, patron saint of England, can boast that his day marks not only his slaying of the dragon but also the birth of Shakespeare himself. Some, but not all, of the major Christian festivals merit mentions in the plays, and a few pagan and ancient Roman celebrations—Hey, gang, it's Lupercal!—get an airing, too.

The search for Shakespeare's favorite holiday ends in vain. He doesn't seem partial to any one celebration, and, indeed, in *King John*, he offers an appealingly New Age formula for making every day a special day:

> To solemnize this day, the glorious sun
> Stays in his course and plays the alchemist,
> Turning with splendor of his precious eye
> The meagre cloddy earth to glittering gold.
> The yearly course that brings this day about
> Shall never see it but a holy day.
>
> —King Philip, *King John*, 3.1.3–8

What a beautiful thought: the sun in his orbit is an alchemist, whose bright rays turn the thin, lumpy earth into magnificent gold; he makes this day special, solemn, and holy, and will do the same every year. These six lines fashion a one-size-fits-all Shakespeare on the Occasion of a Holiday, but on those days that call for something more specific, the list below will serve.

## NEW YEAR'S

Here is Shakespeare's great New Year's resolution to cast off the bad old ways and move into a future resplendent with newness and promise. Turn to it next New Year's Eve, and by the vernal equinox you'll be skinnier, happier, in better shape, and wealthier than you could ever have imagined. And if you aren't, so what? Iambic pentameter goes great with champagne.

> We will . . . like a bated and retirèd flood,
> Leaving our rankness and irregular course,

Stoop low within those bounds we have o'erlooked,
And calmly run on in obedience
Even to our ocean. . . . Away, my friends! New flight,
And happy newness that intends old right.

—Salisbury, *King John*, 5.4.52–61

***In other words:***

Like a flood that has abated and shrunk, we will give up our unruliness and misbehaving ways. We'll drop back below the banks we've overrun, and we'll flow calmly and respectfully toward the ocean. Let's get going, friends! A new journey begins! And it's a happy new journey, because it's aimed at time-tested better ways!

***How to say it:***

- The language in this speech nicely suggests through the metaphor of a roiling, flooding river, the inappropriateness and turbulence of the old behavior your New Year's resolution is meant to undo. It then characterizes the healthfulness of the new behavior toward which you aspire, with such phrases as *stoop low* and *calmly run* and the words *obedience* and *happy*. As you say the speech, give as much vocal color and expressiveness as you can to each side of the image. That is, make *rankness* and *irregular course* really paint a word picture of the terrible habits you're trying to reform, and put into *happy newness* all the joy your reformation will bring.
- Note that the final two lines of the speech rhyme. They happen also to be the final lines of this scene. In his early plays, of which *King John* is one, Shakespeare does this a lot, ending many scenes with *rhyming couplets*. He uses them as a signal to the audience that the scene is over, harnessing their special sound, in particular the sense of closure it conveys, to bring matters to a rousing finish. "The play's the thing / Wherein I'll catch the conscience of

the king" is one famous example; "Never was a story of more woe / Than this of Juliet and her Romeo" is another. Rhyming couplets have a special zing, an uncommon energy, and should be used to give the language punch and vitality.

→ Ignore the ellipses, which mark material I've cut, in this case a few words specific to the state of the dynastic battles that drive the plot of *King John*.

**LET'S FURTHER THINK ON THIS . . .**

Shakespeare's only mention of Valentine's Day is in a bawdy song sung by the mad Ophelia in *Hamlet*, and it's not for a family-oriented book. Fortunately, another Shakespearean Valentine's Day tie-in has filled the breach. Back in the bad old days of the late 1990s, that time of stained blue dresses and disquisitions on what the meaning of the word *is* is, independent counsel Kenneth Starr submitted to Congress his report on his investigations into President Clinton's alleged wrongdoings with White House intern Monica Lewinsky. The nation learned to its surprise that Shakespeare was near the heart of the story. To mark Valentine's Day 1998, Monica placed a personal ad in the *Washington Post*. It read as follows:

> ***Handsome,***
> ***With love's light wings did I o'er perch these walls:***
> ***For stony limits cannot hold love out,***
> ***And what love can do, that dares love attempt.***
> **Romeo and Juliet *2:2.***
> ***Happy Valentine's Day.***
> ***M.***

(*Continued*)

Monica had been transferred from her White House job to a post at the Pentagon, far from the Oval Office. She complained bitterly that her access to the president was being unfairly restricted, and she vowed that she'd find some way to see him, no matter what it took. The lines she placed in her *Post* ad are Romeo's passionate protestation that whatever barriers the Capulet family might place in his way, he'd manage somehow to see his beloved Juliet. Perhaps today Monica recognizes in hindsight that this may not have been the best Bardism to choose—after all, *Romeo and Juliet* doesn't exactly end well. But then again, neither did *The Most Excellent and Lamentable Tragedy of Clinton and Lewinsky.*

## HALLOWEEN

Shakespeare for the Occasion of Trick-or-Treaters at the Door:

> **We talk with goblins, owls, and sprites.**
>
> —Dromio of Syracuse, *The Comedy of Errors*, 2.2.190

## THANKSGIVING

We'll see some Shakespearean expressions of gratitude in Chapter Five. Here, a Bardistic prayer of thanksgiving, suitable for offering after you've made it over the river and through the woods, but before you tuck into that nicely carved bird.

> **O Lord, that lends me life,**
> **Lend me a heart replete with thankfulness!**

For thou hast given me . . .
A world of earthly blessings to my soul.

—King Henry, *Henry VI, Part II*, 1.1.19–22

Oh, and if, when that bird is carved, it looks like fiberboard, all desiccated and inedible, here's a Bardism that will allow you to scoot out gracefully and make your way to the neighborhood pizza joint:

I cannot stay thanksgiving.

—Berowne, *Love's Labour's Lost*, 2.1.192

## CHRISTMAS

The magic of Christmas is explained in beguiling terms near the beginning of *Hamlet*. This lyrical vision of peace and universal serenity would soften the stony heart of Ebeneezer Scrooge himself.

Some say that ever 'gainst that season comes
Wherein our savior's birth is celebrated
The bird of dawning singeth all night long;
And then, they say, no spirit can walk abroad,
The nights are wholesome; then no planets strike,
No fairy takes, nor witch hath power to charm,
So hallowed and so gracious is the time.

—Marcellus, *Hamlet*, 1.1.139–45

***In other words:***

Some people say that every Christmastime, the morning cock crows all night long. What's more, they say that at that time, no ghosts walk around. Nighttime is holy and safe. Negative cosmic forces hold no sway. Fairies don't bewitch, and witches lose their power to cast spells. That's how much that time of year is sanctified and blessed by God's grace.

***How to use it:***

- I once recommended this passage to an artist friend who was seeking something unique for a Christmas card. She painted a gorgeous watercolor of a "hallowed and gracious" winter night that rendered Shakespeare's imagery in visual terms as enchanting as his verbal ones. There was a little rooster in the corner, crowing to the moon, across whose face Santa and his reindeer flew, like E.T. in his bicycle basket. By all means take a leaf from her book and, whether or not you create your own artistic analogue of them, share with your friends and loved ones this splendid vision of why the end of December is always so sweet and blissful a time.

***Some details:***

Scholars report that no source has ever been found for the soldier Marcellus' assertion that cocks crow all night at Christmas, and that there's not much evidence of Elizabethan lore supporting his view that Christmas Eve was a night off for witches, fairies, and evil spirits. No matter. The only evidence Marcellus requires is what he's seen with his own eyes. Just moments prior to this speech, the ghost of old King Hamlet "faded on the crowing of the cock," that is, disappeared when a cock crowed. That's enough to convince Marcellus that benevolent Yuletide energies must be at work. Even Horatio, the German-educated rationalist of the play, dials down his skepticism of the supernatural, conceding to Marcellus at the end of this speech, "So have I heard, and do in part believe it."

It's hard to make much headway with Shakespeare without embracing Horatio's concession. The supernatural is everywhere in the plays. Ghosts, fairies, otherworldly visions, mysterious sounds that emanate unexplained from belowground—the plays overflow with them. For all his precocious grasp of the pragmatic forces that drive human events, Shakespeare still lived in a pre-Enlightenment world in which superstition, folklore, and faith provided more answers than science, ideology, and reason. In my experience, this aspect of his works is the hardest for contemporary artists and audiences to grasp, because it requires a near-complete surrender of the modern world's armature of logic, rationality, and analysis. But in Shakespeare, the boundary between the real world and the spirit world is porous, and the impossible dwells cheek by jowl with the quotidian. If, like Horatio, an actor, director, or audience member can believe it—in part, even—then Shakespeare is a portal to a richer universe in which faith and reason coexist, and in which possibility is limited only by one's powers of language to describe it. Absent an imaginative leap that allows for meaning in the ineffable and substance in the incorporeal, Shakespeare is just melodrama with fancier words.

"There are more things in heaven and earth, Horatio, / Than are dreamt of in your philosophy," says Hamlet to his still-doubting friend. That's Shakespeare speaking, directly to us.

## BIRTHDAYS

One of the very first times I raided my *Complete Works of Shakespeare* for the purposes of public speaking was in preparation to give a toast on the occasion of a theater colleague's fiftieth birthday, many years ago. (He wouldn't want his age revealed, so let's preserve his anonymity and call him "Bob.") I related my search process to the crowd assembled at Bob's surprise party, and I here reprint an excerpt of my remarks as an example of how to deploy Bardisms for a birthday:

When Bob's wife asked me to make a toast today, I figured that since Bob and I both work in the classical theater, some appropriate Shakespearean tribute would just pop right into my head.

No such luck. Although Shakespeare is full of eloquent encomia to great men, almost all of them are made after the great man has died. Now, fifty may be getting up there, but we're not exactly about to call the undertaker. So I started digging around.

The word *birth* appears about one hundred times in Shakespeare (102 to be exact). *Day*, about one thousand. *Birthday*, though, shows up only twice (thrice if you count *Pericles*, but since Shakespeare didn't write all of that play, I'm going to overlook it). Here they are:

Cleopatra says in Act 3 of her play, "It is my birthday."

Cassius in Act 5 of *Julius Caesar* says: "This is my birthday, as this very day / Was Cassius born."

Not much to write home about there. So I changed direction. *Surprise* shows up about thirty times. There's "We may surprise and take him at our pleasure" (that's Warwick in *Henry VI, Part III*) and "You'll be surprised. Muster your wits" (that's Boyet in *Love's Labour's Lost*). Had we gone to Italy to celebrate Bob's fiftieth, I could have used this: "I with a troop of Florentines will suddenly surprise him" (that's the second Lord Dumaine in *All's Well That Ends Well*; don't even ask what the first Lord Dumaine has to say).

Striking out with *birthday* and *surprise*, I turned to *fifty*. Lots to choose from. Falstaff says this in *Henry IV, Part I*: "As I think, his age some fifty, or by'r lady, inclining to three score." But I know Bob's having enough trouble with two and a half score, so I don't want to push him to three prematurely. Charmian in *Antony and Cleopatra* says, "Let me have a child at fifty," but with Bob's kids finally off to college, I'm not sure this one's so apt.

Finally, I decided to shift gears, leave the plays behind, and turn to those poetical repositories of wit and wisdom, Shakespeare's sonnets. Here's the opening of number 104, and with it, I raise my glass to Bob, with love and warmest birthday wishes.

> To me, fair friend, you never can be old,
> For as you were when first your eye I eyed,
> Such seems your beauty still.
>
> —SONNET 104, 1–3

Bob loved it. Everyone wants to know that their good looks remain intact as the years march forward, and despite the absence of any specific mention of birthdays—or, for that matter, surprises, or the birthday boy or girl's age—these three lines fit the bill. Use them with my blessing, and with Bob's, too.

CHAPTER 3

# And Then the Lover

## SHAKESPEARE FOR THE OCCASIONS OF *L'AMOUR*

*And then the lover,*
*Sighing like furnace, with a woeful ballad*
*Made to his mistress' eyebrow.*

The third of Jaques' Seven Ages of Man describes that momentous time when love first blooms, signaling the end of childhood and the imminent start of adult life. Jaques renders the previous two ages, infant and schoolboy, in images of near-photographic realism, and describes the subsequent four, virility through senility, in terms as pitying as they are precise. Only in Age Three, the Lover, does he allow himself—does Shakespeare allow him—a slightly different, somewhat more cavalier tone. Perhaps this is because apparently Jaques was once quite the Casanova: "Thou thyself hast been a libertine," Duke Senior tells him a few moments before Jaques launches into his famous seven-part speech. This revelation always comes as a surprise in the theater. We can well imagine the acerbic, contrarian, and dark-as-Turkish-coffee soul we see before us as a squalling infant, and his diffident and difficult personality suggests that his school days weren't exactly a lark. But a lover? It's an intriguing prospect, and it makes us wonder just who were the women (or men, or both) who once came under his spell, and from whom, if the duke is to be believed, Jaques contracted enough venereal diseases to leave him with plentiful "émbossed sores and headed evils." In the third age of his own life, in other words, Jaques was no swooning swain, but was instead a syphilitic cicisbeo.

Given this squalid past, Jaques' flip fillip here is quite delicious. He depicts the typical lover not as a lothario like himself, but instead as an over-the-top hothouse flower issuing amatory sighs of Bessemer intensity. Pining away, the lover waxes poetical not about his beloved's winning personality, her heartwarming smile, or that magical week they once spent snorkeling in Cabo, but instead about those majestic twin arches of short hair that so beguilingly line the ridges on his inamorata's brow. It's quite mad.

With this outlandish construction, Jaques squeezes into sixteen short words an entire literary tradition of overcooked love poetry. He knows—Shakespeare knows—that something about love encourages poets to turn up the heat. After all, does anyone but a love poet *really* wish, for instance, to die with Wendy on the street tonight in an everlasting kiss, or actually believe that, say, a full moon shining bright strikes the retina in the shape of a big pizza pie? There's a craziness to such images, an excessiveness that neatly manages to capture and express the wild hormonal rush that is first love. The magnificent insanity of a love poem written about an eyebrow lends to the Third Age of Man a certain loony aspect and makes this affectionate, if nonetheless scornful, image the most captivating one in a speech chockablock with stunners.

Consider how Shakespeare—how Jaques—puts the image together. First, note the extraordinarily melodic word music of its second line, and in particular its orotund vowels. The complaining long *i* in *sighing*; the extended, all-consuming *ur* in *furnace*, the woebegone long *o* in *woeful*, and the muffled shriek of *ballad*'s short *a*—*aahhhhyyyeee, ohhhhhhh, urrrrrrrr, aaaaaaaaaa*—together these keening notes make a tone poem of lovelorn agony with more minor-key modulations than a Schoenberg chorale. Next, note where the line ends: After *ballad* but before *made*, or, put another way, smack in the middle of the single idea *ballad made*. This, you will recall from "Seven Steps to Shipshape Shakespeare," is called a run-on line ending, and it creates that important springboard to thought that gives to Shakespearean verse its special feeling of spontaneity and naturalism. The lover writes a ballad . . . *to what?* To his lover's beauty? To his own besotted bliss? To the exquisite mystery of love itself? No. Something much more unexpected. He writes a ballad . . . *to what? . . . wait for it . . . okay, get this! . . . ready? . . .* to his mistress' eyebrow! The line ending after *ballad* gives Jaques an opportunity to find this bizarre and deflating image, to coin it in the moment, to click on the Google in his brain and send it searching for the perfect, most arresting, most memorable image of the silly lengths to which love pushes us.

Many of Shakespeare's observations on love share with Jaques the view that this emotion is one of extremes, and that it drives lovers to sighing, ballad singing, and other, even more outré behaviors. "We that are true lovers run into strange capers," says Touchstone, in the same play as Jaques. The detail in which Shakespeare particularizes these capers in all their lunatic strangeness is what makes his Bardisms on love some of his most poetically efficacious writing. Of course, the excerpts below, which look at love in so many of its manifestations and configurations, which unfold so broad a range of its joys and stings, represent only a tiny fraction of everything

Shakespeare wrote on the subject. Still, they present a rather astonishing demonstration of the powers of a poet who, like Jaques, can conjure the affect he describes even while he's busy describing it. Shakespeare on love, alongside perhaps only Shakespeare on death, is Shakespeare distilled to his very essence. It is Shakespeare expressing emotion at its purest, rendering life at its most recognizable, and composing language at its most fluent, telling, and revelatory.

## SHAKESPEARE ON LOVE

*Love is a spirit all compact of fire.*
—*Venus and Adonis*, 149

"It's made entirely out of fire," Venus says of love in Shakespeare's narrative poem *Venus and Adonis*, and she should know: she's the goddess of love, after all. It's an interesting choice of imagery. Love isn't made of sugar or fields of lavender or the colors of the rainbow, but of something hot and dangerous. Fire is a substance with definite mass and presence, yet it's neither solid nor liquid. It's something in between, something harder to define, ephemeral, impossible to contain. It also happens to be lighter than air. Venus says this line while describing herself as so love-struck by the gorgeous Adonis that she will, "Like a nymph, with long, disheveled hair, / Dance on the sands, and yet no footing seen." That is, she'll be magical, a dancer whose feet never touch the ground. There's an extravagance to this image, a sense of almost drunken abandon. That's why Venus says love is a *spirit* made of fire: she means it's a spirit in the same way that whiskey or gin is one—it's a liquor that intoxicates.

The notion that love is a mind-altering substance underpins *Venus and Adonis*. One of Shakespeare's two long narrative poems, it was his first work to reach print. The twelve-hundred-line poem is based on a story in Ovid's *Metamorphoses* in which Venus decides to sleep with a mortal and chooses the preternaturally handsome Adonis as the best candidate. The majority of the poem relates the increasingly erotic things Venus says as she tries to bed the young man. Though never explicit, some of her more suggestive passages are hot enough to make even Larry Flynt blush. (No doubt this accounted for the poem's runaway success in the buttoned-down 1590s.) The poem introduces some ideas Shakespeare will return to repeatedly in his ensuing two decades of writing. The misery of unrequited love is one. The imprecision of gender stereotypes is another (in this poem it's the woman who's the aggressor and the man who is the coy and demure object of desire). The intense sexual attractiveness of beautiful young men is a third, and a fourth, related to the third, is the fluidity of human sexuality and its resistance to categorization and restraint.

But the most important contribution of *Venus and Adonis* to the rest of Shakespeare's output is the poem's conception of love itself. Like the burning spirit it's compact of, Shakespeare's love is impossible to pin down, ever-changing, and can veer in an instant from being a source of comfort to one of destruction. The love of Venus for Adonis is simultaneously comic and tragic, exalted and silly, pathetic and transcendent. It's fiery love, Shakespeare-style.

## LOVE IS THE GREATEST THING EVER

Venus may be the goddess of love, but not even the considerable expressive gifts she displays in her attempted seduction of Adonis can encapsulate in language everything that makes love so powerful a force in human affairs. For this, we must turn to another character from an early Shakespeare work: Berowne, the anti-romantic romantic hero of *Love's Labour's Lost.*

In the play's first scene, he, the young King Ferdinand of Navarre, and their friends Longaville and Dumaine sign a contract binding themselves to three years of cloistered, full-time study. The four swear to fast one day each week, to sleep only three hours per night, and to have no contact with girls. That last codicil turns out to be the deal breaker. No sooner has the ink on the ascetic contract dried than someone remembers that the beautiful princess of France and three of her ladies are about to arrive in town. So much for the library. The rest of the play is about the ways the young men wriggle out of their commitment to books and into the arms of the gals. By Act 4, everyone realizes they've broken their oaths, and Berowne offers an analysis of what it's all meant. He discourses on how wrong the friends were to forswear women in the first place, and how love itself, not books, is the best education a young man can get. Book knowledge, he argues, resides only in a person's head,

But love, first learnèd in a lady's eyes,
Lives not alone immurèd in the brain,
But with the motion of all elements
Courses as swift as thought in every power,
And gives to every power a double power
Above their functions and their offices.
It adds a precious seeing to the eye—
A lover's eyes will gaze an eagle blind.
A lover's ear will hear the lowest sound
When the suspicious head of theft is stopped.
Love's feeling is more soft and sensible
Than are the tender horns of cockled snails.

Love's tongue proves dainty Bacchus gross in taste.
For valor, is not Love a Hercules,
Still climbing trees in the Hesperides?
Subtle as Sphinx, as sweet and musical
As bright Apollo's lute strung with his hair;
And when Love speaks, the voice of all the gods
Make heaven drowsy with the harmony.
Never durst poet touch a pen to write
Until his ink were tempered with love's sighs;
O, then his lines would ravish savage ears,
And plant in tyrants mild humility.

—BEROWNE, *Love's Labour's Lost*, 4.3.301–23

***In other words:***

Love, discovered by gazing into the eyes of a woman, is not sealed up tight in the brain. Instead, it moves like storms and wind, as quickly as thought itself, into every human faculty. In fact, it enhances the faculties, giving each one powers well beyond its normal functions.

Love makes the eyes see things in special ways. A lover's eyesight is so acute that an eagle, renowned for its excellent vision, would seem blind in comparison. A lover's ears can hear sounds quieter than even thieves can hear, and thieves must be capable of hearing the slightest noise. A lover's touch is more sensitive than the extremely sensitive horns of snails. Compared to love's, the famously discerning palate of Bacchus, god of wine, is clumsy.

When it comes to bravery, isn't love like Hercules, picking golden apples in the last of his twelve labors? Love's as intellectually sophisticated as the Sphinx, with her insoluble riddle. It's as lively as the lute of Apollo, god of music, which was strung with his own hair. And when love talks, the voices of the gods themselves join in, and together they sing a sweet lullaby to the heavens. No poet dares pick up a pen unless his ink is mixed with love's sighs. If it is, then his poetry will soothe wild beasts and infuse tyrants with gentleness and patience.

***How to say it:***

- This speech is great for any occasion on which love is the prime mover: an engagement party, a wedding, a landmark anniversary. It's especially useful in the case of a love that has triumphed against long odds or formidable obstacles. Also, I know of at least one instance when someone sent these lines to a lover to tell her that her love had made him a better person. All you need is a little intro in which you say that you're going to talk about the powerful force that brought everyone together today, or that changed your life: love.

- Like any long speech, this one becomes a bit easier to handle once it's broken up into smaller chunks. Work through the speech in four short, self-contained sections, divided as follows:

    - Lines 1 through 6 set up the central conceit that love endows the human senses with special powers (and feel free to cut *but* in line 1 so you can start with a forceful and direct declaration).

    - Lines 7 through 13 discuss some of these senses and present examples of how love improves them. Think of them as a list: (a) lover's *eye* (precious seeing / gaze eagle blind); (b) lover's *ear* (softest sound / thief can't hear); (c) love's *feeling* (more sensitive than a snail); (d) lover's *tongue* (more refined than Bacchus').

    - Lines 14 through 19 talk about love's effect on more abstract human qualities. Again, Berowne makes a list: (a) bravery (like Hercules and the Hesperides [pronounced *hess-PERR-i-deez*]); (b) sophistication (like the Sphinx); (c) musical ability (like Apollo's); (d) voice (gods join in / lull heavens to sleep).

- Lines 20 through 24 explain love's importance to poetry and suggest its ability to becalm rage and turn evil to good.

→ Berowne uses some great verbs, and you should exploit their power. Here are some I think are most useful: *Lives*; *Courses*; *gives*; *adds*; *gaze*; *hear*; *proves*; *Make*; *touch*; *write*; *ravish*; *plant*.*

## SHAKESPEARE TO SAY "I LOVE YOU"

*Hear my soul speak.*
*The very instant that I saw you did*
*My heart fly to your service.*
—FERDINAND, *The Tempest*, 3.1.63–65

I love you. Three little words that can move mountains. Shakespeare writes many versions of them, some in more than three words, and the mountains he moves are bigger than the whole wide world. Below is a selection of the Bard's vows of love. If you don't know the occasions on which they're best used, then I'm not going to tell you.

### I LOVE YOU

Here's the basic, no-frills Shakespeare on the Occasion of Saying the L-Word.

---

* *Make* is in the plural (as opposed to *makes*) because its subject is "the voices of all the gods" in Berowne's previous line. But wait a minute! He says "the *voice* of all the gods," as though they all share only one larynx. This is one of Shakespeare's syntactical quirks. He often omits the final *s* in the plural of words ending in *–ce*. Why? You'll have to ask him. Meanwhile, it's *voice make*, not *voices make* or *voice makes*.

> Excellent wretch! Perdition catch my soul
> But I do love thee, and when I love thee not,
> Chaos is come again.
>
> —OTHELLO, *Othello*, 3.3.91–93

***In other words:***

You superb little devil! I'll be damned, but I love you. And when I don't, it will be the end of the world.

***Some details:***

Othello clearly means *wretch* affectionately, but decorous eighteenth- and nineteenth-century Shakespeare editors had trouble with the notion that Shakespeare would employ such a coarse word as a term of endearment. Hence they theorized that it must have been an unfortunate misprint. "I make no question but that the poet wrote *wench*," argued one expert, "which was not then used in that low and vulgar acceptation as at present." This is pure supposition, of course, and a later editor offered a commentary on *wretch* that will more than suffice for anyone who would use these lines as a modern expression of love: "Such words of endearment are resorted to when those implying love, admiration, and delight seem inadequate."

## I REALLY LOVE YOU

It's an understatement to say that the marriage of Othello and Desdemona doesn't turn out well. But the spectacular violence in which it goes down in flames does nothing to erase the intense love that set it afire in the first place. Indeed, the depth of the passion that prompted the marriage is precisely what makes its horrible dénouement so tragic. Here's another of Othello's oaths of love for his cherished wife.

> If it were now to die
> 'Twere now to be most happy, for I fear
> My soul hath her content so absolute
> That not another comfort like to this
> Succeeds in unknown fate.
>
> —OTHELLO, *Othello*, 2.1.186–89

***In other words:***

If it were my fate to die at this very instant, it would be my good fortune. I'm afraid that I am so totally and completely joyous right now, that there's no way I could ever experience anything as positive again in the future.

***How to use it:***

- This is an "I love you" to be saved for one of those rare moments when everything in life lines up perfectly. It's for a breathtaking sunset on the beach, for an "I'm the king of the world" howl at the prow of an ocean liner, for some intimate pillow talk, for the dessert course at the Michelin three-star restaurant you visit on your honeymoon.
- By the way, the soul is always female in Shakespeare, regardless of the gender of the body that contains it.

## I ADORE YOU, SO PLEASE LOVE ME IN RETURN

Sometimes we want to say "I love you" to someone we're not sure loves us back. Or to someone we know for sure doesn't love us back. Or to someone we once saw across a crowded room, or on a bus, or wearing nothing but underwear on a billboard in Times Square, who would certainly love us back if only they could somehow meet us. On such an occasion, we can turn to this Bardism, one of Shakespeare's most poignant expressions of hopeless, selfless, stars-in-the-eyes-but-sighs-in-the-heart love.

> So holy and so perfect is my love,
> And I in such a poverty of grace,
> That I shall think it a most plenteous crop
> To glean the broken ears after the man
> That the main harvest reaps. Loose now and then
> A scattered smile, and that I'll live upon.
>
> —SILVIUS, *As You Like It*, 3.5.100–5

***In other words:***

My love is so sacred and so complete, and I am so lacking in your estimation, that I would consider it a bumper crop to gather up the damaged ears of corn that the farmer leaves behind when he harvests the field. Just flash me an offhand smile once in a while, and that will give me everything I need.

**LET'S FURTHER THINK ON THIS . . .**

The debonair composer and lyricist Cole Porter detailed the glories that can redound to a skilled Shakespeare quoter in one of the great songs from his musical *Kiss Me Kate*, based on *The Taming of the Shrew.*

> Brush up your Shakespeare,
> Start quoting him now,
> Brush up your Shakespeare

(*Continued*)

And the women you will wow.
Just declaim a few lines from *Othella*
And they'll think you're a helluva fella,
If your blonde won't respond when you flatter 'er
Tell her what Tony told Cleopaterer,
. . .
Brush up your Shakespeare,
And they'll all kowtow.

The song goes on for six more verses, and as Porter cites increasingly obscure Shakespeare titles, his rhymes get more and more hilariously rococo. When should you quote *The Merchant of Venice*? "When her sweet pound o' flesh you would menace." *Troilus and Cressida*? For "the wife of the British embessida." And a true stroke of genius: what should you do "when your baby is pleading for pleasure"? Why, "let her sample your *Measure for Measure*."

## YOU'RE SO INCREDIBLE THAT ONLY POETRY CAN EXPRESS YOU

One of the surpassing love poems in the English language, which begins with one of the most famous and widely recognized Shakespearean lines of all, serves as the quintessential profession of amorous devotion. Use it to woo your love, and as you do, tip your hat to a poet who knew his work would have staying power.

Shall I compare thee to a summer's day?
Thou art more lovely and more temperate.
Rough winds do shake the darling buds of May,
And summer's lease hath all too short a date.
Sometime too hot the eye of heaven shines,

And often is his gold complexion dimmed,
And every fair from fair sometime declines,
By chance or nature's changing course untrimmed;
But thy eternal summer shall not fade
Nor lose possession of that fair thou ow'st,
Nor shall death brag thou wander'st in his shade
When in eternal lines to time thou grow'st.
So long as men can breathe or eyes can see,
So long lives this, and this gives life to thee.

—SONNET 18

***In other words:***

Should I write a line that says you're like a day in summer? It wouldn't really work. You're more beautiful than a summer day, and more even-tempered. The early part of summer is stormy, and anyway, summer's over as soon as it begins. What's more, some summer days are oppressively hot, and others are overcast and gloomy. In fact, every lovely thing loses its loveliness sooner or later, through some accident, or because it's nature's way to make things plainer and plainer as they age.

But you're different. The summertime of your life will last forever, and you'll never lose your loveliness. Not even Death will be able to boast of conquering you—because my imperishable poetry will make you one with time itself, and you'll go on as long as time does. So long as there are human beings, so long as there are eyes that can see letters on paper—that's how long this poem will live. And this poem will give everlasting life to you.

***How to say it:***

- This sonnet requires a good, strong launch. Be sure you make the question in its first line as real as possible, so that you can spend the next five lines working through the answer to your satisfaction. Imagine yourself a poet, in the middle of composing a poem to your lover. You're about to write something like "You're as beautiful as a perfect day in July." Before setting pen to paper, you ask yourself if that's such a good idea. *Shall I compare thee to a summer's day?* The force of the question makes you really think it through, and you talk your answer out, point by point. *Well, you're prettier than summer. You're more temperate. Summer has storms, it's too hot, sometimes it's cloudy.* Before you know it, you're on line 6, simply by making yourself reason out a real answer to a real question.

→ Note how the sonnet's argument changes direction with that ever-powerful word *But* at the beginning of line 9. The answer to your initial question led you to acknowledge that not just summer but all things lose their beauty over time. Now *but* contradicts that assertion by proposing the one thing whose gorgeousness never fades: your lover. The rest of the poem spells out precisely how he or she pulls off that time-defying trick: by being immortalized in your poetry. By line 14, the answer to *Shall I compare thee to a summer's day?* turns out to be "No, but I'll find a way to write a poem about you anyway." Ask a question, then answer it, and follow that answer in whatever direction it naturally evolves. That's about as good an approach to Shakespeare as any.

→ The verbs do yeoman's service in this sonnet. They are: *compare, shake, shines, dimmed, declines, fade, ow'st, brag, wander'st, grow'st, breathe, see, lives. Ow'st* at the end of line 10 is the present-tense declension of "owe," which in Shakespeare's period was synonymous with "own." (*That fair thou ow'st* means *the beauty you possess.*) In almost every Shakespeare play I've directed, I've simply substituted *own* for *owe* in order to make the sense clear to a modern audience. Doing that here is far trickier, alas, because of the rhyme between *ow'st* and *grow'st.* (*To time thou groan'st.* Yikes!) This is a case where we have to live with an archaic word and rely on the clarity and specificity of our thinking to make its sense emerge.

- Perhaps the most important word in the entire poem is *this*, which appears twice in its final line. It's clear from the context that both occurrences of the word refer to this poem, or this collection of poems, or poetry in general. In order for the reference to be clear, you'll need to point to—physically, with a gesture—the paper or book you're reading from as you really hit each *this*. That won't be hard: you already know to take every word in this line slowly and with strong emphasis because it's entirely monosyllabic. For this reason, both *this*'s are already nice and juicy, so all you need is to give them just a little extra edge in order to ensure they land.

***Some details:***

Shakespeare's plays will forever enshrine him in the pantheon of world literary giants, but they're not the only distinguished collection of verse he wrote. His series of 154 fourteen-line sonnets, of which the Bardism here is number eighteen, is also astonishingly great. Written over many years beginning in the early 1590s, the sonnets weren't published until 1609, although versions of Sonnets 138 and 144 first appeared in a volume called *The Passionate Pilgrim* ten years earlier.

The circumstances surrounding the composition and publication of the sonnets are mysterious. Many scholars believe that Shakespeare never intended the poems to be published at all, because surviving evidence suggests they had been circulated privately to a small group of friends and insiders comprising mostly prominent London literati and connected noblemen. One of these readers might have slipped a manuscript to a publisher without Shakespeare's authorization. This theory is buttressed by the fact that the author's name is given an unusual hyphenated spelling—"Shake-Speare"—on the title page of the

1609 text and throughout the volume. Had Will himself been involved in the publication, his name surely would have been spelled correctly.

Another mystery is the dedication that precedes the poems. It's signed not by Shakespeare but by "T.T."—the initials of the volume's publisher, Thomas Thorpe—and it labels "Mr. W.H." as "the onlie begetter" (literally, sole parent; i.e., inspiration) of the poems. To this day, no one knows who this W.H. was. Literary sleuths adduce all sorts of evidence in support of various candidates (even such luminaries as Oscar Wilde and the philosopher Bertrand Russell turned their considerable minds to the question). Here are a handful of the theories, in increasing order of outlandishness:

- W.H. is any of a number of well-known aristocratic patrons of the arts who supported Shakespeare's early career, including William Herbert, Earl of Pembroke (to whom the First Folio was dedicated), or Henry Wriothesley, Earl of Southampton (Shakespeare's patron and the dedicatee of both *Venus and Adonis* and *The Rape of Lucrece*), whose initials are here reversed to help preserve his anonymity—and yes, there are some fascinating theories as to why he'd want to be anonymous now when he didn't care before, and these sound like cloak-and-dagger stuff worthy of a Jacobean John Le Carré.
- W.H. is some other individual in Shakespeare's life: his nephew, the actor William Hart; his friend the playwright William Haughton; the eminent publisher William Hall; or the young socialite William Hughes.
- "W.H." is an unfortunate misprint for either "W.S." or "W. Sh.": William Shakespeare. Or "W.H." is short for "William Himself": again, Shakespeare. (Those who argue this theory perform some circus-caliber contortions as they attempt to explain why Shakespeare would dedicate a book of his poetry to himself.)

- "W.H." means "Who He," a formulation commonly used at the time by authors who wished to hide their identities. If this theory is correct, then Thomas Thorpe (and/or Shakespeare) was obfuscating on purpose, encouraging a public guessing game about "W.H." in order to confer on the sonnets a certain frisson of notoriety or even scandal, and, as a result, to increase book sales. What I love about this argument is that while it's a 10 on the ludicrous scale, it's also the only theory of "W.H." that's supported by what's actually happened over the course of four hundred years—an endless and complicated cat-and-mouse pursuit of the elusive W.H.

Despite the rampant silliness of some of the speculation, the true identity of W.H. is not without consequence. This is because the 154 sonnets, read in sequence, tell a very personal story, and W.H., as its "onlie begetter," may well have been a leading character in the tale. Most of the poems are addressed by their author to a handsome young man (referred to by scholars as the "Fair Youth"). The first seventeen sonnets compliment the Fair Youth on his uncommon beauty and urge him to preserve and perpetuate it in the form of a child who will resemble him. Sonnet 18 suddenly reveals that the poet not only admires the Fair Youth but also has romantic feelings for him, and the next 108 sonnets chronicle a turbulent relationship between the two men. Frequently this relationship is described in the language of erotic love; indeed, by sonnet 126, the poet has been so hurt by unrequited passion for the Fair Youth that he rejects him and has an affair instead with a woman known as the "Dark Lady." But this affair turns painful when the poet discovers that the Dark Lady is also in love with the Fair Youth and may even have had an affair with him herself! As if all this weren't byzantine enough, a "Rival Poet" enters the picture and ratchets up the complications by vying for the Fair Youth's attention with love poems of his own.

The poet who narrates this melodramatic love story is a middle-aged man confused by the power of his sexual urges, and frustrated and heartbroken over a dashing young man with ice in his veins. By turns jealous, vengeful, desperate, apologetic, abashed, gracious, and finally philosophical and resigned, the poet experiences and describes the whole wide gamut of human emotion. Many of the sonnets seem to revel in the resemblances between this poet and Shakespeare himself, such as number 135, which puns incessantly on the word *will* and all but announces that Will Shakespeare is not only the author of the verses but also their star. Therefore, if W.H. was indeed an actual person, and if he was in fact the Fair Youth of the Sonnets, and if the Dark Lady and the Rival Poet were also real figures from the Elizabethan world, then these 154 sonnets reveal an enormous amount about Shakespeare's personality, emotional and psychological wiring, and private life.

But whether or not we choose to read these 154 poems as a kind of Shakespearean crypto-autobiography, we cannot deny their scope, beauty, and power. Even as they chronicle the vexed romantic interactions of four Elizabethans, the sonnets address countless broader themes: the corrosive powers of time; the enduring beauty of poetry; the disappointments and dissatisfactions of day-to-day existence; the paradoxical ability of sexual passion to generate new life even as it often leaves dejection and humiliation in its wake. The sonnets may well be a glimpse into the heart, mind, and soul of one the greatest geniuses in human history, but they are also one of the most sublime collections of verse ever composed.

## SHAKESPEARE ON LOVEMAKING

*Kiss me, Doll.*

—Falstaff, *Henry IV, Part II*, 2.4.236

In my life as a Shakespeare teacher, I now and then work with high-school-age students. I've learned to look forward to a moment that usually comes while I'm talking about one of the Kate-Petruchio scenes in *The Taming of the Shrew*, or one of the Olivia-Sebastian scenes in *Twelfth Night*, or one of the Rosalind-Orlando scenes in *As You Like It*. Maybe it will be when we get to Petruchio's line about putting his tongue in Kate's tail. Maybe it will be when Rosalind threatens Orlando to be careful about marrying her, because she plans to be the kind of wife who dallies with the pool boy. Maybe it will be when Olivia sees her lover boy's identical twin and, imagining double her fun, exclaims, "O wonderful!" At one of these points, or at any of a million others, I see a light snap on in my students' eyes. "Hey!" it says, in lurid red neon. "This is Shakespeare. And it's got ***sex!***"

"It sure does," I tell them. "And why not? Shakespeare writes about every other aspect of the human experience. Why would he skip this one that's so very, very central to it?"

It disappoints me that the average high schooler doesn't know how much sex there is in Shakespeare—they'd read a lot more of him if they knew—but it doesn't surprise me. The American curriculum typically introduces Shakespeare with plays that seem to me rather bizarre choices for teenagers. *Macbeth* is one, that wholesome study of unhinged ambition, marital perfidy, and violence more brutal than that found in the latest release of Grand Theft Auto. *Julius Caesar* is another, that all-singing, all-dancing journey into political assassination, betrayed friendships, and—a favorite of teenage girls everywhere—

self-mutilation as an attention-getting ploy. Even *Romeo and Juliet*, Shakespeare's hottest play, when taught to kids somehow lurches toward the morality tale and becomes a finger-wagging lecture on the perils of connubial precociousness.

That young people meet a Shakespeare bleached of his throbbing, sweaty, erotic urges is one of the lasting legacies of our English forebears still at the center of American culture: the mutually reinforcing prudishness of Victorian shame and old-school Puritanism. Shakespeare would've burst a blood vessel if he'd known, because animus toward all such restrictive, pleasure-canceling ideologies was one of the driving forces of his dramaturgy.

I say, if we're to presume ourselves worthy of working on this great writer's plays, the least we can do is honor his memory by resuscitating the horny heart that pounds them hormonally to life. Let's put the shagging back in Shakespeare! Let's give some Cialis to *Cymbeline*! Time to cop a feel off sweet Ophelia! Time to coriol-spank a little *Coriolanus*!

To kick things off, then, here's Shakespeare on the Occasion of the Dirty Deed.

## MAY I SMOOCH YOU?

We'll start slowly, with gentlemanly refinement.

> **May I, sweet lady, beg a kiss of you?**
>
> —Ulysses, *Troilus and Cressida*, 4.5.48

***How to say it:***

- You sweet ladies should feel free to swap in *sirrah* for *lady*—and you sweet boys, too, if you're so inclined!

## KISS ME NOW, NOT LATER

"I'll take care of it tomorrow" might work in other areas of your life, but when it comes to your heart, procrastination is obliteration, and when it comes to kissing, a lip-lock lost never returns. In *Twelfth Night*, the clown Feste (*FESS-tee*) sings a song that instructs us to open the door when love rings the bell.

> What is love? 'Tis not hereafter,
> Present mirth hath present laughter.
> What's to come is still unsure.
> In delay there lies no plenty,
> Then come kiss me, sweet and twenty.
> Youth's a stuff will not endure.
>
> —Feste, *Twelfth Night*, 2.3.43–48

***In other words:***

What about love? It's not later on. Laughter comes the moment something's amusing. The future is always uncertain. There's no profit in waiting around, so come and kiss me, my twenty-times sweet one. We won't stay young forever.

***How to use it:***

- We'll hear Shakespeare tell us "there's no time like the present" in Chapter Four. This lyric says something along those lines, but in the specific context of love. As such, wheel it out for a friend who can't decide whether or not to approach the guy she has a crush on, or say it to yourself when you're wondering if you should flash your devilish smile at that cute guy you see on the subway platform each morning.
- The rhyme scheme will point you to the operative words here. Simply say the last word in each line, and you'll understand ex-

actly what Feste is trying to communicate: *hereafter*, *laughter*, *unsure*, *plenty*, *twenty*, *endure*.

***Some details:***

These lines are the second verse of a ditty called "O Mistress Mine," one of the best known of Shakespeare's songs. The first verse:

> O mistress mine, where are you roaming?
> O stay and hear, your true love's coming,
> That can sing both high and low.
> Trip no further, pretty sweeting.
> Journeys end in lovers meeting,
> Every wise man's son doth know.

In other words: "Hey, girlfriend, where are you going? Stay and listen: your lover's coming, and he's got a great voice. Don't take another step, cutie-pie. Everybody knows that voyages end in lovers getting together." Like the second verse above, this one admonishes us to seize love when it comes, not to run away from it or come up with some excuse as to why we can't wait around.

The music for this song survives from Shakespeare's day. It's a lovely English madrigal, and if you're interested in hearing it (or, for that matter, singing it at the next wedding you attend), it's been recorded by a number of famous classical singers, male and female, over the years. Many eminent composers have also turned their hands to this lyric and written memorable tunes, either for specific productions of the play or just for the sake of it. The great singer Cleo Laine has a gorgeous jazz cover (on her early 1960s album *Shakespeare and All That Jazz*—a minor classic), but my current favorites are a dark rendition by rocker extraordinaire Elvis Costello and a ravishing, guaranteed tearjerker by the cult performer/singer/violinist Emilie Autumn. They demonstrate the magic that can happen when a brilliant contemporary artist turns to the past for inspiration and creates something that fuses old and new, yesterday and today.

## SOMETIMES KINKY IS GOOD

Earlier I said that *Romeo and Juliet* is Shakespeare's hottest play. The statement merits clarification. It's his hottest play about teenagers. For love between grown-ups, nothing—and I mean no work in world dramatic literature—beats *Antony and Cleopatra*. That's a bold claim, I know. But this is a play which opens with a speech about the heat generated by "a gypsy's lust" and goes on to include drunken orgies, lots of groping, some quite exotic descriptions of the female anatomy, and even eunuchs who fantasize about what sex might be like if only they had the equipment to experience it. There's also a tiny detour into . . . er . . . shall we say, the rougher side of town . . . when Cleopatra mentions,

> **A lover's pinch, / Which hurts, and is desired.**
>
> —Cleopatra, *Antony and Cleopatra*, 5.2.286–87

## DOING IT

My high school students who delight in the discovery that Shakespeare is a mirror of their randy, gametically supercharged selves also thrill to find that he, like them, loves to talk about sex in the most inventively euphemistic terms. Whole books have been written on the subject of eroticism in the plays, so I'll offer only these few Bardisms, Shakespeare for the Occasion of Getting It On.

First, the Bardism that Don Juan would have pledged, had Shakespeare written him:

> I dedicate myself to your sweet pleasure.
>
> —GIACOMO, *Cymbeline*, 1.6.137

Next, the Bardism the Marquis de Sade would have spoken, in Shakespearean language:

> Fit thy consent to my sharp appetite.
>
> —ANGELO, *Measure for Measure*, 2.4.161

Finally, what both Don Juan and the Marquis de Sade got busy doing, had Shakespeare written their stories:

> Making the beast with two backs.
>
> —IAGO, *Othello*, 1.1.118

***In other words:***

This is a family-friendly book, so I'll skip this part.

***How to use it:***

- If you don't know, you need more than a book on Shakespeare quotations.

***Some details:***

Those will remain private, thank you very much.

## SHAKESPEARE ON GETTING ENGAGED

*We are betrothed. Nay more, our marriage hour . . .*
*Determined of.*

—VALENTINE, *The Two Gentlemen of Verona*, 2.4.172–74

Betrothals in Renaissance England were largely contractual matters, arranged by parents, announced publicly in special church services, and accompanied by elaborate financial negotiations. Thus it can be tricky to find a good Shakespearean version of those four earth-shattering words, "Will you marry me?" Fortunately, early modern lovers—although not necessarily those intending to marry—shared with their counterparts in our era an affection for a certain special token of mutual love: the ring. And it's in the rhetoric of ring giving and ring taking that our search for Shakespeare for the Occasion of the Marriage Proposal yields results.

### PLEASE HAVE THIS RING

All right, so this particular ring presentation is from a homicidal maniac to the vehemently opposed, still-grieving widow of one of his victims. So what? Your lover needn't know the dramatic circumstances. The sentiment is what counts.

**Look how my ring encompasseth thy finger;**
**Even so thy breast encloseth my poor heart.**
**Wear both of them, for both of them are thine.**

—GLOUCESTER, *Richard III*, 1.2.191–93

***In other words:***

Look how my ring wraps around your finger. In just that same way, your body wraps around my heart. Have both my heart and my ring. They're yours.

***How to say it:***

- Technically, this isn't really Shakespeare for "Will you marry me?" because the text makes sense only *after* the ring has been slipped onto your sweetie's finger. If for any reason you don't get that far, bail out of this speech and look for Shakespeare for Drowning Your Sorrows in Booze, to be included in the sequel to this volume!

- Richard, Duke of Gloucester, is nothing if not a capable wordsmith. One of his favorite tools is antithesis ("Now is the *winter* of our discontent / Made glorious *summer* by this son of York"), and he puts it to good use here. Lines 1 and 2 are all antithesis: *Look how* versus *even so*; *my ring* versus *thy breast*; *encompasseth* versus *encloseth*; and *thy finger* versus *my heart*. Rely on those contrasts to help you, but be sure to let each line flow smoothly. Don't let individual antitheses become more important than the larger idea you're trying to express.

***Some details:***

The image of Richard's heart beating in Lady Anne's chest has Shakespeare all over it. This trope—call it cardiac swap—appears a few times in the plays and gets developed at length in a handful of the sonnets. What's marvelous about it is that at the same time as being ravishingly romantic, it's also quite grotesque. My heart is in your chest? Then what's keeping me alive? And what's happened to your heart? And how did this transplant happen? Did some Elizabethan Dr. Jarvik come along and hack you open while you weren't looking? It must have been painful. It must have been bloody. Richard's facility with bizarre and surprising images like this one is part of his charm, and is central to his audacity and inexhaustible self-confidence. Shakespeare's facility with such images is what makes him so hair-raisingly brilliant and so thoroughly indelible.

## SHAKESPEARE ON WEDDINGS

> *As the ox hath his bow, sir, the horse his curb, and the falcon her bells, so man hath his desires; and as pigeons bill, so wedlock would be nibbling.*
>
> —TOUCHSTONE, *As You Like It*, 3.3.66–68

If there's one occasion for which Shakespeare is truly well suited, it's a wedding. Nearly a third of his plays include one, or at least end with the coming together of a couple or two who will soon be headed for one. Here are three pieces of Shakespeare all eminently suitable for reading during the marriage ceremony, or for accompanying a raised glass at the reception, plus one excerpt to ensure the party is a properly raucous affair.*

### A WEDDING TOAST

The standard Bardism for a wedding is this well-known poem that confers a lush and romantic blessing on the couple exchanging vows by exalting their love as true, devoted, and everlasting.

> Let me not to the marriage of true minds
> Admit impediments. Love is not love
> Which alters when it alteration finds,

---

* A special note: The pronouns *he* and *she* run through all my commentary on the excerpts in this section, a fact that may justifiably be construed to suggest that Shakespeare conceived of weddings as unions between *he*'s and *she*'s. Maybe he did. Doesn't mean we do. Should you find yourself in need of some words of wisdom for a match between a he and a he or a she and a she, don't rule the Bard out. Just juggle those pronouns as necessary, and you'll have enough Shakespeare for the Occasion of a Same-Sex Wedding to tide you over.

Or bends with the remover to remove:
O no! it is an ever-fixed mark
That looks on tempests and is never shaken;
It is the star to every wandering bark,
Whose worth's unknown, although his height be taken.
Love's not Time's fool, though rosy lips and cheeks
Within his bending sickle's compass come:
Love alters not with his brief hours and weeks,
But bears it out even to the edge of doom.
    If this be error and upon me proved,
    I never writ, nor no man ever loved.

—Sonnet 116

***In other words:***

I don't want to consider even for a moment that anything whatsoever might somehow block the union of two true-minded people. Love isn't really love if it changes when circumstances change, or if it yields to some attractive temptation. No way!

Love is a permanent beacon, a lighthouse erected forever, that withstands storms without suffering any damage. Love is the North Star that helps every lost little boat navigate its way. (We might be able to determine precisely where in the sky that star is located, but we can't begin to measure its value or the full force of its astrological influence.)*

---

* *Alternatively:* (We can easily determine the size of that vessel, but just by looking at it we can't really figure out the value of its cargo.) *Whose* at the beginning of line 8 can be read to refer back either to *star* (as in the paraphrase above), or *bark* (as in the paraphrase here). The former is attractive because *his height be taken* at the end of line 8 refers to astronomy: "to take a star's height" with a sextant is to navigate a ship by observing the constellations. But *worth*, in its sense of monetary value, seems to fit better with a ship's cargo than with a celestial body. Scholars continue to argue for both interpretations.

Love's not susceptible to time's ravages, although Father Time can indeed undo a person's youthful beauty. Love isn't changed by such little things as hours and weeks; love endures until doomsday itself.

If I'm wrong about all this and you can prove it, then I'm no writer, and no person has ever truly been in love.

***How to say it:***

- The presence of the word *marriage* in this sonnet's first line is not the only reason it's so frequently read at weddings. Another is its opening idea, *Let me not . . . admit impediments.* Many commentators note that this is a direct reference to the part of the marriage service when the officiant asks, in that line so familiar from a million movies, if anyone present knows any reason why this couple should not be joined in matrimony. The speaker of this sonnet answers by saying, "May I never even acknowledge the *possibility* that two such well-matched people might have some reason not to be married!" Keep that in mind when you speak this Bardism. Imagine that the minister or rabbi or justice of the peace has just this minute asked that familiar question. You know this couple well, and you think that the notion of an impediment to this marriage is simply outrageous. This couple's minds are too true and their love is too deep to be affected by any obstacle. After all, you know something not only about these two people, but about love itself. You're a writer—a poet, to be exact—and you've been around. You've traveled (specifically, by boat), you've lived a while, you've observed others in love, and you've loved, too. You therefore know that true love is constant. And you believe this so firmly that you're willing to announce it to the entire world.

- The verbs, as always, are crucial. *Let, admit, alters, finds, bends, remove, fixèd, looks, shaken, wand'ring, taken, come, alters, bears, proved, writ*, *loved*, and, of course, many occurrences of *is*. Try the sonnet one time through, concentrating in particular on the expressive power of these vivid words.

- Next, take a look at the words that come at the end of each line. Read them aloud: *minds, love, finds, remove, mark, shaken, bark, taken, cheeks, come, weeks, doom, proved, loved*. Now read the sonnet again, emphasizing this list. You'll find that the sense of the sonnet starts to emerge much more clearly, because, as a general rule, the energy of each line of Shakespearean verse drives toward the idea at its end.

- What's more, you'll now hear very clearly that there's a rhyme scheme in this sonnet. The first and third lines of each quatrain, or set of four lines, rhyme with each other, as do the second and fourth lines of each quatrain, and the sonnet ends with a rhyming couplet. (Each of Shakespeare's sonnets follows this scheme.) Try to let your audience hear the rhymes, but don't hit them so hard that the sense of the words disappears. (The sonnet has two almost-but-not-quite rhymes: *love* and *remove*, and *come* and *doom*. These are called *near rhymes*. Don't worry about forcing them to rhyme perfectly; just say them as they naturally sound.)

- Remember to stress the contrasting terms: *alters* versus *bends*; *finds* versus *remove*; *worth* versus *height*; *Love's* versus *time's*; *alters* versus *bears*; *I never writ* versus *no man ever loved*; and, in line 2, oddly enough, *Love* versus *love*!

- Finally, really dig into some of the sounds of the words themselves:

  - *Impediments* is, with its four consonant-filled syllables, a long and hefty word. Make each syllable count, letting the weight of the word help infuse it with a sense of irony: as forbidding and formidable as they may sound, *im-ped-i-ments* have no standing in the face of this glorious union of true minds.

- Let the rich and soothing *-ar* sounds in *mark*, *star*, and *bark* be nice and luxurious, suggesting how reassuring and permanent love is, particularly in contrast with the skimpy and tumultuous sounds of *tempests* and *worth's unknown*.

- Allow those *s* sounds in *rosy lips*, *cheeks*, *sickle's compass*, *hours*, and *weeks*, which so vividly describe the sharp swipe of time's cutting scythe, to contrast as fully as possible with the long, melodic vowels of *bears*, *out*, *doom*, and of course, *love*.

- Finish strong by giving each word in line 14, most of which are monosyllables, as much weight as you can: **I. Never. Writ. Nor. No. Man. Ever. Loved.**

→ This sonnet works just fine spoken on its own. But if you want to give it a bit of context or make a few brief introductory remarks, here are some approaches:

  - You might comment on how your friends are ideally matched, and in that sense are indeed a "marriage of true minds," and on how you're certain that theirs will be an everlasting love.

  - You could talk about how every marriage is like an ocean voyage. There are thrills and also challenges, exciting times as well as routine ones, many ups and plenty of downs. But when true love is the star by which the ship navigates, then the challenges, doldrums, and difficulties are far less significant.

  - You could present yourself as an expert on love who's been asked to comment on today's marriage, and you could joke that these are some of your jottings on the matter.

## ANOTHER WEDDING TOAST

Sonnet 116, above, works great prior to or during the marriage service, and is best spoken by one person. This Bardism is better suited to the reception, after the marriage has been consecrated, and it's a good one for a couple to say together to the newlyweds.

JUNO Honor, riches, marriage-blessing,
Long continuance and increasing,
Hourly joys be still upon you!
Juno sings her blessings on you.

CERES Earth's increase, and foison plenty,
Barns and garners never empty,
Vines and clust'ring bunches growing,
Plants with goodly burthen bowing;
Spring come to you at the farthest,
In the very end of harvest.
Scarcity and want shall shun you,
Ceres' blessing so is on you.

—*The Tempest*, 4.1.106–17

***In other words:***

JUNO May you have honor, wealth, marriage blessings, long lives, and a growing family. Hour by hour, may you always have happiness! Juno, queen of all the gods, sings her blessings to you.

CERES May you have the bounty of all that grows on earth, and may you have every abundance. May your barns and granaries never be empty; may your vines sprout bunches of rich, ripe grapes; may all your crops bend with the weight of the good fruits growing on them. May spring always come immediately after autumn, so that your years never suffer winter's chill. Poverty and need will have nothing to do with you. With all this, Ceres, goddess of agriculture, blesses you.

***How to say it:***

- First, even though in *The Tempest* the goddesses sing these lines, you should feel free simply to speak them!

- Two speakers can work together (one as Juno, the other as Ceres), or one person can combine the speeches together into one presentation. In either case, you may wish to omit the goddesses' names and substitute slight rewrites that allow you to speak on behalf of all the wedding guests as you bless the newlyweds. The lines could go like this:

  Line 4: We all sing our blessings on you.

  Line 12: All our blessings so are on you.

  While you've got your red pencil out, you may even consider substituting "produce" or "portions" for line 5's archaic and obscure *foison.* (You wouldn't want anyone to think you're wishing "poison" on the newlyweds!)

- Whether or not you make these minor changes in the text, keep in mind that in offering this Bardism you're giving a priestly benediction. Be as generous of spirit and genuine of heart as you can be. All the wishes you express are positive, happy, hopeful, and warm. Let your real affection for the couple you're addressing infuse the way you speak. The language will be filled with emotion, and your remarks will be moving and quite memorable.

- Lines 1, 2, and 3 comprise a long list of things Juno wishes for the marrying couple, and each new item in the list is somehow bigger or grander or more forceful than the one before. That is, the list builds in intensity as it continues, starting with *honor* and climaxing with *hourly joys*, a phrase so emphatic it's even marked with an exclamation point. (A *build* is precisely what a theater artist would call these lines; a musician would call them a *crescendo.*) A good trick to help find the build is to think the phrase "and not only that but also" between each idea: Honor (*and not only that but also*) riches, (*and not only that but also*) **marriage-blessing**, (*and not only that but also*) **long continuance** (*and not only that but also*) **AND INCREASING**, (*and not only that but also*) **<u>HOURLY JOYS BE STILL UPON YOU!</u>**

Ceres also gives a list with a build, though it develops more slowly than Juno's. Try the "not only this but also" trick at the end of each line of verse and you'll get a sense of how it works.

- Among the many expressive words in these lines, *blessing* is of course the most important. Give it real weight every time you say it. *Still* (meaning "always") in line 3, *never empty* in line 6, and *shall shun you* in line 11 are also crucial ideas.

## AND ANOTHER WEDDING TOAST

In Chapter One, we heard Hermione ask the gods to pour their graces on her daughter's head, and we discussed Shakespeare's obsession with the notion of heavenly precipitation falling on us mortals below. Here's another instance. These three simple and gracious lines will provide a nice finishing touch at the end of the ceremony or reception. (They'll also serve nicely as a toast to a long-married couple, as I know well from saying this Bardism to my parents on their golden anniversary.)

> The benediction of these covering heavens
> Fall on their heads like dew, for they are worthy
> To inlay heaven with stars.
>
> —Belarius, *Cymbeline*, 5.5.351–53

## THEY'RE MARRIED; LET'S START THE PARTY!

Part of what makes Shakespeare so apt for serving at weddings is that his material on the subject strikes the right balance between joy and solemnity. Just like the occasion itself, the passages above combine a good measure of uplift, a dollop of sentimentality, plenty of wit to keep the whole soufflé from collapsing outright, and, sprinkled atop it all tableside, a healthy pinch of wistfulness.

It's the expert deployment of this last ingredient that's so impressive to anyone who's ever experienced the singular emotional complexion of the wedding ceremony. If things get too serious, the whole day melts down faster than the ice sculpture adorning the buffet table. But without some sense of the gravity of the commitment being sworn by bride and groom, the thing starts to feel phony, saccharine, and cloying. Casting a shadow over the altar with such phrases as Sonnet 116's *the edge of doom* and *no man ever loved*, Shakespeare reminds us that "till death do us part" means business. He provides the literary equivalent of the smashed glass that ends every Jewish wedding, the symbolic acknowledgment that loss and endings are no less a part of lives lived in partnership than ecstasy and new creation.

But lest sobering reality do too much damage, Shakespeare comes in again with language that turns us back around. Like the traditional Yiddish shout of *Mazel tov!* ("Good luck!") that banishes from the synagogue the ominous sound of shattering crystal, these lines snap us back from the brink, swing us into happiness, and get us ready for the big celebration still to come.

> Meantime, forget this new-fallen dignity
> And fall into our rustic revelry.
> Play, music, and you brides and bridegrooms all,
> With measure heap'd in joy to th' measures fall.
>
> —Duke Senior, *As You Like It*, 5.4.165–68

***In other words:***

Meanwhile, let's get rid of this sudden seriousness, and dive into some good old-fashioned partying! Strike up the band! And all you brides and bridegrooms, pile on the happiness, and start dancing!

***How to say it:***

- The father of the bride can use this Bardism to help make the transition from the de rigueur remarks about "all those whom we wish were still with us to celebrate this day" to the first rousing chorus of "Hava Nagila." Alternatively, the DJ, bandleader, or best man can use it as a way of getting all the guests up on their feet and boogeying.
- Whoever says these lines must remember that they demand real energy in order to work. Circle the words at the end of each line—two rhyming pairs—and drive through toward them as powerfully as possible. Here's a hint of how it should sound: "Cel-e-brate good times, COME ON!"
- Antitheses: *forget* versus *fall*, *new-fallen* versus *rustic*, *dignity* versus *revelry*, *brides* versus *bridegrooms*. *Forget* and *fall* are also verbs, and they call for some heavy juice.

## SHAKESPEARE ON WEDDING VOWS

*My heart unto yours is knit*
*So that but one heart we can make of it;*
*Two bosoms interchainèd with an oath;*
*So then two bosoms and a single troth.*

—LYSANDER, *A Midsummer Night's Dream*, 2.2. 53–56

It's hard to think of a single wedding I've attended in which the vows taken by bride and groom conformed to the standard formula of "to have and to hold until death do us part." Most couples whose unions I've been fortunate to witness have preferred to depart from the tried and true and have incorporated into their vows music, poetry, their own writings and observations, and in one memorable case interpretive dance.

As always, Shakespeare's at the ready with a rich vein of material for the most special moment of your most special day.

## WITH THIS RING, I THEE WED

Here's a simple Shakespearean statement for bride and groom to repeat to each other at the big moment when the gold bands make their appearance.

> **When this ring / Parts from this finger, then parts life from hence.**
>
> —Bassanio, *The Merchant of Venice*, 3.2.183–84

***Some details:***

Should anyone at your wedding be churlish enough to mention that this line in *The Merchant of Venice* foreshadows the horrible moment when Portia's ring does indeed part from Bassanio's finger, precipitating one of the nastiest spats between any couple in Shakespeare, simply remind them that (a) it works out fine in the end, and (b) nobody likes a smarty-pants.

## FROM THIS TIME FORTH AND FOREVERMORE

Two of my friends offered this Bardism to each other at their gorgeous wedding in a small chapel in the woods of Martha's Vineyard. I include it here in tribute to their long and happy marriage.

> **To you I give myself, for I am yours.**
>
> —Rosalind, Orlando, *As You Like It*, 5.4.106

***How to say it:***

- Some editions of *As You Like It* separate *myself* into two words: *my self*. Though a little pedantic for my taste, this choice at least points to the wonderful doubleness of so much Shakespearean poetry. Rosalind and Orlando give *themselves* to each other—that is, all of what they have, everything they are—but they also give their *selves*—their inmost parts, their secret hearts, the essences that make them who they are. Either way you say the line, it expresses the magnificent idea that takes both Rosalind and Orlando five acts of Shakespeare and all sorts of extraordinary challenges to learn: that love is above all an act of profound generosity, unparalleled self-revelation, and trusting surrender.

## ENDLESS LOVE

Here is a Bardism I consider one of Shakespeare's finest hyperbolic hours, a perfect image of wedding-day love, a love so great it's infinite.

> My bounty is as boundless as the sea,
> My love as deep. The more I give to thee
> The more I have, for both are infinite.
>
> —JULIET, *Romeo and Juliet*, 2.2.175–77

***How to say it:***

- Try to wring all you can out of the important antithesis between *give* and *have*.
- This speech shows how Shakespeare uses the sound of his language to help communicate meaning. First, the vowels. Listen to the echoing *ow* sounds in *boundless* and *bounty*, the repeated *ee* in *bounty*, *sea*, *deep*, and *thee*, and the recurring diphthong *eye* in *my*, *my*, *I*, and *I*. Next, the consonants. Watch how the *v* bounces from *love* to *give* to *have* and how the *b* migrates from *bounty* to

*boundless* to *both*. Finally, the alternation between mono- and polysyllables. The final line employs one of Shakespeare's favorite rhythmic tricks: a monosyllabic line with a polysyllabic word at the end. *The. More. I. Have. For. Both. Are.* go along slowly and emphatically, until *Infinite* springs into the ether, made special not only by its placement at the end of the line, but also by the bold relief that pops out its cluster of three syllables from what comes before. This is Shakespeare at his Mozartian best, a composer of word music as virtuosic as any set out in notes and staves.

***Some details:***

A crucial aspect of this speech is that it's built on paradox. Juliet feels a love that's not only infinite but also continues to grow: the more she gives away, the more she has. Shakespeare loves stuff like this. He's addicted to riddles. You can't get through a dozen lines in *Macbeth* without finding weather that's "both foul and fair," or a prediction that "cannot be ill, cannot be good"; Troilus puzzles at his girlfriend's behavior and concludes that she simultaneously "is and is not Cressid"; Hamlet and Ophelia engage in a long debate about the paradoxical relationship of beauty and honesty; and all those cross-dressing heroines can't take so much as a step in pants without someone making a crack about hermaphrodism. These are just the tip of the iceberg of Shakespeare's obsession with impossibility, indeterminacy, simultaneity, and oxymoron.

He wasn't alone in loving such dizzying intellectual puzzles. Shakespeare's period, for all its social upheavals, political and religious turmoil, and military crises, was distinguished by its great capacity for giddy awe and a real sense of wonder. It's not called the English Renaissance for nothing; the pace of innovation in science, economics, geographical discovery, and art was extraordinary, and as each new idea arrived in Britain, it met with its share of curiosity, amusement, or astonishment. Early modern Englishmen were addicted to optical illusions, astronomical prodigies, and biological oddities, and Shakespeare writes about them all. *Twelfth Night* dwells at length on the distorting effects of mirrors and lenses; *Henry VI, Part I* opens with a comet, and meteor storms break out at least a half dozen times in the tragedies; there are no fewer than three sets of identical twins in Shakespeare's canon, and the mysteries of birth are a constant preoccupation.

Indeed, Shakespeare's contribution to the English attraction to paradox is so prolific that it's hard to know if he was reflecting public taste or shaping it. What's clear is that he brings something new to the table, which we see in the Juliet speech above. Shakespeare finds paradox in *human situations*, in relationships between people, in emotions. After all, he seems to ask, what's more of a curiosity: a newly discovered species of snake that often, when it eats, devours its own tail, or a person whose own appetites prove his horrible undoing? The latter, of course. That's Shakespeare's subject: the wonders, both joyous and terrifying, of being human. And love, the most wondrous of all human experiences, is the ultimate puzzle, the most dizzying trick of the light, and the greatest paradox of all.

## BOTTOMLESS LOVE

Juliet's reference to oceanic love isn't the only deep-water moment in Shakespeare. Here's another, perhaps even better suited to the wedding vow.

> My affection hath an unknown bottom, like the Bay of Portugal.
>
> —Rosalind, *As You Like It*, 4.1.177–78

***How to use it:***

- This nuptial Bardism helped establish my reputation among my circle of friends as the go-to guy for occasion-appropriate Bardophilic quotations. I offered it at the warm and splendid Beverly Hills wedding of my dear friends Karen and Ben, who asked some of their closest pals to read passages on certain themes during their marriage ceremony. My assigned topic was love, so I knew Shakespeare would figure in somehow.

  The Bay of Portugal was the body of water believed in Shakespeare's day to be the deepest on earth. Bridegroom Ben had just published a novel whose hero was a records verifier for a *Guinness Book of World Records*–type volume, so I thought he'd appreciate a way to think about married love in terms of what is (to my knowledge) the only world record in the Bard's canon. Introducing the line, I explained that a modern paraphrase might read, "My love is as deep as the Marianas Trench," the location off Japan now known to be the deepest in any ocean, but that *the Bay of Portugal* sounded much more romantic and exotic, and besides, *bottomless* is a far more mysterious and enticing description of love than "36,201 feet deep." I went on to talk about how surprising and specific details like this one are what make Shakespeare's writing so unique, and, similarly, how the idiosyncratic, day-to-day details we learn about each other are what make us love as deeply as we do. The assembled crowd, and Ben and Karen, were moved. Feel free to borrow my introductory gambit if you decide to use the line in describing a marrying couple, or explain the line in retrospect at a toast during the reception if you incorporate it into your vows.

***Some details:***

One of the ways of studying Shakespeare I find most rewarding is what literary critics call his canonicity, the aspects of his writing that allow us to draw together his many individual efforts into a single, unified body of work. Approaching the canon as a whole, you begin to see echoes and correspondences you can't see when you look at any individual work in isolation. You can watch Shakespeare's craft develop over time. You can identify a set of his core interests running through every work and getting teased out and tried again and again. You can see early false starts and failed ideas developed further and solved better as the canon evolves. The canon has a life of its own—a beginning, a middle, and an end.

Juliet's *my love is as deep as the ocean* and Rosalind's *my love is like the Bay of Portugal* provide one interesting example of the insights into Shakespeare that can be found through his canonicity. Both lines employ an identical simile comparing love with the sea. Juliet's use of it is simpler and more general; love is compared to no specific body of water, and the sea is just plain *deep*. Rosalind is more detailed in both nautical location—the waters off Lisbon—and measurement: *bottomless*, although not a finite number, is a more evocative adjective. Now consider both these lines in the context of Shakespeare's entire output. *Romeo and Juliet* dates from around 1594, and *As You Like It* from about 1599. Watching Shakespeare develop this single image from generality to specificity over that five-year period provides a glimpse into his growth as an imaginative artist, illuminates his method as a writer, and perhaps even opens a door onto him rereading and responding to his own previous work. To consider any products of Shakespeare's mind within the context of all the products of his mind is to glean more than can be gathered from any single line on its own. The whole is greater than the sum of its parts. That's what canonicity is all about.

## SHAKESPEARE ON RELATIONSHIP TROUBLES

> *Men are April when they woo, December when they wed. Maids are May when they are maids, but the sky changes when they are wives.*
>
> —Rosalind, *As You Like It*, 4.1.124–26

"Sweet are the uses of adversity," Duke Senior counsels in *As You Like It*, but the advice might be aimed at the lovers in all the plays who travel bumpy roads toward eventual bliss. Love in Shakespeare meets with crises of every kind: misapprehensions, misunderstandings, slanders, jealousies, and betrayals. And when they're swept away in the delirium of yet another Act 5 series of unlikely reversals, uncanny revelations, and lessons learned, these adversities do indeed serve to render the happiness all the more sweet in comparison.

Yet while Shakespeare knows that shadows make brightness seem even brighter, he also knows that the darkness itself stays dark. The pain is real while it lasts, and it lingers on in the memory. And, of course, sometimes the happy ending never comes. When love founders on life's jagged rocks, it hurts. Truly and deeply, it hurts. Here's a Shakespearean sampler for those Occasions When Love Goes Wrong.

### LOVIN' AIN'T EASY

This famous observation is either a balm to those convinced that their own redemptive Act 5 is just around the corner or a confirmation that what's hard is hard, and nothing's going to change it.

Ay me, for aught that I could ever read,
Could ever hear by tale or history,
The course of true love never did run smooth.

—Lysander, *A Midsummer Night's Dream*, 1.1.132–34

## JEALOUSY IS POWERFUL

Shakespeare's lovers pursue their amours beneath a whole constellation of ill stars. Cranky fathers-in-law abound, and social strictures impose frequently on love's free will, be they based on differences of class, race, or religion. The weather separates lovers in a couple of plays, and villainous lotharios driven by lust or greed or both do their share of damage. In a handful of plays, war stamps its violent boot on Cupid's gossamer wings. Still, no outside force in Shakespeare wreaks more havoc on love than a destructive gale that roars through *Othello*, *The Winter's Tale*, *Cymbeline*, and *King Lear*, and that percolates hot beneath the surface of *Much Ado About Nothing*, *All's Well That Ends Well*, *The Comedy of Errors*, *The Tempest*, *The Two Gentlemen of Verona*, and *Troilus and Cressida*. That devastating storm: jealousy.

Iago, who seems to know everything there is to know on the subject ("Trifles light as air / Are to the jealous confirmations strong / As proofs of holy writ"), describes it in an image whose vivid originality always shocks.

O, beware, my lord, of jealousy.
It is the green-eyed monster which doth mock
The meat it feeds on.

—Iago, *Othello*, 3.3.169–71

***How to use it:***

- Keep this excerpt handy the next time a friend, or your lover, veers into that terrible territory of suspicion, insecurity, and mistrust. One friend swears that a girlfriend who'd grown exhausted with his constant quizzes about her comings and goings once went to the trouble of buying a stuffed monster from a toy store, painting its eyes green, and setting it at the kitchen table with a half-eaten burger in front of it. I've never been able to confirm the story, but I like it a lot.
- Change *my lord* to *my lady* if the girl's the jealous one in your relationship.

***Some details:***

Like the primrose path, the dead doornail, and the milk of human kindness, the green-eyed monster is one of those Shakespearean phrases that's seeped into the lexicon of everyday English. At some time or another, we've all heard it or said it, whether or not we were aware that the Bard wrote it. This strikes me as curious, because unlike Ophelia's path, Pistol's doornail, and Lady Macbeth's milk, Iago's monster isn't exactly the easiest image to understand. Why, for example, are its eyes green? And what exactly does it do when it mocks the meat it eats? Does it sneer, "HA-ha! What a stupid steak *you* are"?

One magnificent nineteenth-century edition of the play offers some answers. The *Variorum Shakespeare* was the brainchild of Philadelphia scholar Horace Howard Furness, and was completed after his death by his son of the same name. Father and son's mad project was to try to cram into a series of single volumes every conceivable textual variant, and zillions of other bits of arcane information, *that had ever been thought* about each of Shakespeare's plays. It was a scheme typical of the Victorian era, a time when thinkers on both sides of the

Atlantic hatched schemes of gigantic ambition and unfaltering self-confidence, and often created achievements to match both. The *Variorum* is a treasure trove of information about Shakespeare—some stupendously valuable, some simply crackpot—and is an indispensable resource to any serious student of the Bard, in the study or on the stage.

The *Variorum Othello* includes no fewer than five full pages of commentary on the "green-eyed" passage. Regarding jealousy's eyes: Shakespeare usually associates jealousy with the color yellow, but the monster's green eyes get support from Portia, who, Furness reminds us, mentions them in *The Merchant of Venice*. One scholar argues that by saying *the* green-eyed monster instead of *a* green-eyed monster, Iago refers to some specific creature widely known to have green eyes and to mock its victim. That monster? Why, "the tyger," of course. Another scholar concurs, but floats the idea that the mocking tiger's not green-eyed at all, but *agreinied*, an archaic word meaning "sportive" or "frolicsome." (That scholar is named Becket, and we'll return to him in a moment.) Regarding *mock / The meat it feeds on*, most scholars agree that a serviceable paraphrase might be, "Jealousy feeds on love, a food it plays with like a child with its pureed veggies." Since Iago uses both the monster and its meat metaphorically, the line therefore really means, "Jealousy laughingly torments the soul of the person who suffers from it." That seems pretty right to me, although Furness recalls an explanation from Lewis Theobald that introduces a very different perspective. The granddaddy of all Shakespeare scholars conjectures that *mock* was a mistaken reading for *make* and that, corrected, the phrase means, "Jealous souls create their own suspicions, and these become a kind of sustaining nourishment for their own paranoia." This brings us back to our agreinied friend Professor Becket. He believes that neither *mock* nor *make* is correct, but that Shakespeare obviously wrote *muck*, meaning *befoul.* A scholar named Jackson supports Becket but argues that if *muck* is correct, then the monster is not a tiger but a mouse, known colloquially as the "little monster." A mouse, Jackson delicately explains, "after it has glutted on a piece of nice meat, leaves as much defilement on the residue as it possibly can."

Mouse droppings? In *Shakespeare*? Furness won't have it. "Some years ago I announced the exhaustion of my patience with Andrew Becket and Zachary Jackson," he snaps, then proclaims that by presenting to the world the self-evident absurdity of their mucking mouse, "my vindication is complete." His bile flowing, Furness moves on to the wonderfully named Lord Chedworth, who holds that Iago's green-eyed monster is "a sort of large dragon-fly, that voids a greenish foam from its mouth, and then gradually sucks it in again." For Furness, this is too much. He petulantly labels this "the last note that I will ever take" from Chedworth, "the sight of whose volume [of Shakespeare commentary] starts a shudder."

At his death, Furness left his books and papers to the University of Pennsylvania, where the Horace Howard Furness Shakespeare Library remains one of the great collections of its kind. I've never been there, but one day I will make a pilgrimage and pay my respects to the professor, whose inability to suffer fools makes him one of the most appealing of the giants in my field.

CHAPTER 4

# Then a Soldier

## SHAKESPEARE FOR THE OCCASIONS OF PROFESSIONAL LIFE

*Then a soldier,*
*Full of strange oaths and bearded like the pard,*
*Jealous in honor, sudden and quick in quarrel,*
*Seeking the bubble reputation*
*Even in the cannon's mouth.*

Jaques' Fourth Age of Man limns a figure recognizable enough to anyone who's ever seen a war movie or even a YouTube clip of steel-spined, high-and-tighted Jack Nicholson barking "You *can't handle* the truth!" straight into the straining solar plexus of the handsomely toothy, toothily earnest Tom Cruise. But while it may be fun to read *As You Like It* during a wee-hours rerun of *A Few Good Men*, you shouldn't push the comparison between the two too far. For one thing, if you did, a produce market's worth of apples and oranges would cascade out of your television; that is, *As You Like It* is *As You Like It*, whereas *A Few Good Men* is, well, *A Few Good Men*. "Comparisons are odorous," as Dogberry says in *Much Ado About Nothing*. For another, the leatherneck whom Nicholson portrays with such barnstorming brio is of a different species—a different *genus*, really—than Jaques' aristocratic soldier. The type Jaques sketches, so familiar in the European Renaissance, indeed so standard in all European societies right up to the moment horses and swords yielded the battlefield to armored tanks and machine guns, is all but extinct in our era of all-volunteer armed forces and the military as the Great Leveler that suborns social status to military rank.

To Shakespeare's audience, an officer and a gentleman was every bit as much the latter as he was the former. Yes, Elizabethan armies had citizen-soldiers, too: the grunts who did the majority of the fighting and dying were recruited from the rank and file of the great unwashed. But Shakespeare's military men, from Coriolanus and Bertram and Benedick and Don Pedro and Macduff to all the titled blue bloods in all the royal families who make war on one another in all the English history plays, are members of a distinct, exclusive, hereditary, and privileged military caste. The bearded, oath-swearing, honor-obsessed gentleman soldier of Shakespeare's plays is one of a handful of character types whose apparent similarities to types familiar in our culture serve paradoxically to render them less, not more, familiar.

To understand what Jaques is talking about—or, for that matter, to make sense of any of the Shakespearean character types transformed by time into quaint figures out of some historical diorama—we need to reconstruct a world that existed four centuries in the past. Traces of a culture long gone survive in Shakespeare's lines, and like clay shards in an archaeological dig, they provide clues about a life and a lifestyle nearly buried by time. Our job is to reassemble these shards into a living whole. Parolles, a character in *All's Well That Ends*

*Well,* is one such archaeological trace. This garrulous, obsessive, self-aggrandizing soldier is detail by detail the man described in Jaques' lines. Read the scenes he's in, and it's easy to suppose that Shakespeare kept a copy of the "All the world's a stage" speech open beside him as he wrote. More surviving shards: older plays, upon which Shakespeare drew as he assembled his indelible gallery of military personages. Plautus, the ancient Roman comic dramatist whom Shakespeare mentions in *Hamlet* and rips off in *The Comedy of Errors*, wrote a play called *Miles Gloriosus* (*The Braggart Soldier*) whose eponymous hero is a type as widely known in the classical world as in the early modern: a hero exactly like the one Jaques anatomizes in his speech. And another shard: contemporary history. Robert Devereux, the Earl of Essex, famous for being the would-be/maybe-was paramour of Queen Elizabeth I and later infamous for leading a rebellion against her that cost him his life, wore a very distinctive beard. Long, thick, orange, and cut square, it set a trend in facial hair that wannabe soldiers imitated up and down England. That trend reached its apogee in 1599, the year Essex went from consort to convict, and the year in which Shakespeare wrote Jaques' famous lines.

A character in a play, an ancient literary form, a short-lived tonsorial fad. Neither revelatory nor particularly meaningful on their own, when taken together they unlock the fourth of Jaques' Seven Ages. The key is what Parolles, Miles Gloriosus, and the hirsute Earl of Essex share in common: they're laughable. Parolles is the comic relief in *All's Well,* the butt of a practical joke whose climax is as prodigiously funny as any sequence in Shakespeare. *Miles Gloriosus* is a knockabout farce whose title character is an absolute and unregenerate buffoon. As for Essex's beard, check out a portrait of the earl and you'll see on his chin a barbigerous bulk that makes the poor fellow look like an Elizabethan cross between two Sams: Uncle and Yosemite. When we piece together these Renaissance shards, we see something otherwise invisible in the Support Our Troops culture we inhabit: the soldier as a subject of lampoon, not reflexive and solemn praise. His oaths make him sound like a madman. His beard makes him look like an idiot. And his worship of honor and pursuit of renown lead him to where only a fool would go by choice—straight into the firing line. It turns out that for Jaques—for Shakespeare—the Fourth Age of Man is as ridiculous as the three that came before it.

Exhuming the bones of a faded culture isn't the only way to sense Jaques' sardonic tone. The words he uses and the way he arranges them also hint at his perspective. The soldier's oaths are *strange*, an adjective that in Shakespeare almost always means "abnormal," "so unusual that it's astonishing"; certainly his pardine chin-beard is all that, too. He's *jealous*—excessively, even suspiciously, vigilant about or devoted to his code of honor. His anger is *sudden*: shocking, surprising, perhaps even unmotivated, and there's a capriciousness in the sound of the alliterative *qu*'s of *quick in quarrel*. These details give us a noisy and eccentric firebrand—I see in my mind's eye a Napoleonic sort, a beribboned, bewhiskered bantamweight of a guy, all chin up and chest out, all hair-trigger and in your face—but it's the next details that tell us he's truly nuts. The fourth line in the image insists that what the soldier values above all is *reputation*, which for Jaques is an attribute entirely devoid of value. It's but a *bubble*, something trivial and empty, something fragile, temporary, and easily destroyed. And *reputation* scans with five syllables here—*REP-you-TAY-shee-un*—a fact that somehow puts the whole idea in quotation marks and lends it an affected, preposterous aspect. More absurd than the bubble itself is the precise location where the soldier seeks it, a place set up by a superbly provocative line ending after *reputation*:

> Seeking the bubble reputation
> *(Where?—Ready?—Really want to know?—Okay, then)*
> Even in the cannon's mouth.

Who but a nincompoop would willingly, recklessly look there?

The Third Age was about swoons and breathlessness, and the Fifth will comprise corpulence and pompous tedium. At least this Fourth Age, despite its fatuousness, is a time of energy and physical vigor. The Bardisms below, then, include not only Shakespeare on the Soldier's Occasions, those life events concerning combativeness, courage, victories, and losses, but they also glance at Shakespeare on the Occasions of Life's Vibrant Years, those times of productivity and achievement, professional conduct, and personal accomplishment.

## SHAKESPEARE ON SOLDIERS

> *To th' wars, my boy, to th' wars!*
> —PAROLLES, *All's Well That Ends Well*, 2.3.262

Most of Shakespeare's soldiers are cut from cloth different from the one Jaques talks about. Their cloth is not buffoonish, but is instead distinctly crimson in hue. In *Henry V*, for example, soldiers "nothing do but meditate on blood." In *Richard II*, they open "the purple testament of bleeding war." In *Macbeth*, their weapons have "smoked with bloody execution." Usually, when Shakespeare thinks *soldier*, he writes *violence*, *blood*, and *death*.

Usually, but not always. Sprinkled throughout the canon are a small number of speeches that portray a third kind of soldier, a man who is neither a foolish braggart nor a killing machine. These speeches frame a figure of upstanding morals, dashing countenance, refined carriage, abundant bravery, and consummate charm. Shakespeare's model soldiers represent the best of the European aristocratic military tradition. They are exemplars of that tradition's highest values, which are summed up in a famous volume scholars know Shakespeare read: Baldassare Castiglione's Renaissance classic, *The Book of the Courtier*.

Castiglione was an eminent Italian diplomat who began his career in the court of the Duke of Urbino, a scintillating place of unparalleled cultural, artistic, and intellectual sophistication. *The Book of the Courtier* distills the essence of Urbino's charms, and spells out the qualities that make it the ideal Renaissance court. Chief among them is the presence of countless Renaissance gentlemen, perfect specimens who are, in short, everything you'd want your son to grow up to be. Their defining attribute, the most important ingredient of the ideal chivalric life, is something called in Italian *sprezzatura*. The word is almost impossible to render in English, except by making reference to the defining characteristics of the Count of Monte Cristo, or James Bond, or, ironically, Shakespeare's own perfect soldiers. *Sprezzatura* has to do with effortlessness, ease in all situations, the ability to make even the most arduous task seem casual, and a knack for seeming to do the most challenging things without devoting to them any preparation or even a moment's thought. Shakespeare's soldiers have *sprezzatura* to spare, and when you have occasion to talk about anyone in the service, you can turn to them for the words you'll need.

## HE DISTINGUISHED HIMSELF IN BATTLE

Here's Shakespeare for the Occasion of the Honorable Discharge, or the Medal-Pinning Ceremony, or even the Admiring Salute.

> **He hath done good service, lady, in these wars.**
>
> —MESSENGER, *Much Ado About Nothing*, I.I.40

***How to say it:***

- If your sprezzaturish soldier is a woman, then start with *She*, and if the person you're talking to is no lady, then substitute *sirrah* (SEER-ah) or *fellow*, or, to avoid gender altogether, try *truly*.

**LET'S FURTHER THINK ON THIS . . .**

When journalistic panjandrum Ted Koppel watched American troops drive their tanks into Iraq at the start of Operation Iraqi Freedom, he quoted *Henry V*—or what he said was *Henry V*; it was actually *Julius Caesar*, but Ted still gets an A for effort—when he turned to the camera and gravely said, "Wreak havoc and unleash the dogs of war." Okay, so the actual quote begins *Cry havoc*, not *wreak*, and it's *let slip* the dogs, not *unleash*. Whatever. A hat tip to Ted for finding a Bardism for the most unlikely of occasions.

## PLEASE DON'T LET MY BELOVED SOLDIER GET INJURED

The folks back on the home front always worry sick about their brave sons and daughters, brothers and sisters, and mothers and fathers on the front lines. This Bardism is Shakespeare's expression of the prayer in their hearts, Shakespeare on the Occasion of a Loved One in Harm's Way:

O you leaden messengers
That ride upon the violent speed of fire,
Fly with false aim, cleave the still-piecing air
That sings with piercing, do not touch my lord.

—Helena, *All's Well That Ends Well*, 3.2.108–11

***In other words:***

Hear me, you bullets, you lead deliverymen that travel fast on a fiery explosion: miss your mark! Split apart the air that closes together again behind you, air that makes a whizzing noise as you fly. Just don't touch my husband!

***How to say it:***

- Helena's metaphor here imagines bullets as messengers made of lead that ride violently and fast not on horseback but instead on fire. It's an image that's typical of her rich imagination, which marks her as one of the most poetical of all Shakespeare's heroines. To bring this speech to life, imagine that wherever you are, you're capable of speaking directly to the enemy artillery being fired on whatever battlefield where your beloved may be fighting. Think of yourself making a cell-phone call to an AK-47 in Anbar Province: "Yo, bullets! Listen up! Make all the noise you want, but don't hit my honey!"

- The monosyllabic phrases on lines 3 and 4 are the most important words in the speech. Take your time with them and give each word in them real weight. *Fly. With. False. Aim! Do. Not. Touch. My. Lord!*

- The vowels in these lines are also indispensable and highly expressive. The long *o* sound that starts the speech; the three long *i*'s in *ride*, *violent*, and *fire*; the long *i*, long *a*, long *e*, *ooooh*, *uhhhh*, and *awww* of lines 3 and 4: these make Helena's speech into a kind of aria of plaintiveness and desperate prayer. Explore them.

- Substitute *lady* for *lord*, or, if some other term is more appropriate to your soldier, use *boy*, *girl*, *man*, or *wife*.

## SHAKESPEARE ON REPUTATION

*The purest treasure mortal times afford*
*Is spotless reputation; that away,*
*Men are but gilded loam, or painted clay.*
—Mowbray, *Richard II*, 1.1.177–79

Shakespeare's was a period obsessed with rank, status, and hierarchy. Among the hoi polloi, one's place in the pecking order determined everything from where one lived to whom one married to what one did on the job. At court, the other end of the social spectrum, the vicissitudes of rank also counted for everything. The game of "who loses and who wins; who's in, who's out," as Lear puts it, was a blood sport. A gaffe could be disastrous, a faux pas could derail a career, and a scandal could—and often did—end in tragedy. Sound familiar? In the Renaissance, as today, when "mistakes have been made," the consequences are dire. That explains why nearly every one of Shakespeare's mentions of reputation comes in the context of the unbearable thought of its endangerment or imminent loss, and why his most vivid passages on the matter remain among the most frequently quoted lines from his plays. For all the differences between our society and Shakespeare's, they have in common a fear of public disgrace and a keen sense of the devastation that follows it.

## NOTHING'S MORE IMPORTANT THAN MY GOOD NAME

If you don't agree with *Richard II*'s Duke of Mowbray, quoted above, that a good reputation is "the purest treasure mortal times afford," then just ask Eliot Spitzer, Gary Hart, Larry Craig, John Edwards, or any of the other beyond-reproach politicos who have in recent years flamed out in public shamefests of their own invention. They'll tell you what it feels like to utter the cri de coeur that shatters forth from *Othello*'s Lt. Cassio, the Act 2, Scene 3 lines that are the last word on a precipitous fall from grace:

> Reputation, reputation, reputation—O, I ha' lost my reputation, I ha' lost the immortal part of myself, and what remains is bestial! My reputation, Iago, my reputation!

Scandal-prone politicians usually have only themselves to blame for their tattered reputations. Cassio, on the other hand, is set up by a bad guy: Iago. Honest, honest Iago. In an irony so typical of how Shakespeare sees the world, this hypocrite, this wizard of deceit, this manufacturer of Spitzerian disgraces, gets the great Bardism on the importance of a good reputation.

> Good name in man and woman, dear my lord,
> Is the immediate jewel of their souls.
> Who steals my purse steals trash; 'tis something, nothing;
> 'Twas mine, 'tis his, and has been slave to thousands.
> But he that filches from me my good name
> Robs me of that which not enriches him
> And makes me poor indeed.
>
> —Iago, *Othello*, 3.3.160–66

***In other words:***

For men and women alike, my friend, a good reputation is the one valuable possession held closer than any other. Swiping my money is like swiping garbage. It's worth something, sure, but it's trivial. It was mine, now it's his. So what? It belonged to thousands of others before I had it. On the other hand, whoever makes off with my reputation grabs something that doesn't make him any richer but that leaves me broke in the worst way.

***How to use it:***

- With this Bardism, you can urge someone to consider the consequences of their actions before they commit to them. Or you can remind someone who would level an accusation that they hold tremendous power in their hands. It's Shakespeare on the Occasion of Castigating a Gossip, as well as Shakespeare on the Occasion of "Governor, what *were* you thinking?"
- The speech's many antitheses are crucial to communicating its sense. *Man* versus *woman*; *purse* versus *trash*; *something* versus *nothing*; *mine* versus *his*; and *not enriches him* versus *makes me poor.* These antitheses all support an overarching opposition that shapes the entire speech: *steals my purse* versus *filches my good name.* Note that the two halves of that juxtaposition are on either side of a very important fulcrum: *But.* This speech is a great illustration of that little word's power in Shakespeare. You can't emphasize it too much. "But" turns an argument around and drives home its central point.
- Substitute *dear my lady* for *dear my lord* if necessary.

## I WANT TO BE KNOWN AS AN HONORABLE PERSON

Shakespeare well knows a storytelling principle that might be called the Gospel According to the Tabloid Journalist: the destruction of a reputation sells more newspapers than the building of one. It sells more theater tickets, too. But unlike the ink-stained wretches of the *New York Post*, the ink-stained Bard of Avon boasts a preternatural command of a key principle of good dramatic construction, namely, that you can't get theatrical value out of a giant's fall in Act 5 unless you've established the giant's spotless bona fides in Acts 1 through 4. Adhering to this principle, Shakespeare makes sure that all his characters who endure devastating public shame—both those who survive it and those who don't—spend a fair amount of time talking up their devotion to the very values whose abandonment leads to trouble. And no value gets more face time with the canon's greatest heroes than that old standby of soldiers, politicians, and people of integrity the world over, honor. Brutus talks (and talks) about it; Hamlet soliloquizes about it; Coriolanus rants about it; Hermione and Queen Katherine swear oaths upon it. All these figures enjoy richly deserved reputations for unimpeachable honor. Only one character, however, delivers an all-occasions quotable on the subject: King Henry V, with Shakespeare on the Occasion of a Deep Commitment to Honor:

> By Jove, I am not covetous for gold,
> Nor care I who doth feed upon my cost;
> It ernes me not if men my garments wear;
> Such outward things dwell not in my desires.
> But if it be a sin to covet honor,
> I am the most offending soul alive.
>
> —King Henry, *Henry V*, 4.3.24–29

***In other words:***

I swear to God, I'm not into money. I don't care how huge an entourage lives off my bank account. I'm not upset if other people use my stuff. These material things aren't my gig. But if it's bad to be addicted to honor, then today I consider myself the wickedest man on the face of the earth.

***How to use it:***

- For all you politicians out there, this is a great speech for that defiant press conference in which you deny all the tawdry allegations against you. You admit to wrongdoing and to being less than perfect, but the crime you cop to is valuing honor higher than anything else in life. It's a perfect piece of political jujitsu—the iambic pentameter version of the Checkers speech, "I am not a crook," and "I did not have sex with that woman" all rolled into one. Of course, the speech also works fine with no ulterior motive: use it to announce to the world exactly how unassailable is your rectitude.

- To use the speech in tribute to the sturdy weave of another's moral fiber, simply change the first-person pronouns to the second person if you're speaking directly to your paragon, or to third-person pronouns if you're speaking about him or her. Some verbs may have to change, too: *I am* in lines 1 and 6 would become *you are* or *he is*; *care I* would become *care you* or *cares she.*

- Henry uses antithesis in an interesting way in this speech. He opposes the abstract idea *honor* in line 5 to the collective idea *outward things* in line 4.

- Line 3's *ernes* is an obscure word. It's an old spelling of *earns*, which in Shakespeare's day could be more or less synonymous with *grieves.* When I directed the play, that's what Henry said: *It grieves me not if men my garments wear.* Feel free to make that change.

## SHAKESPEARE ON VIOLENT CONFRONTATION

*Let's make us medicines of our great revenge*
*To cure this deadly grief.*
—MALCOLM, *Macbeth*, 4.3.215–16

In Shakespeare's plays, as in life, sometimes conflict escalates from the firm but non-violent disagreement of a cold war to the vicious physical confrontation of a hot one. That escalation is accompanied by escalating rhetoric that ratchets up the heat a degree at a time, until it boils over. I despise violence and I'd much rather see disputes resolved over a nice meal than in a back alley, but I've watched enough episodes of *The Sopranos* to recognize that, alas, sometimes a knuckle sandwich is the only food that will do the job. So I here offer a selection of Bardisms I'd call Shakespeare on the Occasions of Violence: making a threat, vowing revenge, and coming to blows.

### I'LL GET BACK AT YOU EVENTUALLY

I wouldn't know much about this, but I understand that certain high school students who prefer books to sports are often picked on by the bully gang. The bespectacled nerds may not be able to hold their own through fisticuffs, but some literary pugilistics can at least generate a buffer of condescension sufficient enough to let them retreat with dignity. Hamlet, hero of brooding bookish types the world over, offers this exemplar of the "Don't worry, you'll get yours" genre:

Let Hercules himself do what he may,
The cat will mew, and dog will have his day.
—HAMLET, *Hamlet*, 5.1.276–77

***In other words:***

Not even the strongest superhero on earth could bar me from my eventual triumph.

***How to use it:***

- Use the rhyme of *may* and *day* to put a nice flourish on your vow of revenge to come, making sure that your vocal energy drives through to the word at the end of each line.
- *Hercules* is the most powerful obstacle you can think of, the perfect image of how even the greatest bar won't stand in your way. Be sure to endow his name with grandiosity and super strength as you say it. The alliterative *h*'s in *Hercules* and *himself* will help you hit a hyperbole home run.
- The monosyllabic nature of the second line will make you take it slowly and deliberately, and spread the iambic stress across each word. But remember that *cat* and *dog*, like *mew* and *have his day*, are antitheses, so those words need special stress.

***Some details:***

Hamlet here appropriates a proverb familiar in Shakespeare's day: "Every dog has his day." Many of the phrases we think of as being Shakespearean coinages were in fact extant proverbs that he merely imported into his dialogue. This practice is one of the ways that Shakespeare makes his lines sound like natural speech; we all spice our conversation with liberal sprinklings of well-known catchphrases, clichés, famous lines from movies, and proverbial wisdom from various sources (even Shakespeare!). Sometimes in the plays, a character who speaks a familiar aphorism will identify it as such and put it in quotation marks, as when the Duke of Gloucester sums up his unceremonious dismissal from King Henry VI's court with "The ancient proverb will be well effected: / 'A staff is quickly found to beat a dog.'" Countless other times, a character will simply say something that he or she assumes the other characters, and the audience, surely recognize as a time-tested truism. Today, four hundred years later, when many of those once-standard maxims are lost to history and linguistic change, we can't as readily identify them as familiar turns of phrase, so we cavalierly attribute them to Shakespeare, in whose plays they seem to appear first.

However, there is one extraordinary scholarly resource, very much in the vein of the Furness *Variorum* I praised in "Shakespeare on Relationship Troubles" above, that helps disentangle the proverbial from the Shakespearean. That is Morris Tilley's 1950 *Dictionary of the Proverbs in England in the Sixteenth and Seventeenth Centuries*, an exhaustive nine-hundred-page compilation. Every bit as monomaniacal as Furness *père et fils* (monomania is a common affliction among professional Shakespeare scholars), Tilley devoted thirty years to his scrupulously detailed and mind-bogglingly comprehensive magnum opus, and, like the first runner at Marathon, he died the moment he crossed the finish line, leaving a protégé to see the completed manuscript through to publication.

Tilley's intention was to do a service to Shakespeare by codifying his mastery of apothegmatic lore, and he succeeded. In honor of his memory, I state for the record that "Every dog has his day" is citation number D464 in the professor's *Dictionary.*

## I'M GONNA MESS YOU UP!

Shakespearean insults are pretty easy to find all over the Web, in books, and even on coffee mugs (I have one, and every morning the witty venom printed on its sides jolts me awake as bracingly as the coffee it contains). Because so many of them are only a mouse click away, I've chosen to include only one, my fave. I call this Bardism a non-threat threat, or Shakespeare on the Occasion of Knowing You'd Better Say Something, But Not Knowing Quite What:

> I will have such revenges on you both,
> That all the world shall—I will do such things—
> What they are, yet I know not; but they shall be
> The terrors of the earth!
>
> —LEAR, *King Lear*, 2.4.274–77

***How to use it:***

- Although in its dramatic context this speech arises from Lear's profound pain and incontinent anger at the ill treatment his daughters Goneril and Regan have dealt him, it nonetheless has a certain comic aspect. There's a flustered incredulity and frustrated impotence to it that lend Lear's fulminations a disconcerting edge of foolishness. This strangely harrowing mixture of the clownish and the enraged is the signature tone of *King Lear*, and this is a speech I cite frequently when trying to explain Shakespeare's insistence that in good drama—as in life—the risible and the horrible generally live side by side.

  Yet I've found myself recommending this speech more for its buffoonish side than its terrifying one. I think it's the kind of speech you quote with a smile in your eyes when for the umpteenth time your children neglect to clean up their rooms. It's for the wife whose husband can't get through his thick head that he needs to put the seat down: "George, if you leave that seat up one more time, I swear to God I'm going to . . . "

- The phrase *on you both* at the end of line 1 can be swapped out for any word or phrase that characterizes the object of your threat: *on you all*; *on you, Frank*; *on those kids*; *on Jane Jones*, and so on. *He*, *she*, or *they* can also substitute for each *I* in the speech should you need to narrate, say, what Pop's going to do when he gets home.

## YOU DON'T SCARE ME, BUB

The Bardism above is for the threatener. Here's something for the threatenee: a dose of offhand dismissal that'll throw some water on whoever's fuming in your face:

> There is no terror, Cassius, in your threats,
> For I am armed so strong in honesty
> That they pass by me as the idle wind,
> Which I respect not.
>
> —Brutus, *Julius Caesar*, 4.2.121–24

***In other words:***

Your threats don't scare me, Cassius. See, I've got the most powerful weapon of all: truth. Your words fly past me like a lazy breeze, and I'm not even paying attention.

***How to say it:***

- Swap in whatever name or other term you need instead of *Cassius* (pronounced either *CASH-us* or *CASS-yus*). If your enemy has a name whose syllable count would ruin the meter of line 1, then I'd suggest *mister*, *buddy*, *bucko*, *boyo*, or the more Shakespearean *sirrah* for a man, and *missy*, *sweetie*, *honey*, or the less contemporary *lady* or *madam* for a woman. I can also image a few gender-neutral, two-syllable curse words that would work here, but this is a family book, so I'll leave them to your imagination.
- Note that line 2 follows the familiar Shakespearean syncopation pattern of monosyllables with a polysyllabic word at the end. This makes *honesty* jump out as a very special and powerful quality. The monosyllabic nature of the majority of the speech conveys just how furious Brutus is, and it's also in keeping with the tone of restraint characteristic of his speech in general. Say lines 3 and 4

through gritted teeth, really holding back from tearing your foe's head off, and making your rage seem all the more gigantic as a result.

## SHAKESPEARE ON WINNING AND LOSING

*It would make any man cold to lose.*
—CLOTEN, *Cymbeline*, 2.3.3

*Winning will put any man into courage.*
—CLOTEN, *Cymbeline*, 2.3.6

Shakespeare's brilliant warriors and soldiers go into battle vowing to win, but only half of them succeed. The victors are without exception quick to credit God for their good fortune. The vanquished spread blame somewhat wider, choosing to curse their foes, their weak-willed rank and file, themselves, or even fate. Curiously, given the fifty-fifty split between winners and losers at war, the plays don't offer a commensurately even distribution of the rhetoric of victory and defeat. There's vastly more of the latter. Perhaps this reflects Shakespeare's view that loss is a more poetic condition than gain, or perhaps, since the majority of the canon's losers die shortly after their fights are done, their thoughts on loss turn out to be thoughts on death, and death always merits detailed consideration. Or maybe it's just that nobody likes going to war, and so even a resounding victory is redolent with the destruction and violence that were its cost. With that cost still fresh in mind, a stemwinder of a victory speech would only seem inappropriately arrogant, callous, and tone-deaf. Still, their paucity notwithstanding, there are some terrific winner's circle pronouncements in Shakespeare, one of which I particularly like. I include that Bardism here, along with one of Shakespeare's most inspirational passages on defeat.

## I WON!

Julius Caesar may have achieved Shakespearean immortality through his famous last words, *Et tu Brute*, but he had at least one good line that, although not included by the Bard in Julius' own play, endures. It was as famous in the Renaissance as it is now, so much so that no less a rhetorician than fat John Falstaff could turn to it when necessary:

> **He saw me, and yielded, that I may justly say, with the hook-nosed fellow of Rome, "I came, saw, and overcame."**
>
> —FALSTAFF, *Henry IV, Part II*, 4.2.36–38

***How to use it:***

- This is a great piece of Shakespeare on the Occasion of Bragging Rights. Use it when you've triumphed over any nemesis, and simply substitute for the first word, *He*, any subject that fits: for example, "That driver's license test saw me, and yielded . . . "

***Some details:***

Falstaff isn't the only Shakespearean character with an affinity for Julius Caesar's famous three-part swagger. Rosalind quotes it in *As You Like It*, labeling it a "thrasonical brag."* The wicked queen in

* The superb adjective means "boastful" and derives from Thraso, the name of a ceaselessly bragging character in an ancient Roman comedy. It's one of those Shakespeare words I'd love to see come back into current use.

*Cymbeline* quotes the hook-nosed fellow's catchphrase as well. And the hippie-dippie Spanish poet Don Armado deconstructs Caesar's boast in a dazzlingly wacky love letter he writes in *Love's Labour's Lost*. For good measure, he also crams in references to King Cophetua and the "indubitate beggar Zenelophon," whoever they may be.

Although the literal translation of "*Veni, vidi, vici*" is "I came, I saw, I conquered," Caesar's catchphrase always shows up in Shakespeare with "overcame" as the English for the third word. This rendering first appears in historian Sir Thomas North's landmark 1579 translation of the Greek historian Plutarch's *Lives of the Noble Greeks and Romans*. Countless other verbal parallels establish that this book was Shakespeare's constant companion as he wrote his Roman history plays. Thus, Shakespeare's repeated use of came-saw-overcame not only sheds light on one of his historical fixations but also drops a tiny hint about his reading habits. Such little details contribute to a picture of Shakespeare the working writer, reading voraciously, rifling through research materials for stories he can dramatize, and bits of raw ore he can refine and cast into precious theatrical metals.

## WE LOST. SO WHAT?

Very few of Shakespeare's bested warriors live to fight another day, and of those who do, only one manages to find inspiration rather than despair in the experience. Lord Bardolph, one of the rebels against King Henry IV who fails to overthrow him in the battle that ends *Henry IV, Part I*, proposes in the first scene of the play's sequel that his gang should make another attempt. He offers this Bardism, Shakespeare for the Occasion of "If at First You Don't Succeed, Try, Try Again."

We all that are engagèd to this loss
Knew that we ventured on such dangerous seas
That if we wrought out life 'twas ten to one;
And yet we ventured for the gain proposed,
Choked the respect of likely peril feared;
And since we are o'erset, venture again.
Come, we will all put forth body and goods.

—Lord Bardolph, *Henry IV, Part II*, 1.1.179–85

***In other words:***

All of us who are part of this defeat knew that we were trying something so dangerous that the odds were ten to one we'd never make it. And yet try we did, because we stood to gain so much. We refused to think about the dangers that we faced. Okay, we've had a setback. Let's try again! Come on! We'll put everything we've got into it this time!

***How to say it:***

- This speech is organized around a powerful central structure that simultaneously employs two related techniques: a build, and also a multiple repetition. That structure is: *we knew we ventured . . . and yet we ventured . . . venture again*. Both techniques turn the entire sequence into one long crescendo. The build, in three parts, is its own kind of escalation: *We knew we ventured . . . and yet we ventured . . .* ***venture again***. To this, the three-peat of *venture* adds additional force: *we knew we ventured . . . and yet we ventured . . .* ***venture again***. Help Lord Bardolph—help Shakespeare—combine the two techniques into a powerful exhortation by letting this double build work its magic. These are only ten of the speech's fifty-seven words, but if you hold firm to them, they will guide you through the argument like so many bread crumbs through the dark wood in a fairy tale.

## SHAKESPEARE ON MOTIVATING THE TROOPS

*But screw your courage to the sticking-place*
*And we'll not fail.*
—Lady Macbeth, *Macbeth*, 1.7.60–61

Two eminent army generals famously quoted from Shakespeare's *Henry V* to their troops: Major General Richard Gale, commander of the British Sixth Airborne Division during World War II, and Major General Ricardo Sanchez, commander of the U.S. Army's First Armored Division at the start of Operation Iraqi Freedom. Both men assembled the troops they were about to send into battle and, to fire them up, raided King Henry's great St. Crispin's Day speech, where they found some of the best military motivational material ever written.

The St. Crispin's Day speech is a long one, and its central section is very specific to England and the English soldiers who fought that day in 1415 on "the vasty fields of France." As a modern motivational address, it serves better as a resource to be cherry-picked, as Generals Gale and Sanchez did, than as a stand-alone number. In that respect, the speech is much like the entire play, which provides such rousing inspiration for warriors that armies have taken to publishing it for distribution to each man on the front lines.

During the war in which General Gale fought, the United States government printed so-called Armed Services Editions of over a thousand titles of classic and popular literature. Formatted to fit in the pockets of combat pants, they proved so popular that by war's end over 120 million books had been provided, free of charge, to G.I. Joes in every theater of the conflict. *Henry V* made it onto the list, more or less, in the form of one chapter in poet and scholar Mark Van

Doren's glorious 1939 volume of commentary, *Shakespeare*.* As America geared up for General Sanchez's war, the Armed Services Editions were revived. This time, *Henry V* was one of only four titles chosen, and fifty thousand copies of it—again pocket-sized—made their way to the deserts of the Middle East. There, Henry's description of his army as "men wrecked upon a sand" surely didn't supply much inspiration to our uniformed men and women, but perhaps the first Bardism below did. It's from *Henry V*, but one play to raid in search of Shakespeare on the Occasion of Inspiring Your Team:

## READY? LET'S ROLL!

Shortly after rhapsodizing on how he and his too-small army are not exhausted and outnumbered but are instead "We few, we happy few, we band of brothers," Henry moves on to the task of getting his men stoked, adrenalized, and ready to charge. The key, as he sees it? Being properly psyched up:

> **All things are ready if our minds be so.**
>
> —King Henry, *Henry V*, 4.3.71

Hamlet expresses a related idea: preparedness matters most.

> **The readiness is all.**
>
> —Hamlet, *Hamlet*, 5.2.160

---

* Van Doren chaired the committee that selected the list of titles the army would publish, and he managed to slip his own book onto it—an ethical lapse, if it is one, that pales in comparison to the one his son Charles committed by being the cheater in chief of the television quiz-show scandals of the 1950s.

Gloucester puts a slightly different spin on Hamlet's notion:

> Ripeness is all.
>
> —GLOUCESTER, *King Lear*, 5.2.11

***How to use them:***

- All three of these short snippets will suit any occasion on which you find yourself at the end of a diving board and about to jump, either literally or figuratively.

***Some details:***

The subtle distinction between Hamlet's *readiness* and Gloucester's *ripeness* has inspired reams of scholarly comment. In context, both lines are about what's necessary in order to accommodate oneself to one's own death. For Hamlet, the younger man, it's a question of being prepared, mentally, emotionally, and in every other way. For the older Gloucester, it's about having fully matured, having lived to the point where the logical next step is to die, to fall, like a piece of fruit from a tree. Wordsworth thought this image was the superior of the two. He famously commented that through Gloucester, Shakespeare teaches us "when we come to die . . . what is the one thing needful," and he adds, wonderfully, "and with what a lightning-flash of condensed thought and language does he teach the lesson!"

## STRIKE WHILE THE IRON IS HOT

Shakespeare appears to have been no procrastinator. For one thing, he turned out an average of two plays each year of his writing life, plus various non-dramatic writing. (That's roughly twenty lines per day, every day, which doesn't sound like much until you consider that those twenty lines include things like "To be or not to be, that is the question.") For another, a conspicuously large number of his characters make speeches about how important it is to seize an opportunity when it comes, and not to hesitate, dawdle, or defer matters until later. Of those many bits of Shakespeare on the Occasion of No Time Like the Present, this is my favorite. (Okay, so it argues for a preemptive and ill-planned military assault. As always, the context can be disregarded so that the content can serve when the occasion arises.) It was also a favorite of my grandma Tillie, of blessed memory, and I quote it here for her.

Knowing his army will soon be outnumbered by enemy forces, Brutus, not only a politician but also a capable military man, urges his commanders to take action now and launch a strike immediately.

> There is a tide in the affairs of men
> Which, taken at the flood, leads on to fortune;
> Omitted, all the voyage of their life
> Is bound in shallows and in miseries.
> On such a full sea are we now afloat,
> And we must take the current when it serves,
> Or lose our ventures.
>
> —Brutus, *Julius Caesar*, 4.2.270–76

***In other words:***

Like the ocean, human lives are governed by tides, and, as with a sea journey, if you set sail at high tide, the voyage goes well. But if you don't, this and every voyage ends with you beached in shallow water, and miserable. It's high tide right now, and we must either set sail this instant, when all the conditions are favorable, or lose everything.

***How to say it:***

- Imagine a number of people gathered together to offer you advice. They counsel restraint, deliberation, slowing down. You know they're wrong, and so you announce your analysis of the situation, and override their objections. Be sure to give the first phrase a real lift. You're consciously speaking in metaphor, using carefully crafted, heightened language in order to make a complex idea clear and immediately graspable. Lay it out clearly: *Life has tides*. Then unpack what you mean by it: *and flood tides are preferable to ebb tides*. Then drive your point home with the switch to monosyllables: *We. Must. Take. When. It. Serves. Or. Lose.*
- Stress these key antitheses: *taken at the flood* versus *omitted*; *leads on to fortune* versus *bound in shallows*; *take* versus *lose*.

## SHAKESPEARE ON WORK

*I cannot draw a cart, nor eat dried oats;*
*If it be a man's work, I'll do it.*
—Captain, *King Lear*, 5.3.39–40

Workingmen abound in Shakespeare's plays. A cobbler and a carpenter open *Julius Caesar*, two gravediggers ply their trade in *Hamlet*, a gardener and his assistant tend to fruit trees in *Richard II*, and a tailor makes Kate a dress in *The Taming of the Shrew*. There's also a tailor in *A Midsummer Night's Dream*. His pals, a bunch of "rude mechanicals" with showbiz dreams, include a carpenter, a bellows mender, a weaver, a tinker (an Elizabethan handyman), and a joiner (a woodworker who specializes in framing buildings). The play's list of characters reads like the program at a tradesmen's convention.

For the most part, Shakespeare treats these working characters with affection and respect, although he now and then indulges in a few condescending jokes at their expense: their breath reeks of garlic, they're not the sharpest bunch. These wisecracks would have amused the aristocrats in his audience as much as it would have irritated his working-class, glovemaker father. But although Shakespeare's aspirational yearnings, royal patronage, and material successes may have aligned his attitudes with those of the high end of the social scale, he never forgot his origins in a working family and a market town. Throughout the canon he nails the technical lingo of workingmen's crafts with such accuracy that sometimes it feels like he must have moonlighted at Ye Olde Home Depot. And if Shakespeare's father was indeed put out by his son's sometime snootiness, William the good papa's boy apologized by shouting out to his father's trade in dozens of places, including *Twelfth Night*, *Hamlet*, and Sonnet 111. In that poem, he observes how our work defines who we are: "my nature is subdued / To what it works in, like the dyer's hand." The leather dyes that John Shakespeare could no more wash from his skin than Lady Macbeth could Duncan's imaginary blood from hers gave his boy a way to talk about what his own job had become to him: a permanent mark, a badge of identity, an essential and indelible part of who he was. Dad had to have appreciated that filial salute.

## I'M REPORTING FOR DUTY

Given the relentless and breakneck writing pace he maintained all his life, Shakespeare clearly knew what it meant to work hard. This knowledge wends its way into his plays in some terrific passages about rolling up our sleeves, putting our noses to our respective grindstones, and doing the hustle we all must do in order to buy baby those new shoes.

First, Shakespeare on the Occasion of the Expert Coming in to Save the Day:

> The strong necessity of time commands
> Our services a while.
>
> —Antony, *Antony and Cleopatra*, 1.3.42–43

***In other words:***

The fierce urgency of now demands that I get to work.

***How to use it:***

- Use this speech when you're the hero arriving to the rescue, as when a firefighter strides over to a wailing child staring up at her cat stuck high in a tree. Or use it as Antony does, as an excuse to make a quick exit from someplace you'd rather not be. Or use it when your employees can't quite figure stuff out and you need to swoop in to get the job done.

Second, Shakespeare on the Occasion of Whistling While We Work:

> To business that we love we rise betime,
> And go to't with delight.
>
> —Antony, *Antony and Cleopatra*, 4.4.20–21

***In other words:***

We get up early in order to do stuff we love, and we do it joyfully.

***How to use it:***

- This is the Bardism you need when your partner moans that the alarm has gone off before sunrise. "I know you want to sleep, but

I love my job, so I've got to wake up early." It also serves to rouse an oversleeping teenager who'd rather not get ready for school, work, that ice-fishing trip you've been planning, and so on. Or the lines can be bent to a more ironic reading than the one Shakespeare intends. Scheduled to start that house-painting job at 5:00 A.M.? Let Antony express how "happy" you are.

Third, the motto of Elizabethan FedEx, or, Shakespeare on the Occasion of It Absolutely, Positively Has to Be There Overnight:

> I'll put a girdle round about the earth
> In forty minutes.
>
> —Puck, *A Midsummer Night's Dream*, 2.1.175

***In other words:***

I'm gonna run like heck. (Literally, I'll tie a belt around the planet in less than an hour.)

***How to use it:***

- Puck's famous line also lends itself to irony. I've seen many productions where he sneers the words at his boss, the fairy king Oberon, then lopes slowly offstage like someone being paid by the hour. On the other hand, many Pucks play this moment with genuine, even overeager, enthusiasm. In that sense, it's a great line for that first week on a new job, when pleasing the boss is your highest priority.

## KNOCK YOURSELF OUT, I'LL CHILL

If the three hardworking Bardisms above have tired you out, don't despair. Here's another that will justify a little break.

**I were better to be eaten to death with a rust than to be scoured to nothing with perpetual motion.**

—FALSTAFF, *Henry IV, Part II,* 1.2.198–200

***In other words:***

I'd rather rust away than wear myself down to nothing by working too hard.

***How to use it:***

- My own teenage nephew once out-Shakespeared me with this line. When I asked him on a gorgeous spring day why he was inside playing Xbox rather than getting some fresh air outdoors, he answered matter-of-factly with this Falstaffian blow-off. I could only congratulate him in response. Use it, as he did, as the national anthem of the United States of Couch Potatoes.

CHAPTER 5

# And Then the Justice

## SHAKESPEARE FOR THE OCCASIONS OF LIFE'S MIDDLE YEARS

*And then the justice,*
*In fair round belly with good capon lined,*
*With eyes severe, and beard of formal cut,*
*Full of wise saws and modern instances;*
*And so he plays his part.*

The wars ended, the brave soldiers return home and resume their civilian lives. There are families to raise, homes to build, businesses to run. Step by step society walks forward, in the Renaissance as in our own time, as yesterday's moony youth matures into today's conquering hero and then tomorrow's seen-it-all elder. So steady is this progression, so stable, that society anticipates it, formalizes it, and frames it with the trappings of institution. Rules evolve and structures for governance develop. Bylaws describe procedures, mechanisms resolve disputes, insurance mitigates risk, and soon all that might be turbulent acquires, like the actors under Hamlet's tutelage, "a temperance that may give it smoothness." In such a world, change comes not fast and furious but slow and steady, and moderation—conservation—is the watchword, protecting, defending, and reassuring. Safety first: there is a tide in the affairs of men, to be sure, but it ebbs just as certainly as it floods, and the law of entropy—that everything tends slowly toward stasis—applies to human interactions no less than it does to the interplay of subatomic particles.

Entropy is a law whose jurisdiction is the Court of Midlife, where the attorneys who argue cases are members of the Middle-Aged Bar Association and the presiding judge is the Honorable Justice Jaques' Fifth Age. Justice JFA, as he's known, is serious-minded, as witness his intense gaze. A tad overweight—that happens when the odometer clicks past forty—he's nonetheless appearance-conscious, sharing with the soldier of Jaques' Fourth Age a taste for distinctively styled facial hair. Not shy about speaking his mind, he's ready for any subject with both time-tested wisdom and also the latest cutting-edge theory. All in all, he seems to be everything you'd want in a judge, the very model of modern jurisprudential probity.

But wait—this judge springs from Shakespeare's (well, from Jaques') imagination. And just as a Jaquean baby is merely bodily fluids and noise, a schoolboy always a truant, a lover by definition a silly twit, and a soldier perforce a bragging idiot, so for Jaques an apparently unimpeachable jurist is in fact anything but. The four seemingly beguiling lines with which he—with which Shakespeare—paints a word portrait of a figure of Solomonic wisdom and integrity turn out on closer inspection to encode enough subversive detail to freeze a gavel in midstrike.

Consider the capon that lines the Justice's round belly. It sounds from the context as though it's some kind of delicacy, the sort of rich dish served in the wood-paneled dining room of the club to which the Justice belongs, and that's partially correct. A capon is a male chicken whose meat is uncommonly tasty and moist thanks to its very high fat content. The bird is fat because it's raised to be much more sedate than the typical cock, normally so aggressive that it's bred for fighting as often as for eating. Caponization, the process that becalms the bird, is achieved by castrating the poor thing at a young age and then encouraging its couch-potato (coop-potato?) lifestyle until it's all chubby and ready for slaughter. Caponization is illegal in most countries today (although capon meat itself is not, oddly) making capon a boutique dish that's as expensive and hard to find as a cheeseburger made of Kobe beef, but in the Renaissance, capon was the decadent repast that everyone craved. Priced beyond the reach of most mere mortals, and certainly above the pay grade of a civil servant like a justice of the peace, it became the ideal gift to present when looking for a favor. One anonymous wag of the period makes plain in a fun piece of doggerel that in law courts, capon was the bribe of choice:

> Now poor men to the justices
>     With capons make their errants,
> And if they hap to fail of these,
>     They plague them with their warrants.*

So redolent with chicken fat was the air in the chambers of many local magistrates that they came to be known as "capon justices," and in a parliamentary debate on the issue only a year after Jaques' speech was first spoken at the Globe, an MP railed, "A justice of the peace is a living creature that for half a dozen chickens will dispense with a dozen of penal statutes."

---

* *Errants* is the same word as *errands*, but its *t* makes a happier rhyme with *warrants*. *They* in the final line refers, of course, not to *poor men* but to the hungry—and vengeful—Justices.

In the unlikely event that Shakespeare's audiences weren't up on the latest trends in judicial bribery, then the latest trends in judicial facial hair would have given them another clue about the Justice's true character. Jaques' irritation at men's beardly vanity—his soldier was "bearded like the pard" in emulation of the great military man the Earl of Essex; now his judge sports a "beard of formal cut," that is, trimmed with a special, and presumably pretentious, appropriateness to its wearer's vaunted station—was common among satirists of the period. One of the greats, the pamphleteer Philip Stubbes, penned an attack against the affectations of the smarter set called *The Anatomie of Abuses*, and he rants in it that a conspiracy among barbers is responsible for the beardly excesses of the day. Stubbes catalogues the many absurd styles a man could request: the French cut, the Spanish cut, the Italian cut, the Dutch cut, the new cut, the old cut, the bravado cut, the mean cut, the gentleman's cut, the common cut, "and infinite like vanities which I overpass." It's easy to imagine Jaques—and Shakespeare—leafing through Stubbes with a belly laugh and a notebook at the ready, and then deploying snippets of his hilarious venom when choosing to detail the most venal of the Seven Ages of Man.

And just in case Jaques' descriptions of the Justice's diet and look don't sufficiently convey the fact that he's a bungler, the things he says surely will. He's got old material and new; the old (*wise saws*) are canned sayings, clichés, overused to the point of becoming trite; and the new (*modern instances*) are, like everything else *modern* in Shakespeare's canon, trivial, ordinary, commonplace, the kind of self-consciously up-to-date insight that's absurd on its face if not altogether meaningless. Justice Fifth Age dispenses wash-and-wear advice of the TV talk-show variety: "There's no time like the present" passes for eternal wisdom, and "Pink is the new black" represents the cutting edge in words to live by. The very sounds of Jaques' description echo with the Justice's pomposity and windbaggery. The sonorous vowels that dot the speech—"fair round belly" resounds with *aaaayyy*, *owwwww*, *ehhhhh*, and "eyes severe and beard of formal cut" features *aaaayyy*, *eeeeerr*, *eeeeerr*, *awwwwr*, *uhhhhh*—signal even to a listener who speaks no English that something about this fellow isn't quite right. And the whopper vowels in "wise saws" are hewn roughly at their ends by buzzing *z*'s, telling us unmistakably that while this sad-eyed fellow may be an expert in the law, he's also no slouch at bloviation. No wonder Jaques, for whom wit and pith are the ultimate values, finds him contemptible.

To be sure, the subversive significance of capons, formal beards, old saws, and modern instances isn't necessarily accessible to today's Shakespeare fans, or Shakespeare quoters. As one editor of *As You Like It* remarks of the capon as bribe, "The allusion here was probably more intelligible in the time of Shakespeare than it is at present." That's undoubtedly so, but for me, retrieving these lost nuances of meaning is part of the fun of working on the Bard's plays. To exhume from beneath the lines such details as the barbers whose crazy tastes in beards made them into Elizabethan versions of Edward Scissorhands is to travel backward in time to a Tudor England in which the familiar "ye olde" image of thatched roofs, thick beams lacing geometric patterns through walls of white stucco, and smiling wenches yo-ho-ho-ing tankards of ale in the friendly confines of the Publick House becomes something more complex, something more real. Something more like life.

That's how I like my Shakespeare: recognizable, actual, and alive. That Shakespeare, and not the one on the porcelain plate for sale in a Stratford souvenir stand, is the one who comes to mind when I read in the morning paper of a local official who sold his influence to the highest bidder—for cash, not capons, but what's the difference? That

Shakespeare, and not the one mummified by some BBC recording from 1950, is the one whose voice rings in my ear when I read an interview with, say, Supreme Court Justice Antonin Scalia (he of the eyes severe), in which wise saws and modern instances express his views on important matters of yesterday and today. The living Shakespeare is the one who makes you say, "That's it, exactly!" Shakespeare alive is Shakespeare for all occasions, and Shakespeare for the Fifth Age of Man is Shakespeare for the real events of midlife: events concerned with sophisticated things, mature themes, and matters monetary, dietary, and judiciary.

## SHAKESPEARE ON MIDDLE AGE

*I am declined*
*Into the vale of years—yet that's not much.*
—Othello, *Othello*, 3.3.269–70

Shakespeare died in 1616 at age fifty-two, and it's a commonplace in discussions of the Bard's life and times that while fifty-two seems terribly young in comparison to our modern life spans of eight decades or more, in comparison to the average Renaissance life expectancy of thirty-five or so, Shakespeare enjoyed a respectably long run. But that fixation on thirty-five as life's terminus can be misleading. History records countless individuals who lived decades longer than Shakespeare, some in his own family, and the dramatis personae of the playwright's own canon would fill to capacity the waiting room of any Jacobean geriatrician.

In truth, the period's average life expectancy is more accurately understood as an expression of how unlikely it was to make it out of childhood in the first place. After all, mathematics yields an average life expectancy of thirty-five when one person dies at sixty-five and another at five—the lower number makes all the difference. Shakespeare's day knew infant mortality rates that were shockingly high, and various incurable childhood diseases claimed half of all English children by the time they reached four. Half of the half of girls who survived puberty died giving birth to the next generation, and half of the half of boys who were their peers died either in one of the endless military conflicts of the age, or of the plague or some other epidemic disease, or from primitive and ineffectual medical practices, or of malnutrition, or lack of proper sanitation, or from some noxious agent in the food supply, or, or, or, or. Death was woven prominently into the fabric of every life, and in such a context, Shakespeare's survival into middle age must be reckoned a triumph of endurance and a cause for celebration.

## I'M BETWEEN OLD AND YOUNG

One vivid Shakespearean take on middle age acknowledges how hard it is to define anything that's in the middle: it's neither one extreme nor the other, neither what came before nor what's coming after. Jaques' Fifth Age? Think of it in terms of other periods of life that are a bit easier to pin down. If life is a journey, then middle age is a kind of layover between the young soldier's foolish excesses, the behavior of man's Fourth Age, and the nostalgic senior citizen's overly sentimental effusions, the dotage of man's Sixth.

> KING LEAR **How old art thou?**
> KENT **Not so young, sir, to love a woman for singing, nor so old to dote on her for anything. I have years on my back forty-eight.**
>
> —*King Lear*, 1.4.33–35

***In other words:***

KING LEAR How old are you?

KENT I'm not that young that I get infatuated with a woman for some pretty feature like a nice voice. And I'm not that old that I start getting all mushy and sentimental about any random thing. I'm forty-eight.

***How to say it:***

- Note how indirectly Kent answers Lear's question. Rather than just stating his age straight out, he offers instead a wry riddle. There's wit about his first sentence, an ironic and winking sense of humor. The second sentence, on the other hand, is plain, hard fact. Imagine the difference between "Well, I'm old enough to vote but not old enough to collect Social Security" and "I'm thirty-nine years old." There's a shift of tone between the two sentences. When you quote this speech, embrace that shift, and have fun with the witty way you stall before pronouncing your true age.
- Kent makes expert use of a series of antitheses: *young* versus *old* is of course the central one, along with *to love* versus *to dote*, and *for singing* versus *for anything.*
- It would be easy enough to offer a female-gendered equivalent of this speech, but since it's extraordinarily ungentlemanly to ask a woman her age, I'll spare my women readers on the shy side of fifty the awkwardness of having a way to answer.

## LIFE IMPROVES WITH AGE

The conventional wisdom of our new millennium holds that "forty is the new twenty" and "sixty is the new forty." Shakespeare would, I think, have found both phrases most amusing—and not unfamiliar. He wrote his own version of the wise saw that life begins in middle age, and put it in the mouth of an optimistic and entirely sincere young woman to pronounce to the world.

> The heavens forbid
> But that our loves and comforts should increase,
> Even as our days do grow!
>
> —DESDEMONA, *Othello*, 2.1.190–92

***In other words:***

May God ordain no other course than this: that as we grow older, our loves may grow deeper, and our material comforts, greater.

***How to use it:***

- This is an ideal bit of Shakespeare for use as a birthday toast to someone in midlife, or on any other occasion that marks a milestone of the middle years: retirement, the purchase of second home, and so on.
- Rely on the passage's three verbs (each of which falls at the end of a verse line) to help you through it: *forbid*, *increase*, and *grow*. Stressing these will in turn help you mark the structural symmetry that shapes Desdemona's wish: that *good things remain abundant* even as *we get older.*

## SHAKESPEARE ON JUSTICE

> *In law, what plea so tainted and corrupt*
> *But, being seasoned with a gracious voice,*
> *Obscures the show of evil?*
>
> —BASSANIO, *The Merchant of Venice*, 4.2.68

It's obvious from Shakespeare's plays—brimful of legal language, legal principles, lawyers, judges, and trials—that he knew a lot about the law, and one of the most striking details about his life is how large a proportion of the scant record of it consists of legal documents. Apparently his intimacy with what Hamlet calls quiddities, quillets, cases, tenures, and tricks—lawyerly arcana—derived from his own lived experience. His name appears on many real estate papers, most having to do with the lease, purchase, and sale of the Globe Theatre and the land on which it stood, and on a mortgage for a property he owned in the City of London. His officially notarized last will and testament survives, in which he leaves his wife his "second best bed," whatever that odd phrase might mean. Surviving court records show that he was the plaintiff in a number of lawsuits, most involving the recovery of debts owed him.

He also testified in a trial or two, including one rather melodramatic case involving a marriage contract that went awry. In the years just prior to his retirement to Stratford, Shakespeare's London address was a spread of rented rooms in the Silver Street home of French immigrants named Christopher and Marie Mountjoy. Mary, their daughter, fell for a young apprentice in Christopher's millinery shop. When he asked for Mary's hand in marriage, Shakespeare, clearly a close friend of the family, officiated at a ceremony in which the young couple formally pledged their troth. The wedding followed, and then, in a twist straight out of one of Uncle Will's plays, the couple's loving relationship imploded in an angry dispute over the size of Mary's dowry. The groom sued, and Shakespeare was summoned to court to swear out a deposition in the matter.

His statement survives, as does his signature on it, one of only six that historians consider authentic. Scholars who've analyzed it claim that it's difficult to miss Shakespeare's displeasure with the whole affair. "Wm Shakspe," he scrawled, scarcely legibly, as though his body was out the door before his hand finished writing, as though he managed only barely to stop himself writing his own famous line from *Henry VI, Part II*: "The first thing we do let's kill all the lawyers."

## POETIC JUSTICE IS THE BEST KIND

As consistently and prolifically inventive a wordsmith as Shakespeare was, he could now and then outdo even himself. His finest hours are those famous phrases that still appear in the everyday lexicon of English speakers born four centuries after his death—"it's Greek to me," "the primrose path," "my pound of flesh," "to give the devil his due." Here's another: a Bardism for those very enjoyable moments when some jerk gets his long-overdue comeuppance.

> Let it work,
> For 'tis the sport to have the engineer
> Hoist with his own petard.
>
> —Hamlet, *Hamlet*, 3.4.185.4–185.6

***In other words:***

Bring it on. It's great fun when a bomb maker is blown sky high by his own device.

***Some details:***

Your edition of Shakespeare may call Hamlet's *engineer* an *enginer*, a spelling that perhaps better conjures the word's Renaissance meaning. An *enginer* invented and built *engines*, or mechanical devices, and specifically engines of war, or weaponry. Just a few years before Shakespeare wrote *Hamlet*, some creative enginer whose name has been lost to history created a new gizmo for breaching walls or doors. It was a small case packed with explosive materials under pressure and sealed tight, so that when it was set off, it did serious damage. (Understandably, workplace accidents in engineers' ateliers were common—so much so that Shakespeare could refer to them in a popular play. Whether or not anyone joined Hamlet in finding such mishaps amusing is harder to guess.) This crafty inventor called his creation a *petard* (the final *d* is silent), in tribute, I like to think, to his ten-year-old son, because the word comes from the Middle French *peter*, which means "to fart." That little piece of information bestows a whole other level of meaning on being hoist with your own petard, but, as Polonius says earlier in the play, "let that go."

### LET'S FURTHER THINK ON THIS . . .

Perhaps the least likely Shakespeare quoter I've come across is the so-called twentieth hijacker of 9/11 infamy, Zacarias Moussaoui, a man who was certainly "hoist with his own petard." Throughout his trial in a Virginia federal court, Moussaoui served as his own counsel, and in that capacity he talked and lectured and harangued and grandstanded for months and months. His courtroom monologues were often all but incomprehensible, and his legal moves sometimes bizarre and contradictory. One such was his decision to withdraw his initial guilty plea after consulting various Islamic legal texts. Oddly, though, when he entered his revised plea of not guilty, it was not the Islamic canon he cited. Instead, Moussaoui said this: "Somebody say [*sic*] to be or not to be, that is the question. And today I say guilty or not guilty, that is the question." The jury say guilty, and now Moussaoui has all the time he'll need to grab a book from the library at the Supermax prison in Florence, Colorado, and learn just who that somebody was who say "To be or not to be, that is the question."

## BE MERCIFUL, NOT HARSH

Were there a list of the Shakespeare Top Ten, this speech would surely be on it. One of the gems of the Bard's middle period, it is a superb instance of his gift for writing verse that works simultaneously in its dramatic context and also when lifted out of it. In context, it's a plea made by one character that another temper his righteous anger and unrestrained appetite for revenge. Out of context, it's a glorious reminder that justice need not always be harsh, and that compassion, learned from God, is one of man's highest values.

> The quality of mercy is not strained.
> It droppeth as the gentle rain from heaven
> Upon the place beneath. It is twice blest:
> It blesseth him that gives, and him that takes.
> 'Tis mightiest in the mightiest. It becomes
> The thronèd monarch better than his crown.
> His sceptre shows the force of temporal power,
> The attribute to awe and majesty,
> Wherein doth sit the dread and fear of kings;
> But mercy is above this sceptred sway.
> It is enthronèd in the hearts of kings;
> It is an attribute to God himself,
> And earthly power doth then show likest God's
> When mercy seasons justice.
>
> —PORTIA, *The Merchant of Venice*, 4.1.179–92

***In other words:***

Mercy is never forced. Instead, it drops gently like rain from heaven. It creates two blessings: it blesses both the person who acts with mercy and also the person who benefits from mercy. And it's most powerful when powerful people exercise it. On a king, it looks better than even his crown. The royal scepter is a symbol of worldly power, it's a feature that's awe-inspiring and majestic, and those qualities are what make a king strong and fearsome. But mercy is a higher sort of power. Its throne is the king's soul. It's a characteristic of God himself. And worldly power most closely resembles Divine power when mercy moderates stern justice.

***How to say it:***

- Use this speech on any occasion when some martinet in your life needs to be reminded that even the strictest rules sometimes need bending. Use it also in any situation that calls for moderation, temperance, and a middle path. (Oh, and should you ever happen to be found guilty of a crime, wheel this out when the judge asks if you have anything to say before sentencing.)
- I teach this speech when showing student actors how central the concept of antithesis is to Shakespearean thought, and how, for artists in the theater, antithesis refers not only to dictionary opposites but also to ideas whose meanings, though unrelated, are juxtaposed oppositionally by a given speaker. Portia conjures a number of paired concepts, pitted against each other, as she communicates her argument. They include: *not strained* versus *droppeth* (not strict opposites but used in opposition); *him that gives* versus *him that takes* (direct opposites); *mightiest* versus *mightiest* (the same word used as two different parts of speech); *His scepter* versus *mercy* (two abstract ideas, compared antithetically); *earthly power* versus *God's* (*power* is implied as the object of *God's*, thus two varieties of power are presented as antithetical), and, most important of all, the speech's major antithesis, *mercy* versus *justice* (in which the opposition implies that justice is necessarily tyrannical, inflexible, and harsh). As always, stress the terms being compared, and the speech will make instant sense.

- A few key verbs are also crucial to Portia's complex moral argument: *strained*, *droppeth*, *blest*, *blesseth*, *becomes*, *enthroned*, *show*, and most powerful of all, *seasons*. Indeed, that last verb makes line 14 the most important of the whole speech. Portia wants Shylock to know that justice can be qualified, adjusted, toned down, and, by analogy with the verb's sense in the context of cooking, *enhanced* by being helped with a salty, peppery pinch or two of mercy.
- Yet one other approach to this speech is to use the Paper Trick, covering the whole speech with a blank sheet of paper, then revealing it one line at a time as you say it. This will connect you to Portia's thought process, and will help you lay the speech out for your listeners with remarkable ease and clarity.

## SHAKESPEARE ON WITTY PEOPLE AND BORES

*When shall we laugh? Say, when?*
—Bassanio, *The Merchant of Venice*, 1.1.66

*More of your conversation would infect my brain,*
—Menenius, *Coriolanus*, 2.1.83–84

"I am not only witty in myself," Sir John Falstaff announces in *Henry IV, Part II*, "but the cause that wit is in other men." This outsized self-regard is typical of the Fat Knight, and given how hilarious he is, it's well earned, too. But it's also, in my experience at least, not at all typical of the truly wittiest people I know. My friends with the best funny bones tend also to be expert and thoroughly disarming self-deprecators, and not Falstaffian show-offs. In fact, Sir John excepted, most of the people I've met who are given to incessant pronouncements of their own hilarity prove in the end to be notable only in terms of how tiresome they are. On those occasions when a person of one or the other extreme enters your life—seated next to you at a dinner party or in an airplane, giving the keynote at a board meeting or business conference, maybe even on a date—these two Bardisms will prove themselves worth knowing.

## THAT'S ONE FUNNY DUDE

The word *wit* is in contemporary English almost always linked with humor, and a *witty* person is one whose silver tongue can fire off jokes and light banter with dazzling speed and prolific abandon. In Renaissance English, however, *wit* described not merely comedic gifts but also—indeed primarily—intellectual prowess overall. One's wit was one's brainpower, one's powers of observation, one's insight, and one's capacity for taking the quickest possible measure of a person or situation. For Shakespeare, wit has yet one more important connotation: it refers not just to the acuity of a person's perceptiveness but also to his capacity for expressing his thoughts about what he perceives in trenchant, keen, and memorable terms. Shakespeare talks about wit in many places in the canon, and he certainly deploys it in large doses. But in one speech in *Love's Labour's Lost*, he provides a pretty good working definition for the concept.

A merrier man,
Within the limit of becoming mirth,
I never spent an hour's talk withal.
His eye begets occasion for his wit,
For every object that the one doth catch

The other turns to a mirth-moving jest,
Which his fair tongue, conceit's expositor,
Delivers in such apt and gracious words
That agèd ears play truant at his tales,
And younger hearings are quite ravishèd,
So sweet and voluble is his discourse.

—ROSALINE, *Love's Labour's Lost*, 2.1.66–76

***In other words:***

I've never spoken with a cheerier guy (as cheery as good manners allow, anyway). His eyes light on things that activate his sense of humor. And everything his eyes see, his humor converts to some hilarious notion, which his facility with language—the public address system for his humor—pronounces. The things he says are so truthful and captivating that mature people neglect their responsibilities just to listen to him. Young people are absolutely swept off their feet by the liveliness and perfection of his rap.

***How to use it:***

- Quote this Bardism in tribute to, or by way of introduction to, any wag, wordsmith, or comedian you know.
- Some gentle rewrites—of the male pronouns to female, or of the third person to the second—will expand the number of occasions on which this piece of Shakespeare applies. An e-mail thanking someone for a great night out? Mention that it was fun because "So sweet and voluble is your discourse." Setting someone up with your hoot of a best girlfriend? "A merrier gal, / Within the limit of becoming mirth, / I never spent an hour's talk withal."
- Rely on the passage's antitheses to help you through it: *eye* versus *wit*; *the one* versus *the other*; *object* versus *jest*; *catch* versus *turns*; *agèd ears* versus *younger hearings*; *play truant* versus *are ravishèd.*

***Some details:***

*Love's Labour's Lost*, a play that contributes a handful of Bardisms to this book, is one of Shakespeare's least-produced comedies, which is a shame because it's an absolute delight. Its scarcity on the American stage is understandable, however: almost all of it is written in the vein of Rosaline's speech here. Everyone in the play speaks this kind of rhetorically elevated and formally exquisite language, and the play's many poetic meters, elaborate rhymes, and highly wrought structures ricochet about like the "paper bullets of the brain" Benedick discusses in *Much Ado About Nothing*. As if all this weren't complex enough, the characters add to the mix ceaseless wordplay, an endless series of literary allusions, and a vocabulary that's as baroque as can be, including the longest single word in Shakespeare: *honorificabilitudinitatibus*.* This wild stuff comes together to make a kind of word music that's unique in Shakespeare—and devilishly hard for contemporary actors to pull off.

It was also, surely, heavy lifting for Shakespeare's own actors. They had an advantage over their twenty-first-century counterparts, though, because they'd had some experience with this kind of language. John Lyly, an author and playwright almost completely forgotten today, skyrocketed to fame in the 1580s and early 1590s thanks to a series of plays that sound conspicuously like *Love's Labour's Lost*. His popular book *Euphues, or the Anatomy of Wit* lent Lyly's overly decorative and archly self-conscious style its name: euphuism. Around the time Shakespeare first arrived in London, a whole school of Lyly imitators—the so-called euphuists—had taken London's literary scene by storm, and it's no exaggeration to say that had they not so powerfully expanded what was possible for authors to do with the English

* Meaning, approximately, "capable of gathering honors."

language, Shakespeare as we know him would not have existed. Most critics read *Love's Labour's Lost*, therefore, as the Bard's deliberate and warmhearted homage to Lyly, and an acknowledgment of the debt the young playwright owed his trailblazing forebear.

## THAT'S ONE BORING DUDE

Rosaline's eloquent description of a witty man hasn't much of a counterpart on the boredom end of the spectrum. One good reason why not: you don't need the playwrighting acumen of the Bard of Avon to know that boring characters don't really belong on a stage. The heroes of the classical dramatic canon are princes, kings, soldiers, and lovers, not CPAs and dentists. Yet Shakespeare knows that boredom and bores have their dramatic uses. Boredom is a way of building anticipation in advance of a great event (cf. the French generals bored off their rockers in the great scene that takes place on the night before the climactic battle in *Henry V*); bores are wonderful foils for short-tempered men of action who'd sooner die than spend a moment in the company of some droning fool. One such action hero is Hotspur, the aptly named hothead whose rebellion is chronicled in *Henry IV, Part I.* Here he complains about the obnoxious verbosity of Owen Glendower, the Welsh warlord, magician, and windbag whom the exigencies of politics have forced him to befriend.

O, he is as tedious
As a tired horse, a railing wife,
Worse than a smoky house. I had rather live
With cheese and garlic, in a windmill, far,
Than feed on cates and have him talk to me
In any summer house in Christendom.

—Hotspur, *Henry IV, Part I*, 3.1.155–60

***In other words:***

Oh, he's as boring as a knackered nag, a nagging wife. He's harder to take than a room full of smoke. I'd rather subsist on the Stinky Food Diet and live in a noisy factory in the middle of nowhere than eat delicacies and live in any Hamptons house in the universe if I'm forced to listen to *him*.

***How to say it:***

- Use this Bardism to explain to the friends who set you up on a blind date precisely why you won't go out with the guy a second time. Use it to tell your spouse why you don't want to go to dinner with her best friend and her mind-numbing husband. Or change the gender of the pronouns and use it to tell your shrink why Marian the librarian just isn't the girl of your dreams. (Should you rewrite the speech so that *she* is as tedious as a tired horse, then you might also want to compare her unfavorably to a *snoring husband* rather than a *railing wife*.)

***Some details:***

This speech offers some interesting examples of one of Shakespeare's standard rhetorical devices. He likes to build excitement and energy in his language by grouping ideas in threes and arranging these groupings so that each idea of the three is somehow bigger or more outlandish than the one that came before. Theater artists call these groupings *three-part builds*. We've seen one or two already and observed how they create very flashy effects with great economy.

The first of Hotspur's three-part builds here describes Glendower as harder to endure than (1) a tired horse, (2) a railing wife, and (3) a smoky house. Each image is more extravagant, crazier, and further over the top than the one that comes before. The next three-part build is the content of line 4: Hotspur would rather live (1) on an exclusive (and nasty) diet of cheese and garlic, (2) in a windmill (which would be a very cramped and loud place to live), and (3) in the middle of nowhere. Again, the images get more grandiose as they continue. Finally, Hotspur proposes that this backwoods existence of *windmill con formaggio e aglio* would be preferable to a life of (1) eating delicacies, (2) listening to Glendower, and (3) living in the loveliest country house in the world. Speaking each of these three-part lists, you can feel their intensity build, and Hotspur's disgust crest, as you continue. Allow each one to have its own little crescendo, and allow the speech as a whole, which is, after all, a three-part build of three-part builds, to heat to a boil as you move through it.

O, he is as tedious
As *a tired horse, a railing wife,*
Worse than ***a smoky house***. I had rather live
*With cheese and garlic, in a windmill,* ***FAR,***
Than *feed on cates* and have *HIM TALK TO ME*
In ***ANY SUMMER HOUSE IN CHRISTENDOM!!!!!!***

## SHAKESPEARE ON THANKS

*For this relief much thanks.*
—Francisco, *Hamlet*, 1.1.6

Given the number of life occasions for which Shakespeare provides us just the right words, it seems reasonable to expect that the people for or about whom we say those words might want to requite our efforts with some of their own. Here, then, a handful of Bardisms of gratitude. Use them in speeches, toasts, or as some Shakespeare on the Occasion of Finally Sending that Thank-You Card You've Been Procrastinating About for Too Long.

## THANKS A MILLION

First, the most basic Shakespearean expression of appreciation:

> This kindness merits thanks.
>
> —PETRUCHIO, *The Taming of the Shrew*, 4.3.41

Next, a slightly more elaborate way to put it:

> I can no other answer make but thanks,
> And thanks, and ever thanks.
>
> —SEBASTIAN, *Twelfth Night*, 3.3.14–15

Here's some Shakespeare for when you need a moment to figure out exactly the right way to say thank you; this, a promissory message that your gratitude will come in the form of some future good turn:

> I will pay thy graces / Home both in word and deed.
>
> —PROSPERO, *The Tempest*, 5.1.70–71

***In other words:***
I will repay your kindness in full, both with words and actions.

Should you feel yourself for some reason unable to express your thankfulness through future recompense, or should you be acknowledging the largesse of someone more well-heeled than yourself, either in material wealth or magnitude of generosity, the Melancholy Dane is ready to pen your Hallmark card:

> Beggar that I am, I am even poor in thanks, but I thank you.
>
> —Hamlet, *Hamlet*, 2.2.265–66

If you need to thank two people, then listen to the plainspoken Vincentio:

> Many and hearty thankings to you both.
>
> —Duke, *Measure for Measure*, 5.1.4

***How to use it:***

- Substitute *all* for *both*, and you're set to thank a group of any size.

Finally, in case you're moved to up the rhetorical ante and really unfurl a thicket of thanks, a mellifluous *merci*, a doozy of a *danke*, and a goodness-gracious *gracias*, you can always pick up your trowel and lay on these five lines:

> For your great graces
> Heap'd upon me, poor undeserver, I
> Can nothing render but allegiant thanks,
> My prayers to heaven for you, my loyalty,
> Which ever has and ever shall be growing.
>
> —Cardinal Wolsey, *Henry VIII*, 3.2.175–79

***In other words:***

In exchange for all the huge kindnesses you've done me—someone who doesn't deserve them—all I can offer is my faithful gratitude. And also my prayers to God on your behalf. And my devotion, which always has and always will grow greater.

## SHAKESPEARE ON APOLOGIES AND FORGIVENESS

*I desire you in friendship, and I will one way or other make you amends.*

—Sir Hugh Evans, *The Merry Wives of Windsor*, 3.1.74–75

Shakespeare stopped writing in 1612, left London for Stratford, and lived there in quiet retirement until his death four years later. His last playwrighting efforts before decamping to the countryside were collaborations with John Fletcher, the popular dramatist fifteen years his junior, who succeeded him as the house writer of his theater company, the King's Men. Scholars differ over how much and which parts of their joint efforts *Henry VIII* and *The Two Noble Kinsmen* Shakespeare wrote, and no one knows how much of *Cardenio* is his, because that play, based on an episode in Cervantes' *Don Quixote*, is lost.

Shakespeare's final solo effort was *The Tempest*, written in 1611. It centers on Prospero, the deposed Duke of Milan, who, during his enforced exile on a remote island, has mastered the occult arts and become a magus, or sorcerer, capable of casting spells, conjuring storms, rendering himself invisible, commanding troops of spirit-world minions, and even raising the dead. The play opens with him stirring the titular tempest and shipwrecking his enemies on his island. With them in his power, Prospero plots revenge. But just as he is about to loose his pent-up rage and inflict a terrible punishment upon them, his better instincts, prodded awake by his sensitive servant Ariel, take over, and he decides that the quality of mercy is indeed not strained: "The rarer action is / In virtue than in vengeance." (*Rarer* here is synonymous with "more extraordinary," hence, "superior.") Pronouncing an eloquent "I quit!"—"This rough magic / I here abjure"—he plunges his sorcery books into the sea and breaks his magical staff, renouncing his black art forever and granting forgiveness to those he wanted dead only moments before.

Critics who insist on the futility of reading Shakespeare's works autobiographically tend to trip over *The Tempest.* It's impossibly tempting to view Prospero as a Shakespearean self-portrait—he stages performances, he reads voraciously, he has daughter trouble—and to see the Bard's abjuration of his own magic just a year after writing Prospero's as a sure case of his life imitating his own art. Yes, yes, the whole theory may well be nothing more than romantic speculation, but life and art rarely come together this neatly, so what's the harm?

But whether or not *The Tempest* is Shakespeare's self-conscious curtain call (his Swan of Avon song?), it is an indisputable end point, not only of the greatest canon of plays ever written in English but also of a debate that rages throughout the thirty-five plays that came before it. It's a spiritual debate, a philosophical one, an ethical, moral, and existential one. *Is virtue in fact preferable to vengeance?* Hamlet wrestles with the question for five long acts and votes no. Macbeth and Othello ponder it too, but both men are so addicted to violence that virtue for them is hardly a possibility. Lear's universe comes unmoored from its moral anchors before he can even frame the question coherently. Yet after writing all these plays—all this blood, all this death, all this nihilism—Shakespeare ends his career by writing for Prospero his most Christian line. If it's harmless to read *The Tempest* as Shakespeare's farewell to the theater, then I say it's positively uplifting to read the play as his declaration that what the whole thing's all about—all the characters, all the stories, all the antitheses, all the iambic pentameter—is this: Turn the other cheek. Embrace goodness. Issue apologies, and accept them. Love. *Forgive.*

## I APOLOGIZE

For an all-purpose apology that manages to be gracious and flattering at the same time, here's the Prince of Denmark.

> Give me your pardon, sir. I've done you wrong;
> But pardon't as you are a gentleman.
>
> —Hamlet, *Hamlet*, 5.2.163–64

***How to say it:***

- Transgendered, the lines might read *ma'am* for *sir* in line 1, and *gentlewoman* for *gentleman* in line 2.

## I FORGIVE YOU

This plainspoken line is the great Shakespearean response to apologies simple or elaborate.

> I have forgiven and forgotten all.
>
> —King of France, *All's Well That Ends Well*, 5.3.9

***Some details:***

This Bardism always reminds me of the actress Irene Worth. Born in a tiny Nebraska town, she went on to become one of the grandes dames of the twentieth-century British and American stage. (She changed her name from Harriet Elizabeth Abrams and pronounced Irene with three syllables: *i-REE-nee*. The theater is a place of all sorts of transformations.) I had the honor of working with her only once, at a benefit evening in which celebrity actors—Kevin Kline, Sigourney Weaver, Christopher Walken, Robert Sean Leonard, and others—read Shakespeare's sonnets. At one rehearsal an actor in the group worked through Sonnet 60, which begins:

> Like as the waves make toward the pebbled shore,
> So do our minutes hasten to their end;
> Each changing place with that which goes before,
> In sequent toil all forwards do contend.

Ms. Worth sat nearby, listening. She walked over to the actor and said, in her seismically resonant, British-inflected voice, "Darling, just do this: *always* stress the word *all*." When Irene Worth said the word *all*, it really was all—the sun, the moon, the stars; yesterday, today, and tomorrow; everything in God's creation. Ms. Worth wasn't saying that *all* should sound grand. She was saying that the breadth and size of the idea the word communicates cannot be ignored or given short shrift. The Bardism that organizes this book makes her case—*All* the world's a stage / And *all* the men and women merely players—as do these others:

> How *all* occasions do inform against me . . .

> He was a man, take him for *all* in *all*,
> I shall not look upon his like again.

> *All* my pretty ones?
> Did you say *all*? O hell-kite! *All*?
> What, *all* my pretty chickens and their dam
> At one fell swoop?*

Remember Irene Worth. Always stress *all*.

---

* Italics mine. Citations: Hamlet, *Hamlet*, 4.4.32; Hamlet, *Hamlet*, 1.2.186–87; Macduff, *Macbeth*, 4.3.217–20.

## SHAKESPEARE ON PARTIES

*Good company, good wine, good welcome*
*Can make good people.*
—Guildford, *Henry VIII*, 1.4.6–7

We established at the opening of this chapter that the rotund Justice who stars in Jaques' Fifth Age enjoys a good meal. He also likes to opine about every subject under the sun. Add a cigar or pinch of snuff and a snifter of brandy or glass of port and you've got yourself one middle-aged party animal. Despite the fact that this fifty-something frat boy appears in *As You Like It*, he'd feel at home in any of the dozen or so Shakespeare plays in which the Bard includes a party scene. *Romeo and Juliet* gets rolling with one; *The Taming of the Shrew* ends with one. Mark Antony gets drunk at one; Cassio gets blotto at one. Beatrice and Benedick flirt at one; Timon gets his revenge at one. Henry VIII meets his wife at one; he then meets another wife at another one.

Shakespeare's parties feature all the energy, spontaneity, fun, and unexpected drama that we find in real-life gatherings and celebrations. That means that for we band of brothers (and sisters) who, four hundred years on, continue to turn to our *Complete Works* for words to suit the occasions of our lives, there is in that volume a splendid assortment of Bardisms for every party we throw, attend, or even bolt. Below, the highlights.

### LET'S PARTY!

Just prior to setting out for Alexandria and his final showdown with his mocking and disrespectful enemy, Octavius Caesar, Mark Antony decides to throw a big going-away blowout for his men, himself, and Cleopatra. His clarion call to his fellow revelers is a forerunner of the classic *Animal House* chant of "To-GA! To-GA! To-GA!"

> Come,
> Let's have one other gaudy night. Call to me
> All my sad captains. Fill our bowls once more.
> Let's mock the midnight bell.
>
> —Antony, *Antony and Cleopatra*, 3.13.184–86

***In other words:***

Come on! Let's party hearty one more night. Gather all my serious-minded friends. Pour some wine again, and let's stay up all night!

***How to use it:***

- Any of the short sentences that make up this speech could serve as the headline to a party invitation, or the subject line of an e-vite to this weekend's big debauch. I always hear in Antony's call to "mock the midnight bell" my own childhood joy at being given permission on New Year's Eve to stay up past twelve, so I've recommended that passage to friends planning all-night revelry.
- This is not a speech for the faint of heart. It's big and boisterous—the full-throated cry of a man who's clambered up onto the bar to announce to everyone that drinks are on him.

***Some details:***

Antony wants his *bowls* filled because such were the vessels from which wine was drunk in the Renaissance. In addition to those, Shakespeare's characters drink wine from *stoups* (i.e., tankards), *chalices* (i.e., goblets), and *cups*, but never from glasses, as we do today. This may be because the Jacobean world was a lot less genteel than our own and preferred a major guzzle to a dainty sip. But it may also be because Renaissance wine was not quite the quality beverage we imbibe today. Jacobean oenophiles routinely did things no connoisseur today would dream of: mix sugar into their wine, dip toast into it like donuts into coffee, float chopped fruit in it, or heat it to steaming. Preparations like these called for containers suited to heavier duty than crystal stemware.

**LET'S FURTHER THINK ON THIS . . .**

When Fleetwood Mac was inducted into the Rock and Roll Hall of Fame, Mick Fleetwood summoned the band onstage to perform their hit "Say You Love Me" by crying, "If music be the food of love, play on!"—the opening line of *Twelfth Night.* There's not another livin' soul around who didn't think it was a superb Shakespearean shout-out.

## WELCOME TO MY SHINDIG!

Once the invitations have gone out and the RSVPs have been counted, the host's next public duty is to extend a gracious welcome to his guests. Here are three Bardisms for the job. First:

> You're welcome, my fair guests. That noble lady
> Or gentleman that is not freely merry
> Is not my friend. This, to confirm my welcome,
> And to you all, good health!
>
> —Cardinal Wolsey, *Henry VIII,* 1.4.36–39

***In other words:***

My gorgeous guests, welcome! Any lady or gent who's not up for a good time is no friend of mine. I raise this glass as proof of my welcome, and I drink to your health!

***How to use it:***

- *This* at the midpoint of line 3 is what's known as an *index word*. It indexes, or indicates, or points to, some specific thing. Here, *this* refers to the glass (or bowl, or stoup, or cup) that you're raising to your guests. This Bardism is therefore ideal for that moment during the party when the host rises to thank everyone for coming, and to instruct everyone to have a ball.
- The four monosyllables that begin line 3 are the center of the speech. Let each one ring out, but in good humor—you don't really mean that you're going to end your friendship with anyone who's a downer at your party. It's playful hyperbole.

Second, if your gathering features food, you can rise and offer this Shakespearean *bon appétit*, as Cardinal Wolsey does in *Henry VIII* just a few dozen lines after welcoming his guests with the lines above.

> A good digestion to you all, and once more
> I shower a welcome on ye—welcome all.
>
> —CARDINAL WOLSEY, *Henry VIII*, 1.4.62–64

Third, Cardinal Wolsey's party in *Henry VIII* is a very posh affair. The scene's stage directions specify that there are multiple tables, including one very long one; dinner takes place "under the cloth of state," or royal insignia of the king; there's music, supplied by "hautboys" or oboes, as well as a "drum and trumpet"; and cannon fire accompanies the arrival of the most prominent guests. Don't despair if your party isn't quite so grand.* Instead, remind your guests that your parsimonious provisioning needn't mean they'll have a bad time:

> Small cheer and great welcome makes a merry feast.
>
> —BALTHAZAR, *The Comedy of Errors*, 3.1.26

***In other words:***

As long as you provide a warm welcome, you can have a fab party even without an elaborate spread.

## DON'T TELL ME WHAT FUN I CAN AND CAN'T HAVE

It's inevitable that wherever there's a celebration, there's some stiff who wants to shut it down. Here's Shakespeare for the Jerk Who Harshes Your Buzz.

> Dost thou think because thou art virtuous there shall be no more cakes and ale?
>
> —SIR TOBY, *Twelfth Night*, 2.3.103–4

***In other words:***

Do you really believe that just because you don't like parties, no one else should be allowed to have a good time?

---

* On the contrary, be glad. The cannon that discharged in this scene ignited a fire at the Globe Theatre on June 29, 1613, that burned the structure to the ground. Had Cardinal Wolsey's party been a bit more modest, theatrical history might well have taken a different course.

***How to say it:***

- This is Shakespeare's great cry of "Who the hell do you think you are?!" Use it when your downstairs neighbor starts pounding on his ceiling with a broom to get you to stop Riverdancing with your friends. Wheel it out, too, for any stick-in-the-mud who believes his way is superior to yours, and for every know-it-all who would restrict you with her self-imposed rules and regulations.
- The line calls for some serious scorn. To find it, stress the second *thou*, and put *virtuous* in the most dismissive, ironic quotation marks you can. To get a feel for the power of Sir Toby's famous citation of *cakes and ale* as the ultimate in sensual pleasures (and where would Somerset Maugham be without it?) substitute your favorite gustatory indulgence—the more decadent, the better—then multiply it by one hundred. Despite their many resemblances, Sir Toby is not Homer Simpson (although they both like to burp a lot—indeed, *Belch* is Toby's last name), and he's talking about more than just donuts and beer. *Cakes and ale* means every one of life's pleasures, from the simple to the sublime. Toby's fury arises from his disbelief that anyone would dare force him to rein in his hedonistic appetites.

***Some details:***

*Thou* in Sir Toby's line refers to Malvolio, his nemesis, and the steward, or servant-in-chief, at Toby's niece Olivia's house, the stately home where Toby lives. Three times in *Twelfth Night*, Malvolio is called a "Puritan." Modern audiences hear the label as a description of Malvolio's dour personality, and indeed in his joyless demeanor and fervent opposition to frivolity of any kind, he is puritanical. But Shakespeare's audience understood the word differently. For them, "Puritan" was a relatively new label for a strain of Protestantism that believed in strict religious discipline, and the reform of Church of

England doctrine and ritual in the direction of severity and simplicity. The word thus had a distinctly derisive strain, and it was used by mainstream Protestants as a cudgel to marginalize what they regarded as a growing threat.

And what a threat it turned out to be. In 1600, when *Twelfth Night* was written, the Puritans may have been nuisances, Malvolio-like party poopers, but a mere four decades later, they would be revolutionaries whose political and economic power would overthrow the English monarchy, plant the seeds of the governmental system that rules the United Kingdom today, and, not incidentally, export to the New World many of the political thinkers who would sire the United States of America. As a character in a play, Sir Toby has ample reason to despise Puritans: they loathed the theater—fulminated against it, in fact—and in one of their first acts upon seizing power in 1642, they shut down London's theater industry. The fifteen words of this one line of Toby's suggest that Shakespeare saw it coming. With the eerie foresight that great playwrights often display, he captured here what was really the central political story of England in his generation: the mighty struggle for power between the Puritans and their adversaries.

CHAPTER 6

# The Lean and Slippered Pantaloon

## SHAKESPEARE FOR THE OCCASIONS OF OLD AGE

*The sixth age shifts*
*Into the lean and slippered pantaloon,*
*With spectacles on nose and pouch on side,*
*His youthful hose well saved, a world too wide*
*For his shrunk shank; and his big manly voice,*
*Turning again toward childish treble, pipes*
*And whistles in his sound.*

Hearing testimony, weighing precedent, reviewing case law, and handing down verdicts, the Justice of Jaques' Fifth Age lives life at a sedate, deliberative pace. No surprise there: with an all-you-can-eat buffet of good capon at his constant disposal, and an inexhaustible supply of old saws and modern instances ready for pronouncement across the dinner table, why should he hurry? Instead he ambles and meanders, just as middle age, the phase of life he represents, often fills a long stretch, perhaps even lasting a few decades. The Justice presses pause on Time's shuffling iPod, and if life is indeed an (Elizabethan) cabaret, old chum, then the Fifth Age is its intermission.

*Intermission* is a theater term, of course: the pause between acts of a play. Jaques says the Sixth Age *shifts* into place, and that's a theater term, too. On its surface, the word's meaning, something like "moves or transfers from one place or state to another," is obvious enough—it has a physical, material aspect suggesting the bodily changes that happen between middle and old age. But in the theater, a "shift" is a change of scenery, a rearrangement of props, furniture, and other bits and pieces, that moves or transfers the action of the play from one place to another, and that carries the story, and the audience, forward into the next series of events.

This theatrical sense of "shifts" builds on the metaphoric line that Shakespeare—okay, Jaques—develops from the beginning of the Seven Ages speech through its end: the world is a stage; the men and women, actors who exit and enter; and each age, a role to be performed. The Justice, just prior to the scene shift into Age Six, "plays his part," and when he finishes delivering his lines, stagehands emerge from the wings, shift some stuff about, and—presto!—a new scene, and a new Age of Man, begins. Its star, like those of the five preceding scenes, is a human type we recognize, but this time, he bears no generic label such as infant, schoolboy, lover, soldier, or justice. This time, his label is specific, a brand name, the moniker of a figure from—wouldn't you know?—the theater itself. The Sixth Age's seismic shift lurches it into the time of the pantaloon, *il pantalone*.

*Il pantalone* is a stock character in the Italian *commedia dell'arte*, the popular, semi-improvised comic theater tradition that evolved in sixteenth-century Venice and endured for over two hundred years. Derived from previous vernacular entertainments, especially the New Comedy of ancient Rome, the *commedia* was all the rage in Italy and well enough known in Renaissance England that its character types appear in comedies by most of the major playwrights of the day. Some even show up as the dramaturgical skeletons on which the personalities of the others of Shakespeare's Seven Ages avatars are built: *commedia*'s *innamorato* is the lover, sighing and silly; *il capitano*, the swaggering military man with more bluster than bravery; and *il dottore*, the doctor, the learned, self-serious, middle-aged gasbag.*

But while Jaques—okay, Shakespeare—certainly has that group of characters in mind in this speech, the only one he names and describes in perfect Italianate detail is *il pantalone*. In the classic *commedia* scenarios, *il pantalone* is always old, and usually withered or otherwise infirm. He always wears slippers, sometimes eyeglasses, and generally carries a pouch, whose contents he jealously guards, usually by hunching over it in a bent-knee, curved-spine posture that makes him look even older than he is. With his traditional red hose, black cape, and mask with a huge hooked nose, *il pantalone* is quite a sight. He's the very stereotype of crotchety, dyspeptic old age.

I suppose by now I needn't point out that the pantaloon is also an utter fool. (He wouldn't feature so prominently in this speech chock-full of folly if he were a man of wisdom and perspicacity.) His main folly: an unholy devotion to filling his pouch with cold cash. His isn't any garden-variety cheapness. No, it is instead a miserliness so hardcore that it flouts the desires of every other character in every story the pantaloon appears in, and thus becomes the engine that drives the entire *commedia* form. *Il pantalone* won't part with a penny—not to his underpaid and overworked servant, *arlecchino* (aka the motley-wearing

---

* If this collection of nutcases sounds suspiciously similar to the passengers shipwrecked on Gilligan's Island, that's no accident. The seven stranded castaways owe their identities to stock *commedia* characters.

clown, Harlequin); not to *il capitano*, who'd like to borrow a couple of bucks so he can grab a bite to eat after a hard day of vanquishing enemies; and most definitely not to his handsome ward, the *innamorato*, who needs some dough in order to make headway with his *innamorata*. Such a tightwad is the pantaloon that he'd rather make do with worn-out old possessions than spend any coin on new gear. Hence the "well-saved" hose from his younger years: they may be way too big for him in his shriveled old age, but he isn't about to part with capital for something as frivolous as legwear that actually fits. Piping and whistling his way through complaints, irritations, and assorted senior moments, the pantaloon is as cockamamie—and as noisy—as any of the other dramatis personae who populate Jaques' morose and tedious *teatrum mundi*.

And yet, I can't hear Jaques paint his word portrait of the preposterous pantaloon and his baggy trousers that flap in the wind without thinking of an image of an entirely different nature. A few summers ago I tuned into CNN to watch its coverage of the sixtieth anniversary of D-Day and the Allied invasion of Normandy. By then, the ranks of surviving veterans—never large to begin with, given the staggering carnage of that ferocious battle—had thinned, and those happy few of the Greatest Generation who'd made the pilgrimage to Omaha Beach were in their seventies, if not older. Some had spectacles on their noses, some carried pouches on their sides: bags containing cameras, passports, and the other trappings of international travel and ceremonial commemoration. Some spoke to reporters, and yes, it was plain to hear how the timbre of their once manly voices was now noticeably squeaky and reedy. But what caught my eye and lumped my throat was this: many of these well-saved Private Ryans insisted on walking those famous French sands in the very uniforms they'd worn there six decades earlier. Their shanks were shrunken now, to be sure, and their government-issued combat fatigues were at least one world too wide. But these men were no pantaloons, no foolish dotards. Quite the contrary: they were conquerors. Applied to them, Jaques' patronizing language took on another dimension, and Shakespeare, out of context and remembered on an occasion he could neither imagine nor intend, elicited not laughter and derision but admiration, sympathy, deference, and warmth.

Jaques' Sixth Age imagery requires more words than any of the five before it or the one after it. Its text is full of alliteration (*shrunk shank*, *world wide*), antithesis (*manly* versus *childish*), and even rhyme (*side* and *wide*). Its music plays the same symphony of atonal asininity that Jaques conducts so masterfully from the instant he gives the downbeat of "All the world's a stage." Its tone, however, stakes out new territory. There may be an unmistakable foolishness about the old, cheapskate pantaloon, but there's a sadness about him, too. There's a sense of lost vitality and irretrievable youth, of a life with fewer sunrises ahead than sunsets behind, of physical malady and spiritual malaise, and of an end drawing ever more rapidly near. The Sixth Age, that is, is the age of wistfulness. Its substance is reminiscences, valedictories, and, alas, hospitals. It's a time of observing, taking stock, and watching the clock wind down to stillness. The pantaloon is cranky and parsimonious, but he's got a perfect excuse: how else to fill all the time he must spend waiting, waiting?

Of the pantaloon and what's on his mind, Shakespeare has much to say, and he says it in the Bardisms collected in this chapter.

## SHAKESPEARE ON OLD AGE

*I am old, I am old.*
—Falstaff, *Henry IV, Part II*, 2.4.244

In a surprising passage midway through *Henry VI, Part II*, King Henry fantasizes about the life he might have led had he been born a regular Joe instead of *le roi*. He imagines himself a "homely swain" (i.e., a simple shepherd), and contrasts the responsibilities and worries of leadership—paranoia about disloyal underlings, the burdens of statecraft and warfare—with a shepherd's far less stressful preoccupations: tending the flock, shearing their woolen coats in springtime, sitting around and meditating, taking a nap. In the end, Henry concludes, the shepherd's peaceful existence "would bring white hairs unto a quiet grave."

But the king never reaches the white-haired time of life, and he goes to his grave in tumult, not quiet. Such is the fate of most of Shakespeare's kings, and for that matter, most of his senior citizens, and with good reason: the shepherd's senior years may be pleasant and calm, but who would want to watch a play about them? The turbulent dotages of Lear and Gloucester, Falstaff, Polonius, Prospero, and dozens of other characters provide Shakespeare the stuff of memorable drama. For these figures, old age is a time of yearning for an ease and grace that they sorely desire, but that events stubbornly refuse to provide. Still, the Bard grants to a handful of his éminences grises a moment of respite in which to frame their advanced age with a consoling sense of acceptance, and in at least one case, a proud sense that geriatric needn't mean defunct. Shakespearean superannuation is no picnic, but at least it's good for a few comforting turns of phrase.

## WE WERE YOUNG ONCE UPON A TIME

Here are some Bardisms for those sepia-toned moments when a mournful nostalgia warms the heart and mists the eyes. First, a lament about how the years separate one from joys fondly remembered:

> **Where is the life that late I led?**
>
> —Petruchio, *The Taming of the Shrew*, 4.1.121

Next, a mournful admission that one's mortal coil seems no longer to shuffle off to Buffalo with quite the energy it once did:

> **You and I are past our dancing days.**
>
> —Capulet, *Romeo and Juliet*, 1.5.29

And then, two sparkly-eyed reminiscences about tripping the light fantastic back in the day:

> **Jesu, Jesu, the mad days that I have spent!**
>
> —Shallow, *Henry IV, Part II*, 3.2.29–30

> **We have heard the chimes at midnight.**
>
> —Falstaff, *Henry IV, Part II*, 3.2.197

***How to use them:***

- These brief lines are well suited to a toast to bygone times, or when reminiscing about past fun with friends and family, or for commiserating with a pal about the slower pace of life's later chapters.
- Petruchio's *late* means "lately," or "once upon a time"; Shallow's *Jesu*—a term he uses interchangeably with *Jesus*—is pronounced *JAY-zoo.*

***Some details:***

Falstaff's wonderful metaphor of his party-boy youth—he stayed up late enough to hear the church bells chime midnight—supplied Orson Welles with the title for one of the best Shakespeare films ever made. *Chimes at Midnight* is a 1965 screen adaptation of Welles' *Five Kings*, his famous stage condensation of Shakespeare's English history plays. The film tells the stories of *Henry IV, Parts I and II* and *Henry V* and features not only Welles' own finest performance as Falstaff but also countless sequences that show his unparalleled mastery of filmmaking. Scene after scene, he translates Shakespeare's text into cinematic terms so evocative that Shakespeare himself couldn't have imagined them better. The climactic battle sequence is an extraordinary tour de force, and its camera work and editing have been studied, emulated, and stolen wholesale in just about every war movie made in the past four decades (directors Mel Gibson and Steven Spielberg explicitly acknowledged their borrowings from Welles for the battles in, respectively, *Braveheart* and *Saving Private Ryan*). *Chimes at Midnight* is difficult to find because of legal entanglements dating back to the shenanigans Welles pulled, in his post–*Citizen Kane* disfavor, in order to get the movie made, but now and then it shows up on television. See it if you can.

## I'M IN GOOD SHAPE FOR MY AGE

One Shakespearean character who manages to grow old gracefully and without too much Sturm und Drang is Adam in *As You Like It*. Perhaps his happy fate is a function of the actor who played him: theater lore holds that William Shakespeare himself trod the boards in the role. He'd have been in his thirties at the time—less than half the character's age—so it's hard to credit the legend too far, but it's fun to imagine him pronouncing this delightful Bardism, Shakespeare on the Occasion of the Spry Old Fox.

> Though I look old, yet I am strong and lusty,
> For in my youth I never did apply
> Hot and rebellious liquors in my blood,
> Nor did not with unbashful forehead woo
> The means of weakness and debility.
> Therefore my age is as a lusty winter,
> Frosty but kindly.
>
> —Adam, *As You Like It*, 2.3.48–54

***In other words:***

I may look old, but I'm still vigorous and full of beans. That's because, when I was young, I made sure not to take anything that would inflame my passions and stir me up to no good. And I didn't go crazily chasing after all sorts of things that would in the long run be bad for me. The result is that in my old age, I'm like a bracing winter's day: cold, but enjoyable.

***How to use it:***

- I've pressed this speech into service on two very different occasions. The first was when a pal told me that his seventy-five-year-old dad had just won a tennis tournament held in his Florida retirement community. "Tell him to say this when he accepts his trophy," I advised, and Papa did, to general approbation. The second was when a student of mine asked for something to read at her uncle's seventieth-birthday party. I advised her to substitute *he* and *his* for Adam's *I* and *my* and to present the passage as Shakespeare's tribute to her hale and hearty uncle. She reported that the speech was met with gales of laughter: apparently her uncle's youth was not quite as abstemious as Adam's, so the lines about having avoided rebellious liquors took on an amusing irony. *Lusty* also prompted giggles, especially from my student's aunt, who gave her husband a knowing—and appreciative—wink!

➔ The pronouns *she* and *her* will render Adam's text suitable for Eve.

## SHAKESPEARE ON GRANDPARENTHOOD

*Thy grandam loves thee.*
—King John, *King John*, 3.3.3

Few events mark the beginning of the Sixth Age of Man as definitively as the birth of a grandchild, yet grandparents in the *Complete Works* are thin on the ground, and what few there are hardly embody the cookies-and-cardigans warmth I associate with my own parents' parents. At the same time, dynastic issues are everywhere in the canon; in practically every single play some part of the story turns on what's bequeathed by an ancestor to his or her progeny, be that their moral values, some political imperative, or money and real estate. For Shakespeare, each generation is a product of all the generations that precede it, and so firmly is this genealogical principle embedded in his works that his briefest glance in its direction communicates it with force and clarity. The Bard doesn't need to put a forefather onstage in order to convey his presence in the lives of his descendants;

merely mentioning his name or one of his famous exploits summons everything that person could have wished to leave his dynasty. And that, I think, is why Shakespearean grandparents are so scarce in the flesh. The very DNA of the plays encodes the essence of "grandparentness," so Shakespeare can economize on ink and vellum by not writing the actual people. Put another way, in Shakespeare's dramaturgy, the idea *grandma* is a perfectly sufficient substitute for Grandma herself.

In life, of course, no such grandmotherly substitution is imaginable. Paradoxically enough—and fortunately for those Shakespeare quoters in need of a Bardism for Mom's mom—in two lines out of the thousands and thousands he wrote, Shakespeare managed to express, even absent a grandma, just what grandmas are all about.

## GRANDPARENTS HAVE A LOT OF LOVE TO OFFER

Those two lines are spoken by Richard III as he labors to persuade a horrified Queen Elizabeth to allow him to marry her young daughter. Richard imagines a future in which his bride will bear him children who will call him father and the Queen grandmother. And those grandchildren, although sired by a man she hates, will nonetheless, Richard assures the Queen, be "even of your mettle, of your very blood," and so will "be a comfort to your age." It's a bold rhetorical move that yields Richard what he seeks, and yields us Shakespeare on the Occasion of a Visit to Granny's House.

> **A grandam's name is little less in love**
> **Than is the doting title of a mother.**
>
> —King Richard, *Richard III*, 4.4.273.12–273.13

***In other words:***

The word Grandma has in it the same amount of love as the very love-filled word Mama.

***How to use it:***

- Feel free to change the gender of the lines—*grandam* becomes *grandsire*, and *mother* becomes *father*.
- These lines can help grandparents convey to their families exactly how intense is their love for their grandkids. They can also serve as an expression of affection and gratitude to Gram and Gramps for the quantity and quality of their love. Perhaps most useful of all, they can mediate the kinds of disputes that arise when Granny lets the kids chow down on Pop-Tarts in direct contravention of Mom's prohibition against excessive sugar intake. (Disputes, I should add, I know nothing about.)

## SHAKESPEARE ON TRIBUTES

*Give me a staff of honor for mine age.*
—Titus, *Titus Andronicus*, 1.1.198

The Sixth Age of Man is a time when work wraps up and life slows down. The lean and slippered pantaloon walks more slowly, talks more slowly, and often thinks a bit more slowly than he did back in the high-energy salad days of Ages Three and Four. A mentor of mine once told me that the reason people slow in old age is because taking a more leisurely approach to time is their hard-earned reward for seven long decades of hurtling, hustling, and bustling. Looked at in this way, retirement isn't the end of a career in the workforce, it's the beginning of a new career of unhurried experiences and easygoing pleasures. This explains why a gold watch is the standard retirement gift: the retiree deserves to tell the hours of his repose in style. For those occasions on which that gold watch is presented, for those moments when the reward that is the Sixth Age's slower pace is publicly bestowed, indeed, for those situations when words of tribute of any kind are called for, Shakespeare's ready for action.

## YOU ARE A VERY SPECIAL GUY

One of the great things about Shakespeare's words of tribute is that they manage to be moving and heartfelt without being sentimental. Here are two wonderful examples.

First, no character treads the line between true feeling and treacle better than Hotspur, the no-nonsense soldier we've met before. His tribute to Lord Douglas, his Scottish comrade in arms, is one of my favorites: matter-of-fact, yet full of love.

> By God, I cannot flatter, I do defy
> The tongues of soothers, but a braver place
> In my heart's love hath no man than yourself.
>
> —HOTSPUR, *Henry IV, Part I*, 4.1.6–8

***In other words:***

I swear to you, I'm incapable of flattery. I've got no time for smooth-talking yes-men. But I will say this: I hold no man in higher esteem than I do you.

***How to use it:***

- I once heard the chairman of a college English department bid farewell to a retiring professor with these words, and they brought a tear to the eye of everyone in the room. The strength of the first phrase, which insists that the speaker isn't given to hyperbole and excessive praise, somehow makes the lines especially emotional.

- This Bardism is an ideal retirement tribute, but it works equally well as a commendation on a job well done, or even as an expression of warmth and gratitude between close friends.
- Hotspur's final line is built according to a favorite Shakespearean pattern: a polysyllabic word at the end of a line of monosyllables, as in "To be or not to be, that is the question." Give each of the eight single-syllable words its own deliberate weight (In. My. Heart's. Love. Hath. No. Man. Than.) and you'll find that the longer, two-syllable word *yourself* jumps out of your mouth and takes on a special emphasis.
- Address this speech to a woman by adding the letters *wo* to *man* in its last line.

Second is Duke Vincentio, the measured hero of *Measure for Measure*. Here he publicly acknowledges the excellence of Angelo, his meritorious subordinate.*

O, your desert speaks loud; and I should wrong it
To lock it in the wards of covert bosom,
When it deserves, with characters of brass,
A forted residence 'gainst the tooth of time
And razure of oblivion. Give me your hand,
And let the subject see, to make them know

* Actually, not so meritorious. Angelo is the bad guy of this play, and the Duke flatters him here in a ruse designed to prime him for his eventual comeuppance. You needn't share this bit of dramatic context with your own meritorious colleague.

That outward courtesies would fain proclaim
Favors that keep within.

—Duke Vincentio, *Measure for Measure*, 5.1.9–16

***In other words:***

Those things about you that are praiseworthy are very noticeable, and I'd be dishonoring them to keep quiet about them, and to hide my affection for them. They should have lasting monuments erected to them, strong fortresses that will withstand time's ravages and never fall into obscurity. Let me shake your hand, and let everyone see me do it. They'll understand that this gesture of politeness shows how deeply I feel about you, and how many good turns I intend to do you.

***How to say it:***

- This speech is perfect for public ceremonies of acknowledgment and appreciation. The Duke praises his deserving associate before the citizenry over whom he reigns; you're more likely to be praising yours before your employees, co-workers, or friends. Feel free, then, to replace line 6's *the subject* with some more appropriate collective phrase: *my colleagues, my family, this gath'ring, the comp'ny*. Note that the speech is appropriate for honorees of either gender.
- Some highly charged language expresses the passion and energy of this lavish tribute. The honoree's deserving doesn't mumble or huff, but *speaks loud*; it deserves to be written in *brass*, the medium of all great monuments, so that it will defy *time's* devouring *tooth,* and stand fast against *oblivion's* determination to *raze* it. Allow these powerful words their full expressive rein.
- The Duke's verbs are vivid and should be given their due: *wrong, lock, deserves, give, see, know, proclaim.*

- Note the physical business that the speech demands: the Duke takes Angelo's hand on line 5. I remember seeing a production in which the Duke clutched Angelo's hand in both of his and then pressed it to his heart. The actor playing the role obviously felt that this gesture was more of an *outward courtesy* than a mere handshake would have been. Feel free to borrow that interpretation.

## SHE IS A VERY INSPIRING WOMAN

If you're looking to stroke the ego of a female friend, peer, or partner in crime, you can't do better than this extravagant Bardism, spoken about Queen Margaret after she gives a stemwinder of a pep talk to the troops under her command in the Wars of the Roses. Margaret is one of a small number of women in the plays who do military service, and the only one whose oratory rivals anything screamed out by Henry V.

> Methinks a woman of this valiant spirit
> Should, if a coward heard her speak these words,
> Infuse his breast with magnanimity
> And make him, naked, foil a man at arms.
>
> —Prince Edward, *Henry VI, Part III*, 5.4.39–42

***In other words:***

I think a woman whose character is as upstanding as this one's could fill a coward with courage simply by saying the kinds of things she always says. She could inspire a naked man to defeat an armored soldier.

***How to use it:***

- This speech is about a woman whose work or great achievements have to do with her powers of speech. Introduce your remarks by citing some of the special and stirring things your honoree has said, then move into this Bardism to explain how inspirational you find her. However, if you need to talk about a gal whose gifts are not merely of gab, worry not: some minor tweaks to the second half of line 2 will save the day. Again, begin by describing what it is that's so unique and motivating about this woman—her deeds, her work, her example, say—and then point out, with some gently rewritten Shakespeare, that if a coward *saw* her *do these deeds*, or *make this work*, or *reach this goal*, or *set this standard*, he'd become magnanimous and invincible.

- Be sure to draw the contrast between the craven *coward* of line 2 and the *magnanimity* he'd gain from your fine female friend's inspirational ministrations.

## SHAKESPEARE ON HEALTH AND MEDICINE

*Self-love, my liege, is not so vile a sin*
*As self-neglecting.*

—Dauphin, *Henry V*, 2.4.74–75

No doubt there are a host of entirely normal physiological changes associated with growing old that result in the Sixth Age's shrunken shank and piping, whistling voice. On the other hand, these traits may also be symptomatic of ailments that can beset the pantaloon in the December of his years. Illness and infirmity, so dreadfully prominent as life winds down, and an unwelcome intrusion even on life's most vital years, are widely considered in the Bard's works. There are characters who catch cold, who suffer accidents and injuries, who speechify on their deathbeds (folklore held that the gift of prophecy was given to the dying in the moments before they expire), even, in *Henry IV, Part II*, a character who feigns illness in order to get out of doing something he doesn't want to do (that's Northumberland, who calls in sick to the Battle of Shrewsbury, thus hanging his own son out to dry—and die—at enemy hands). There is also a smattering of physicians and surgeons in the canon, very few of whom actually manage to cure anyone of anything, perhaps dramatizing Shakespeare's core belief that the physical ravages of old age no more yield to human intervention than do any of time's other savagely destructive powers.

The Bardisms below are Shakespeare for Occasions of Aches, Pains, and Visits to the Doc.

## A TOOTHACHE IS SERIOUS BUSINESS

Compared with the miraculous practice of today's doctors, medicine in Shakespeare's period, known as physic, was just this side of voodoo. But Renaissance doctoring, however primitive, was like a visit to the Mayo Clinic compared to Renaissance dentistry, a practice about which the adjective *barbaric* is a compliment. Although by the late sixteenth century dentists had begun to professionalize themselves through standard training and practices, in most parts of England it remained nearly impossible to receive anything resembling decent dental care. The medieval approach to mouth care continued: dentistry was handled by barbers, who maintained alongside their combs and scissors a veritable torture chamber of hammers, pliers, levers, saws, and other blunt instruments for cutting, drilling, and extracting teeth. Pain-free dentistry? Hardly. But despite the agony of getting dental care, patients sought it out on doctors' orders: physicians often prescribed tooth extraction as a cure for a whole host of diseases that we know today to be entirely unrelated to the mouth.

People often ask me: "If time travel existed, would you like to go back to Shakespeare's London?" My answer: "Only if I was sure I didn't have any cavities."

> There was never yet philosopher
> That could endure the toothache patiently,
> However they have writ they style of gods,
> And made a pish at chance and sufferance.
>
> —LEONATO, *Much Ado About Nothing*, 5.1.35–38

***In other words:***

Not even the most thoughtful and analytical person can put up with the agony of a toothache, even if their writings have transcended human concerns, and even if they've blown a raspberry at bad luck and suffering.

***How to say it:***

- Feel free to interpret the toothache in this passage metaphorically. Leonato's observation works in the context of any inconvenience that's grown so annoying that it can no longer be ignored.
- End at line 2 if you'd like. Lines 3 and 4, though, are well suited to the stoic in your life who doesn't usually complain about anything, but whose impacted wisdom teeth have him climbing walls and cursing like a stevedore.
- Use the Paper Trick on this passage and you'll find that it unfolds elegantly, line by line by line. Observe the phrasing break at the end of line 3, and you'll discover how absolutely perfect is Leonato's choice of the word *pish* to express the philosopher's disdain for every misery, a cavalier dismissal that's useless in the face of root canal.

## MY BODY MAY BE SHOT, BUT MY MIND'S OKAY

Here's some Shakespeare on the Occasion of Heroically Punching Your Time Card Even Though You Really Should Be Home in Bed. It may not fully satisfy the guy in the next cubicle who's slathered himself in Purell in order not to catch your flu, but it should at least keep him quiet for a moment.

> **I am not very sick, / Since I can reason of it.**
>
> —IMOGEN, *Cymbeline*, 4.2.13–14

***In other words:***

I'm obviously not seriously ill, since I'm still okay enough to talk about my condition.

---

### LET'S FURTHER THINK ON THIS . . .

When movie star Charlton Heston announced in 2002 that he'd be leaving public life because he'd been diagnosed with Alzheimer's disease, it seemed entirely fitting that he ended his statement by quoting Prospero from *The Tempest*. "Our revels now are ended," the actor said, then skipped a few lines to the really meaty bit: "We are such stuff / As dreams are made on and our little life / Is rounded with a sleep." Heston chose exactly the right character (an elderly artist), at precisely the right moment in his life (contemplating his imminent death), and from just the right play (a work very much concerned with endings and the emotional and psychological preparations they require). We were moved by his plight, stirred by his words, and appreciative of his efforts to locate Shakespearean rhetoric appropriate to the occasion.

---

## NATURAL CURES ARE THE WAY TO GO

What we'd today call self-help books constituted a small literary subgenre in the English Renaissance, and home remedy manuals filled a significant niche within the category. Sufferers of everything from headache to ingrown toenail could consult various early modern versions of the *Physician's Desk Reference* and learn how to prepare concoctions, boluses, and poultices to treat their pains. All the necessary ingredients were as close as the nearest garden: Shakespeare's pharmacopoeia was Mother Nature. Friar Laurence, the homeopathic healer, clergyman, and (unfortunately idiosyncratic) relationship counselor in *Romeo and Juliet*, makes the Bard's most sustained comments on the powers of natural medicine when he first appears in the play:

> O mickle is the powerful grace that lies
> In plants, herbs, stones, and their true qualities,
> For naught so vile that on the earth doth live
> But to the earth some special good doth give.
>
> —Friar Laurence, *Romeo and Juliet*, 2.2.15–16

***In other words:***

Let me tell you, there's goodness and effectiveness in plants, herbs, rocks, and their inherent properties, and it's strong. Even the worst living things on earth have some good to contribute.

***How to say it:***

- When you quote these four lines, try to take note of the fact that they comprise two rhyming couplets (the Friar's speech is thirty lines long, all of it in rhyme). *Live* and *give* obviously rhyme. *Lies* and *qualities* make a so-called near-rhyme: they are almost but not quite the same sound. The rhymes give the passage a slight sense of quaintness, of expressing tried-and-true wisdom. Let your listeners hear it.

- I sometimes recite these lines at the cash register when I visit health food stores to stock up on echinacea, Chinese herbs, and other remedies. It's a habit that irritates my wife but most of the time earns a smile from the yogi hemp-head true believer who rings up my purchase.

## WE CAN'T DO ANYTHING MORE FOR HIM

When natural cures fail and modern hospital technology throws up its hands, turn to Cerimon, the Hippocrates of *Pericles*. His Bardism on medical futility couches some harsh news in kindness and eloquence.

> **There's nothing can be ministered to nature**
> **That can recover him.**
>
> —Cerimon, *Pericles*, 3.2.7–8

***How to use it:***

- Swap in *her* if need be.
- Certainly useful to the *Grey's Anatomy* set, Cerimon's brief statement might also prove valuable when applied metaphorically to anyone incorrigible: a madcap friend who won't stop joking; a professional daredevil determined to encase himself in ice for a week; an adventure tourist bent on a bungee-jumping expedition around the world.

## I'M GOING TO SUE FOR MALPRACTICE

Cerimon possesses at least the dignity to report on his own professional impotence in person. Other Shakespearean physicians are far less respectful to their charges. In this blunt and sobering Bardism, Lucrece complains that inattentive doctors are the moral equivalents of venal judges and cruel tyrants. Use it not only on those—I hope rare—occasions when the doctor's orders aren't doing the trick, but also whenever your struggles are overlooked by those who should be paying attention.

> The patient dies while the physician sleeps;
> The orphan pines while the oppressor feeds;
> Justice is feasting while the widow weeps;
> Advice is sporting while infection breeds.
>
> —*The Rape of Lucrece*, 904–7

***In other words:***

The sick person passes away while the doctor snoozes. Starving children go hungry while the corrupt leader responsible for their privation parties down. Those in the criminal justice system are out having lunch instead of busy prosecuting the murderer of the bereft widow's husband. Disease spreads like wildfire while the experts are on the golf course.

***Some details:***

Shakespeare sustained his theater career alongside an entirely separate and equally successful life as a poet. Yes, his thirty-eight magnificent plays are his claim to fame today, but had you asked a Londoner of the early seventeenth century who William Shakespeare was, he'd have answered, "He's the brilliant bloke who wrote that gorgeous and titillating *Venus and Adonis*." That poem, from which we quoted in Chapter Three, was more successful by a mile than even his best-selling published plays: there were nine separate printings of it during Shakespeare's lifetime, and a handful more in the two decades after his death. *Venus and Adonis*, along with *The Rape of Lucrece*, Shakespeare's other great narrative poem, quoted here, show that Shakespeare was and is not only the world's greatest playwright, but that he's one of the geniuses of non-dramatic English poetry, too.

While it's likely that Shakespeare turned to poetry in order to help pay the bills during the plague years of the early 1590s, when he would have been on forced furlough from his regular gig at the government-closed playhouses, it's by no means clear that he regarded poetry as a secondary calling. Quite the contrary: of the more than three dozen of his works that reached print, the only two we can be certain he personally supervised through the publishing process were *Venus and Adonis* and *The Rape of Lucrece*.

Both poems are over a thousand lines long. Both are inspired by stories Shakespeare found in the work of his favorite classical author, Ovid—stories to which he'd return many times throughout his career. Both are about lust and its consequences, and both link sex and death in ways that would make Dr. Freud dance a jig. In the first, the wicked Tarquin, a member of Rome's ruling family, rapes Lucrece, wife of the General Collatine, while the latter is away in battle. Lucrece, horrified and ashamed, commits suicide. When Collatine returns to Rome and learns what's happened, he raises a revolt against the Tarquins, which leads to the foundation of the Roman republic. In *Venus and Adonis*, a handsome young man, Adonis, refuses the rapacious sexual advances of Venus, the middle-aged goddess of love. He goes off to hunt and is gored to death by a wild boar. Venus is so devastated that she curses love, which is why to this day love and pain are always intertwined (one example: "It [i.e., love] shall be cause of war and dire events, / And set dissension 'twixt the son and sire"). Both poems show flashes of the genius Shakespeare will manifest steadily later in his career, and both deploy dramatic effects in an unusually sophisticated way—no surprise given that their author already knew a thing or two about playwrighting. I teach material from both poems in my acting classes, and my students enjoy it. I recommend taking a look at them sometime.

## SHAKESPEARE ON NEWS

*What news on the Rialto?*
—SHYLOCK, *The Merchant of Venice*, 1.3.33

Arthur Miller articulated a fundamental principle of good dramatic construction in one of his many essays about his writing process. "Every line of dialogue in a play," he pronounced, "must deliver new information. If it doesn't, then it must be cut." Miller's plays—the early ones, anyway—abide scrupulously by this rule, and are as lean and tightly composed as any of the masterpieces of world dramatic literature. Miller's model during that first phase of his career was one of the pillars of the canon, Henrik Ibsen, the father of modern drama. Norway's favorite son was another writer fanatical about cutting away the fat until all that's left is dialogue that drives the play forward, that delivers news.

Shakespeare's artisanship is less disciplined than either Miller's (a carpenter by avocation, whose love of precision and handicraft is as visible in every mortise and tenon he joined as it is in his characters' speech) or Ibsen's (an abstemious Scandinavian whose revulsion at excess is evident in his life as well as his work). Yet for all the Bard's sprawl and ornament—his piling on of metaphor and linguistic filigree, and his refusal to say something once when he can say it three times—he is in his own way a devout preacher of Miller's "new information or cut it" gospel. Witness the hundreds and hundreds of times he writes the word *news*. That little syllable catapults his plots forward as characters ask "What's the news with thee?" or demand "How now, what news?" or declare "This is the news at full." Indeed, Shakespeare delivers so much *news* that he could bring a smile to the stony visages of Miller and Ibsen, tongue-tie Brian Williams, Katie Couric, and Charlie Gibson, and pick up a Pulitzer or two, all without breaking stride. Here's a selection of some of his stop-the-presses bulletins: Bardisms for the news junkie.

## BREAKING DEVELOPMENTS . . .

If I ran the Federal Communications Commission, I'd mandate that television stations replace the familiar stentorian bark of "We interrupt this program for a special report" with this more poetic formulation. Use it to announce your unfolding story.

> **With news the time's in labor, and throws forth**
> **Each minute some.**
>
> —Camidius, *Antony and Cleopatra*, 3.7.80–81

***In other words:***

There's so much news that it's like the world is a woman pregnant with it, and she's in the delivery room giving birth to more by the minute.

## I'VE GOT GOOD NEWS!

There's no more delightful duty than to be a messenger carrying wonderful news. Celebrate your felicitous info by announcing it thus:

> Tidings do I bring, and lucky joys, / And golden times, and happy news of price.
>
> —Pistol, *Henry IV, Part II*, 5.3.89–90

***In other words:***

I've got something to say, and it's about joyous good fortune, and beautiful moments, and giddy news that's really valuable.

## IT'S ONE THING AFTER ANOTHER

Alas, not all news is good, and bad news has an irritating habit of clustering together and hitting like a tsunami. "When sorrows come, they come not single spies / But in battalions," says Claudius to his wife in *Hamlet*. She echoes him a few scenes later with this Bardism, Shakespeare on the Occasion of the World Coming to an End.

> One woe doth tread upon another's heel,
> So fast they follow.
>
> —Gertrude, *Hamlet*, 4.7.134–35

***In other words:***

The bad news is coming on so fast and furious that each piece trips over the one in front of it.

## SHAKESPEARE ON WEATHER

*So foul and fair a day I have not seen.*
—Macbeth, *Macbeth*, 1.3.36

Just as he's standing by with a pithy phrase for life's red-letter days—the weddings we love and the funerals we don't—Shakespeare's also ready with tidbits for the everyday moments that make up the majority of the days of our lives. No subject of conversation better suits those quotidian occasions—standing on line at the grocery store, whiling away the wait at the bus stop, greeting a neighbor across a picket fence—than that old standard, the weather. The Bard's a past master on the topic, as these Bardisms attest. Use each to comment on the meteorological event it describes, or as a gloss on some metaphorical version of said atmospheric condition.

### IT'S THE DOG DAYS OF SUMMER / IT'S THE DEAD OF WINTER

As the mercury soars, bear this Bardism in mind:

> Fie, this is hot weather, gentlemen.
> —Falstaff, *Henry IV, Part II*, 3.2.90

And as the mercury plunges, remember this one:

> 'Tis bitter cold, / And I am sick at heart.
> —Francisco, *Hamlet*, 1.1.6–7

### HERE COMES THE SPRINGTIME THAW

Worried that winter will never end? Or that some other, more personal stretch of icy cold and early dark might never lift? Queen

Margaret has some words of encouragement that will help you await the arrival of warmer days.

> **Cold snow melts with the sun's hot beams.**
>
> —Queen Margaret, *Henry VI, Part II*, 3.1.223

## THAT WAS QUITE A DELUGE

Here's Shakespeare on the Occasion of Touring the Storm Damage. For the more poetically inclined, it's also a Bardism about how the whips and scorns of time leave us looking a little green around the gills.

> **Much rain wears the marble.**
>
> —Gloucester, *Henry VI, Part III*, 3.2.50

***In other words:***

Rain can erode even things as durable as marble.

## 'TAIN'T A FIT NIGHT OUT FOR MAN NOR BEAST

"This disturbèd sky / Is not to walk in," advises the sage Cicero in *Julius Caesar* when he spots Cassius running around, shirtless, in the middle of a storm. I've taken the Roman orator's counsel to heart on many occasions, even quoting it when urging my wife to take an umbrella with her into a cloudy Brooklyn day. Cicero's words might have benefited other Shakespearean characters had they heard them: King Lear on the heath, the sailors in the opening scene of *The Tempest*, and the eponymous hero of one of Shakespeare's lesser-known late plays, *Pericles*. Here's his Bardism for a raging storm.

Yet cease your ire, you angry stars of heaven!
Wind, rain, and thunder, remember earthly man
Is but a substance that must yield to you,
And I, as fits my nature, do obey you.

—Pericles, *Pericles*, 2.1.41–44

***In other words:***

Let up a little, you furious heavens! Wind, rain, and thunder, please bear in mind that man is made of weak stuff that must bow down to your force. I, as such a man, surrender to you.

***Some details:***

Shakespeare's contemporary Ben Jonson dismissed *Pericles* and its plot full of coincidences and melodramatic contrivances—shipwrecks, storms, resurrections, reunions—as "a mouldy tale . . . and stale." Perhaps so, but it's fresh in one sense, at least: the play is the first of Shakespeare's late-career experiments with a form critics label tragicomedy or romance. *Cymbeline*, *The Tempest*, and *The Winter's Tale* are also in this genre, and if they seem the more accomplished plays, that's not only because by the time he wrote them, Shakespeare had gone through the practice round of writing this one, but also because at least half of *Pericles* is believed to be by someone other than the Bard.

Collaborative playwriting was not uncommon in the period, and Shakespeare shared authorship with others in more than one of his plays. In the case of *Pericles*, he chose a distinctly minor-league partner: the second-tier playwright and pamphleteer George Wilkins, about whom little is known (he once gave a deposition in a lawsuit in which Shakespeare was also a witness; he wrote a novel called *The Painful Adventures of Pericles, Prince of Tyre*, which the play follows in many places; he was a small-time pimp). Why Shakespeare would choose such an unlikely and unwholesome writing partner is one of the many things about his life and career scholars can only guess at. Some believe that Wilkins came to Shakespeare's theater company with the idea of dramatizing his *Pericles* novel, and that when Shakespeare found in it some themes he was already exploring at the time, he jumped on board and made the thing work. Others argue that the play we know today is Shakespeare's polish of Wilkins' own draft, or that Wilkins finished an incomplete Shakespearean original. However the play was written, Shakespeare and everyone else in his orbit knew it was lesser stuff, which is why the play wasn't included in the First Folio of 1623. The mystery of its composition notwithstanding, the play has its charms—the Pericles/Marina father/daughter reunion is one of Shakespeare's best scenes—and its stageworthiness has been proven many times over the centuries. As for the woebegone George Wilkins, wherever he is today, he can enjoy the knowledge that his name endures as a footnote in the life of a genius. If that seems like cold comfort, it's at least better than disappearing entirely, which is certainly the fate of those Jacobean whoremongers who didn't have the good fortune to co-author a play with the immortal Bard.

## GLOBAL WARMING

As thrilling as it can be to listen to Shakespeare talk about something in his experience that we recognize as identical in ours despite the centuries that have passed—the beauty of a flower, the giddy whirl of new love—it's also delightful to hear him prophetically address a phenomenon that hadn't yet occurred in human history when he was alive. He does so in this excerpt. Greenhouse gases, rising sea levels, melting polar ice, and Al Gore are all things Shakespeare didn't, and couldn't, know about, and yet here he talks in unequivocal terms about the harmful effects of climate change. Like so many of the Bardisms in this book, this one demonstrates the uncanny way a shift of context brings new and vivid meaning to a four-hundred-year-old passage of poetic text.

> The seasons alter: hoary-headed frosts
> Fall in the fresh lap of the crimson rose,
> And on old Hiems' thin and icy crown
> An odorous chaplet of sweet summer buds
> Is, as in mock'ry, set. The spring, the summer,
> The childing autumn, angry winter change
> Their wonted liveries, and the mazèd world
> By their increase now knows not which is which.
>
> —Titania, *A Midsummer Night's Dream*, 2.1.107–14

***In other words:***

The seasons are changing. White-tinged frost now falls on the red rose, and the icy crown of Hiems, god of winter, now sprouts a sweet-smelling garland of summer flowers that seems to mock him. Spring, summer, abundant autumn, tempestuous winter: they're exchanging their usual appearances. And the astonished world, seeing them spin out of control, can't tell them apart.

***How to use it:***

- Wow your dinner companions by laying out this beauty of a speech when the talk turns to carbon footprints and the Kyoto Protocol. It's also great for the next news report of some climate-change-fueled megastorm, or, more simply, for a hot winter day or cold summer one.

- Some strong antitheses make this speech work. The image of frost in the lap of a rose is opposed to the equally odd image of flowers set in the crown of Hiems, the god of winter. Think *frosts / rose* versus *Hiems' crown / flowers*. Note also that *which* versus *which* in the final line is also an antithesis.
- Two verbs are crucial here. *Change* at the end of line 6 needs special emphasis, and *knows not* gives the entire speech its kick on line 8. (And note the gong-like monosyllables with which Titania drives her point home: Now. *Knows*. *Not*. **Which**. Is. **Which!**)

***Some details:***

The evocative image *childing autumn* on line 6 of this rich bit of poetry is a hard one to paraphrase. *Childing* seems to be related to giving birth, and so, linked to autumn, the time of harvest, likely means something like "abundant," or "yielding a large crop." Titania—well, Shakespeare—is the first person to use the word in this sense in English, according to the *Oxford English Dictionary*. Of course, there's every possibility that the *OED* got it wrong and that Shakespeare himself wouldn't recognize this sense of *childing*. That's because there's every possibility that he actually wrote a different word. Although Titania says *childing* in the first two published texts of *A Midsummer Night's Dream*—a 1600 quarto and the First Folio of 1623—in the Fourth Folio of 1685 she says *chiding*, making the phrase *chiding autumn* mean, roughly, "harsh November."*

This is just one of literally thousands of cases in which an oddball

---

* The terms *quarto* and *folio* refer to page sizes. The process of printing books involved laying out multiple pages on one large sheet of paper called a *broadsheet*. Folded once, to make two pages with four sides, it was called a folio. Folded again, to make four pages with eight sides, it was called a quarto.

Shakespearean word changed its spelling—and therefore its meaning—between the printed versions of his works that appeared during his lifetime and after his death. Unlike writers today, who demand and receive final approval of their texts before any printing presses roll, Renaissance authors neither expected nor enjoyed such proprietary rights in their work. This was particularly true of playwrights, who wrote for performance, not publication, and who sold their plays outright—along with all artistic control of them—to the theater companies that produced them. These companies in turn sold the texts to publishers, who were in no small hurry to supply printed copies of the latest hit script to a public eager to read its favorite plays. Unfortunately, Renaissance printing technology wasn't built for speed, and to call the laborious process of book manufacturing in the period error-prone would be an understatement. With no author on hand to supervise, print-shop workers could—and did—introduce changes in the texts, based on their own quirks of punctuation and spelling, exigencies of format and space on the page, misreadings and other mistakes, or even simple preference. When a published play text sold especially well, publishers would market subsequent print runs—which meant starting again from scratch, sometimes months or even years later, and introducing yet another set of unauthorized changes.

Thus, Shakespeare may have written *childing* in 1595, only to have the word get the *l* beaten out of it by a sloppy typesetter in 1685. Or he may have written *chiding*, only to have the word gain an *l* of an extra letter through a mistake in 1600 repeated by a new generation of printers when the First Folio was prepared two decades later, but then corrected sixty years after that. There's no way to know for sure because Shakespeare's manuscript of the play doesn't survive (none of his manuscripts does, except maybe a fragment of a page of a lost play called *Sir Thomas More*). So which is right, *childing* or *chiding*? You decide. Shakespeare's dead; he won't know what you've chosen. However, he will, I suspect, appreciate the care you're taking with his words. After all, the process by which Renaissance play texts made it into print shows that just as Shakespeare in the theater is the product of collaboration among many artists and craftspeople—director, actors, designers, technicians, crew—so Shakespeare on the page includes contributions from many people beyond the Bard himself. There's no reason why you too can't be one of his artistic partners.

CHAPTER 7

# Mere Oblivion

## SHAKESPEARE FOR THE OCCASIONS OF THE END OF LIFE

*Last scene of all,*
*That ends this strange eventful history,*
*Is second childishness and mere oblivion,*
*Sans teeth, sans eyes, sans taste, sans everything.*

"An old man is twice a child," Rosencrantz tells Prince Hamlet, who moments earlier mocked the elderly Lord Polonius as a "great baby" who is "not yet out of his swaddling-clouts." The maxim "old men are twice children" was a commonplace in the Renaissance, but I like to think that Rosencrantz alludes not to the conventional wisdom but instead to Jaques' Seventh Age.

Of course, I can't prove that *As You Like It* was on the Masterpieces of World Drama syllabus at the Danish school Rosencrantz and his sidekick Guildenstern attended. But one of the things that happens when you spend as much time with these characters as I do is that they become very real people in your imagination. And as real people, they can go and read the same plays, even Shakespeare plays, that other real people read. To my mind, Hamlet's read *Richard II* and *Henry V*, Coriolanus knows *All's Well That Ends Well*, and Desdemona could ace an exam on *Much Ado About Nothing*. The characters may not be able to read ahead to the ends of their own plays, but I see no reason to deny them the glories of all the others. Besides, I can support this unorthodox theory on postmodern grounds: Shakespeare's company employed a small number of actors—a core group of sixteen, who played all the principal roles in any given play. Thus Laertes "is" Macduff "is" Hotspur, because the same fellow played all three. And Hermia "is" Celia "is" Hero for the same reason. In this sense, Rosencrantz may not literally know Jaques or have ever heard him speak, but "Rosencrantz"—in the form of the actor who played him—certainly heard "Jaques"—in the form of the actor who played him—list the Seven Ages on that great day in theater history when *As You Like It* premiered. Jaques was likely played by Richard Burbage, who also played Hamlet—apparently he was especially convincing as a melancholy cynic with an ironic bent. Shakespeare's company, unlike most of today's thespians, performed a different play every day, so it was theoretically possible that Burbage-as-Jaques could tell his castmates about how life tends toward second childishness on Tuesday, and then on Wednesday, as Hamlet, he could listen to one of them tell him about how an old man is twice a child. Such was the funhouse mirror existence of a Shakespearean actor in the English Renaissance.

My twenty-year run in the contemporary Shakespearean theater has given me the chance to watch our era's Burbages at work, and although I've seen them give performances of jaw-dropping excellence and stirring emotional truthfulness, I don't know if it's even possible for them to inhabit Shakespeare's words, to *live* them, in quite the same manner Burbage and company did. For those artists—the Founders, if you will—"all the world's a stage" wasn't just a line in a speech, it was a way of life. In Shakespeare's theater, the boundary between onstage and off was permeable and the frontier line separating these realms, ever changing. Not all the sophistication of our modern theater can conjure such a reality. Our culture—scientific, rational, accountable—is ineluctably different from that of the English Renaissance, and it simply won't allow for such contingent and elusive constructs.

In the English Renaissance, world and stage were two shifting points on a single continuum, and experts on the period show us how deeply this notion penetrated the entire worldview of Shakespeare's day. Theater historians and archaeologists argue that the very architecture of the Globe Theatre itself encoded the idea. There, the audience and the actors occupied the same space, under the same open roof, lit by the same gray afternoon light of the overcast London sky. Above the theater's main entrance gate, custom holds, was a crest showing Hercules bearing the earth on his shoulders, and the Latin motto "*Totus mundus agit histrionem*," or "The entire world is a playhouse." This striking assertion helps make clear why Jaques' *last scene of all* ends a strange, eventful *history*: the word was not merely a synonym for "story." Like *shifts* in Jaques' Sixth Age, *history* also carried with it a theatrical undertone, because during the English Renaissance, chronicle plays—works that depicted human lives unfolding against epic tapestries of large national themes—were labeled by that generic term (as in Shakespeare's *The History of King Lear*, *The History of Henry IV*, and *The Comical History of the Merchant of Venice*). "History" the recorded facts and "history" their dramatization are interchangeable. All the world's a stage, all people are actors, and all of life is a play. If that's true, then a playhouse is a stage upon a stage, an actor is a person playing the part of a person playing a part, and a drama is an artistically crafted version of a life that's already artistically crafted.

The theater of the English Renaissance was a kind of Dreamland, a Coney Island fantasy palace populated by exotics and attended by people whose real life was, at least according to the sign above the theater door, as fictional as the story they were watching. When the play ended, both groups—actors and audience—simply went away, and ended, too. The players disappeared into some unseen backstage nowhere, and the audience returned to its world, which was—fasten your seatbelts—a stage!

To be sure, man's Seventh Age is not about the endless feedback loop of life and theater. Instead, it's about the end of this strange, eventful tale. The Seventh Age is death. But to Jaques—all right already, to Shakespeare—death and the end of a play are two ways of looking at the exact same phenomenon. In his last play the Bard makes the connection clear. "Our revels now are ended," *The Tempest*'s Prospero announces when the play he presents at the wedding party of his daughter and son-in-law concludes. "These our actors," he continues, "were all spirits and / Are melted into air, into thin air." Jaques was written nearly a dozen years earlier, and so he doesn't have Prospero's poetic precision on the subject. But what Prospero spells out is what Jaques implies in describing the *last scene of all* as *mere oblivion*. *Mere* is Elizabethan for "utter, total, absolute." Death is in this sense a process of annihilation, or, more accurately, sublimation: the direct transformation of solid into gas, the melting of what we are, into air. Into thin air.

Jaques' last line is chilling enough when read as a literal description of the final moments of life; we die toothless, blind, and incapable of discernment of any kind. But if we read his four repeats of *sans*, that series of bass notes that toll this magnificent speech to a close, as forerunners of Prospero's vision of the nothingness that follows the final curtain's fall, then *sans everything* leaps beyond the literal. Jaques' last word—*ev-ry-thing*—with its intimation of infinity, tells us that the Seventh Age may be a time of physical decay, but it is also, stunningly, a time of metaphysical transformation and limitless possibility.

We *are* such stuff as dreams are made on. That is, our origins are the material of fictions. Life is evanescent and ephemeral, and after all its sevenfold dramas, and all the turmoil, and all the pomposity and self-importance, and all the foolishness, it ends where it began. In the dark, on a bare stage, our story over, yet somehow ready to begin again, thanks to some impossible-to-name power: magic or art or God or "Shakespeare" or faith or the essence of theater itself, that cascades over the edge of the stage with Niagara force.

Here, then, Bardisms for the Seventh Age. Shakespeare on the Occasions of Oblivion, and for that spark whose flicker kindles new light.

**LET'S FURTHER THINK ON THIS . . .**

Vincent "the Chin" Gigante, longtime boss of New York's notorious Genovese crime family, was sentenced to twelve years in prison after a long trial on charges of conspiracy to murder, extortion, and racketeering. His family objected that Gigante was suffering from Alzheimer's disease and therefore incompetent to stand trial; after all, he was famous for shuffling down the streets of Greenwich Village in a ratty blue bathrobe and jabbering to himself like a madman. Prosecutors countered that it was all an act, and U.S. district judge Jack Weinstein agreed, saying "the Chin" was faking his illness in order to escape justice. "One man in his time plays many parts," wrote Weinstein in his opinion, quoting Jaques in support of his view that Gigante's second childishness and mere oblivion were simply second-rate theatrics. "The Chin" died in prison in 2005, sans everything.

## SHAKESPEARE ON DEATH

*Thou know'st 'tis common—all that lives must die,*
*Passing through nature to eternity.*
—Gertrude, *Hamlet*, 1.2.72–73

Love and death: for sheer quantity, these two subjects top the Bardisms list, although it can be a challenge to specify which comes in first and which second. Ranked by line count, love probably wins, but only by a nose. Ranked by potency—by poetry's power to stun, to clobber, to stop all motion cold—death gets the edge, but that's perhaps more a reflection of death's frightful and tenacious hold on the imagination than it is a comment on the relative weakness of Shakespeare's love poetry. One of art's great subjects is the intersection between humanity's terror in the face of death and its ecstasy in the face of romance—where would Italian grand opera, the nineteenth-century English novel, Bosch and Breughel, or all of Greek tragedy be without this theme?—and art often concludes that death is the more overwhelming force.

This, I think, is the reason *King Lear* and *Hamlet* are reckoned the greater Shakespearean efforts than, say, *As You Like It* or *Twelfth Night*, despite those two hardly being chopped liver, as my grandmother would have put it. (And it's also why the life-affirming comedies are way, way more fun to watch.) I laugh myself to joyous tears at the multiple wedding that concludes *As You Like It*, and my heart leaps when the twins Viola and Sebastian appear together in the final scene of *Twelfth Night*. But as intense as those reactions always are, something of another magnitude happens when Lear howls over his daughter Cordelia, dead in his arms. "Why should a dog, a horse, a rat, have life," the king wails, "and thou no breath at all?" and the agony is so profound that I can barely look at it. When Fortinbras enters at the very end of *Hamlet* and gapes at the carnage strewn about the marble halls of Elsinore, I share his disbelief at the devastation. When I staged the murder of Desdemona in a production of *Othello*, I left every rehearsal feeling shaken and drained—the violence in the scene is too mighty, the airless, Stygian darkness in Desdemona's bedroom too real. Shakespeare knows the force of death, understands its workings, comprehends its annihilating power, and, as always, finds words to express all this in surprising, even shocking, detail—detail so vivid and material that we, like Lear, want to wash our hands before we go on. "Let me wipe it first," he tells Gloucester, who has asked to kiss the royal palm, "it smells of mortality." The Bardisms below render in verse various aspects of that cataclysmic scent. I've found that they provide some comfort when the ugly whiff wafts across one's path.

## DEATH IS PART OF THE NATURAL COURSE OF LIFE

Gertrude, quoted above, labels death *common*. She means something like "typical," or perhaps "widespread," "experienced by everyone," and hence "ordinary." Gertrude's notion—that all living things die—is, in a word, common in Shakespeare: "But kings and mightiest potentates must die, / For that's the end of human misery," says the heroic general Talbot, nearly rhyming (*Henry VI, Part I*, 3.6.22–23); doddering Justice Shallow expresses the notion in the comically repetitious phrases of a nutty old man: "Certain, 'tis certain; very sure, very sure. Death, as the Psalmist saith, is certain to all; all shall die" (*Henry IV, Part II*, 3.2.33–34). And in a little-known late play, written in collaboration with dramatist John Fletcher, Shakespeare articulates "everybody dies" in a lyric that combines cartography, urbanism, and commerce in a remarkable and vivid metaphor:

FIRST QUEEN Heavens lend
A thousand differing ways to one sure end.
THIRD QUEEN This world's a city full of straying streets,
And death's the market-place, where each one meets.

—*The Two Noble Kinsmen*, 1.5.13–16

Here's another iteration of the "death is common" idea, a Bardism that puts a quite terrible thought into moving and even beautiful poetic form.

This is the state of man. Today he puts forth
The tender leaves of hopes; tomorrow blossoms,
And bears his blushing honors thick upon him;
The third day comes a frost, a killing frost,
And when he thinks, good easy man, full surely
His greatness is a-ripening, nips his root,
And then he falls.

—WOLSEY, *Henry VIII*, 3.2.353–59

***In other words:***

Here's how a person's life runs. Today he cautiously indulges his hopes, those fragile things that are like the newest buds on a branch. Tomorrow he flourishes, and collects all sorts of splendid successes and tributes that he displays proudly. On the third day it suddenly gets cold, deadly cold, and at the very moment when this trusting person is convinced that glory is upon him, that's when he's cut down and crashes to the ground.

***How to say it:***

- Wolsey is a cardinal, and his years of Sunday mornings in the pulpit have taught him a thing or two about crafting a good speech. This one deploys a marvelously artful three-part build: (1) *today* this happens, (2) *tomorrow* that happens, and (3) *the third day* something else takes over. Try to let the speech intensify as it moves forward, and let this three-step process carry you through.

- As you do, take care to emphasize the verbs in the passage: *puts forth*; *blossoms*; *bears*; *comes*; *killing*; *thinks*; *is a-ripening*; *nips*; *falls*. Note how they chart the speech's sobering message of promise turning to decay. In particular, observe how the verbs associated with the frost that descends in the deadly third step of the speech are stark, sharp, and haunting. *Nips* is especially powerful. It's such a small word, the action of a gardener's pruning shears, and yet it carries with it enough force to take down *greatness*. And can there be a verb more devastating in context than *falls*? It knots my stomach every time I read it.
- Certainly applicable on any occasion calling for some insight into death and its ways, this Bardism is also perfect whenever arrogance meets comeuppance. That showboating baseball player who at the crucial moment chokes like Mighty Casey knows what Cardinal Wolsey's talking about, as does that politician who believes his own polls and veers too close to the boundaries of ethical conduct, as does that yahoo in your office whose last month's sales results make him certain that he can coast to this month's gold star status.
- Change the gender-specific words as necessary: *woman*, *she*, and *her* allow this Bardism to speak to the Gertrudes who need to hear it.

***Some details:***

Repeating *frost* in line 4, Cardinal Wolsey employs one of Shakespeare's favorite playwright's tricks. When a word appears twice, or even more times, in close proximity or in a row, Shakespeare is instructing his actors to intensify. That's the theater equivalent of the musician's *crescendo*: an increase in volume, force, and size. Leontes has a great repeat in *The Winter's Tale* when he sees what he's sure is open flirtation between his wife and his best friend: "Too hot, too hot," he says. Every actor who's ever played the role has taken Shakespeare's advice about repeats and increased in intensity between the first and second iteration of the phrase. The heat between Leontes' wife and his best friend is not just hot, it's "too hot . . . **too HOT!**" In *Richard II*, the über-patriot John of Gaunt calls his beloved England "this dear, dear land." Again, every actor I've ever seen give the line has said, "This dear, **dear** land." Most good Macbeths say "Tomorrow, and *tomorrow*, and **tomorrow**," and I can't remember a Lear who didn't say "Never, *never*, ***never***, ***never***, ***NEVER***!" Repeats mean build in intensity. After all, Cardinal Wolsey's not describing a crisp December morning in Vermont, nor the inside of his Sub-Zero freezer. He's talking about an icy blast that wipes out the crop: "The third day comes a *frost*, a ***killing frost.***"

## LIFE IS A SLOW MARCH TOWARD DEATH

Shakespeare's greatest formulation of death's pervasiveness and life's status as merely a preamble to its inevitable end is this entry in the Shakespeare Top Ten, familiar to most of us from when Miss Baxter forced us to memorize it in eighth-grade English class.

> Tomorrow, and tomorrow, and tomorrow
> Creeps in this petty pace from day to day
> To the last syllable of recorded time,
> And all our yesterdays have lighted fools
> The way to dusty death. Out, out, brief candle.
> Life's but a walking shadow, a poor player

That struts and frets his hour upon the stage,
And then is heard no more. It is a tale
Told by an idiot, full of sound and fury,
Signifying nothing.

—MACBETH, *Macbeth*, 5.5.18–27

***In other words:***

One after another after another, our days crawl slowly along, until the very last moment of human history. And all the events of our pasts are merely signposts that guide us—silly us—toward our deaths. End already, you short, shining life. You're nothing but a phantom, a zombie, a bad actor that shouts and hams it up while he's onstage and, when he exits, disappears forever. Life's a story told by a moron. It's noisy and eventful, but it doesn't mean a thing.

***How to say it:***

- I could teach a semester-long verse-speaking class using only these ten lines. There's a three-part build (line 1) and a pair of two-part repeats (lines 2 and 5). There are great verbs (*creeps*, *lighted*, *out*, *struts*, *frets*, *is heard*, *told*, *full*). The thoughts emerge beautifully one line at a time (cover the page with a paper, read each line one by one, and see for yourself how clearly the speech unfolds). There are complex puns and locutions (*tomorrow* and *yesterday* are named outright, while *today* is glanced at in another form at the end of line 2). The language leaps to and fro from pedestrian to heightened and back again. It's really got everything that makes Shakespeare Shakespeare. The best way to speak this speech and allow all its poetic detail to resonate is to take it slowly, deliberately, and as simply as possible.

  Do take note, though, of how the language here has an aspect that moves it beyond its simple function of conveying meaning: the words operate in an almost physical manner. Their sounds, their shapes, their existence in three dimensions lifts them beyond the level of mere semantic or lexical communication and into a realm of material presence. The very vowels and consonants in the passage knit together to communicate as much information as the meanings of the words they constitute.

Okay, okay. This is getting a little ethereal, a bit touchy-feely, and awfully hard to quantify. But the phenomenon I'm discussing—the way a word's sound seems to embody its sense—is widely recognized in literature and even has its own very impressive name: *onomatopoeia*. Most of us think of that term as applying to words such as *buzz* or *clang* that sound exactly like what they are. Grammarians, and for that matter poets, use it in a wider sense. For them, onomatopoeia refers to those aspects of a word that give it a life of its own, an aural presence that transcends meaning. This is Shakespeare's understanding of the term, and since he's interested in the ways a word's physical dimension generates a sense beyond sense, so must his interpreters be.

Say only the vowel sounds in the speech, and then say only the consonant sounds (both are common rehearsal exercises). The long vowels in *creeps*, *day*, *time*, *player*, *stage*, *tale*, *told*; the pained *oo* in *fools* and *poor*; the injured *ow* in *out*, *hour*, and *sound*—these form a kind of tone poem of grief and loss. The mass of alliteration (what grammarians term repeated consonant sounds), including the initial letters *p* in *poor* and *player* and the *t*'s in *tale told,* are also worth noting. But the three occurrences of the consonant pattern *s-f*, in *struts and frets*, *sound and fury*, and *signifying* truly blow my mind. In those three paired *s*'s and *f*'s can be found everything anyone might need to know about what Macbeth is going through at this, his lowest moment. *Sss. Fff. Sss. Fff. Sss. Fff.* It's a symphony of suffering, a susurrus of futile finality. And it happens on a level totally apart from the meaning of what Macbeth is saying. When you try the speech again, this time reintegrating the consonants and vowels, the taste of *sss fff* will remain in your mouth, adding richness to the metaphors, deepening your empathy with Macbeth, and amping up the power of this language to move an audience.

***Some details:***

The literary excellence of this most famous of Macbeth's utterances has earned it pride of place in many books about Shakespeare, but the speech has also, oddly enough, found its way into a rather less likely body of literature: studies about the American presidency.

No commander in chief was more of a Bardophile than the sixteenth president of the United States, Abraham Lincoln. Honest Abe's devotion to Shakespeare and his works surpassed that of even the noted presidential Shakespeareans John Adams, his son John Quincy, Thomas Jefferson, and John F. Kennedy, all of whom are on record declaiming iambic pentameter in the Oval Office.

Lincoln's favorite Shakespeare was *Macbeth*, and his obsession with the play is well documented. He is known to have carried a worn copy of the drama with him in the years he traveled up and down Illinois practicing law, and witnesses attest to many spontaneous White House references to and recitations from the play so passionate that they sometimes moved the great man to tears. "Tomorrow and tomorrow and tomorrow" gripped Lincoln's imagination in a particularly strong—and, given what the speech talks about, a particularly odd—manner. One contemporary recalled in his memoir that he visited Lincoln late one night during the terrible summer of 1864, one of the most violent periods in the Civil War. Lincoln was asleep at his desk, "ghastly pale, rings under his caverened eyes." His Shakespeare lay open beside him. Lincoln started awake and immediately read aloud Macbeth's remarkable speech, with its imagery of life as bad acting and of human endeavor as mere empty sound that punctuates our inevitable march toward death. When he finished, Lincoln said of this extreme nihilism and utter hopelessness that "it comes to me tonight like a consolation." It's hard to think of a more revealing, or chilling, insight into the terrible psychic burdens borne by a president in wartime.

Some of Lincoln's successors shared his fixation on this speech. Ronald Reagan cited Shakespeare frequently during his presidency, quoting everything from the ever-popular "There is a tide in the affairs of men" and the pro-democracy catchphrase "the people are the city" from *Coriolanus* to the title of one play in a witty blast at Jimmy Carter, whose economic policies Reagan found to be "a tragic comedy of errors." Reagan's most detailed remarks about Shakespeare, however, centered on *Macbeth*. At an appearance at a Tennessee school, the president recited the "Tomorrow and tomorrow and tomorrow" speech from memory when a teacher asked him his favorite line in the canon. Unlike Lincoln, who was rattled to the point of despair by the bleakness of Macbeth's vision, Reagan construed the lines as a reinforcement of his trademark "Morning in America" optimism. "I hope that none of you ever get that pessimistic or that cynical about life," he told the students assembled to hear him. "I think that humankind is very important, and their lives are not as futile as he [i.e., Macbeth, or perhaps Shakespeare] would have us believe."

Another president who gravitated toward Macbeth's great soliloquy of wretchedness: Bill Clinton. At a White House poetry event, the president recalled the lines—flawlessly—and commented wittily that *Macbeth*, which is, after all, about murdering your way to power and then getting murdered once you have it—was "hardly designed to entice me to a public career," but added that through the play, "I learned about the dangers of blind ambition, the fleeting nature of fame, the ultimate emptiness of power disconnected from higher purpose." He returned to the passage in his autobiography, noting that he'd looked it up while in the Arkansas governor's mansion. He found it still "full of power for me, a dreadful message." But there were no Lincolnesque caverened eyes for Bill Clinton; instead, his sparkled with a Reagan-like commitment to seeing the bright side: "I was always determined [that Macbeth's bleakness] would not be the measure of my life." Bill Clinton was perhaps the one president who understood the playwright as fully as Lincoln did before him. "Old Will had it right," he discovered. "Life is comedy and tragedy." He added, "Mr. Shakespeare made me a better president." It's a sentiment that a select few of the men in this most exclusive of clubs would share.

## SHAKESPEARE ON THE LOSS OF LOVED ONES

*O you gods!*
*Why do you make us love your goodly gifts,*
*And snatch them straight away?*
—Pericles, *Pericles*, 3.1.22–24

The Bard's philosophical meditations on death expertly take the measure of a phenomenon that obsesses us all but that few of us can comprehend in any concrete way. That's one of the great favors Shakespeare the poet does us: he "gives to airy nothing / A local habitation and a name," as Duke Theseus puts it in *A Midsummer Night's Dream*; that is, he renders in accessible human scale things that in themselves are simply too large for everyday understanding. But Shakespeare the dramatist does us favors, too. He knows that the most effective plays revolve around how the outsized, ineffable forces at work in the universe—the forces to which poets give labels and addresses—impact private, individual lives. His history plays provoke us when they consider war in the abstract, but they move us when they dramatize war separating parent from child. His romantic plays tickle us with some memorable phrase about a lover's eyes glowing bright, but they swoop our hearts to heaven when they put those bright eyes on stage in front of us, radiating a passion intense enough to power an urban electrical grid. And so it is with his tragedies. They tell us much about what death is, how it works, why it comes, and how inescapable is its grip, and we learn from these passages. Yet when the plays dramatize death, when they show it walking into a home and taking a family member away, then our response moves into another zone. Then we feel, then we remember, then we grieve, then we mourn.

Here are some Bardisms about the personal nature of death. They're to be consulted at those painful times when death takes that terrible step from literary conceit to palpable presence.

## THE DEATH OF A HUSBAND

Widows wander through Shakespeare's canon bearing witness to the human follies that summon death to curtail the world's supply of husbands and fathers. Many of these widows declaim their stirring jeremiads about the Angel of Death long after their spouses' demise. However, one very notable woman watches life ebb from her beloved while cradling him in her arms. Cleopatra's in-the-moment narration of Antony's death is as moving a piece of dramatic poetry as any I know, and it's the Bardism I recommend, quietly and respectfully, to anyone who's lost a husband, father, or revered mentor.

Noblest of men, woot die?
Hast thou no care of me? Shall I abide
In this dull world, which in thy absence is
No better than a sty? O see, my women,
The crown o' the earth doth melt. My lord!
O, withered is the garland of the war.
The soldier's pole is fall'n. Young boys and girls
Are level now with men. The odds is gone,
And there is nothing left remarkable
Beneath the visiting moon.

—Cleopatra, *Antony and Cleopatra*, 4.16.61–70

***In other words:***

Will you die, you finest of men? Don't you even care about me? Do you want me to live in this boring world, which, without you, is about as glamorous as a barnyard? Look, my companions: the world's most glorious ornament is ruined. My man! The laurel leaves of victory have dried and cracked, the flags have drooped. With the only real man gone, there's no difference between those who remain and children. Nothing distinguishes between greatness and mediocrity anymore. Nothing special is left on the entire face of the earth.

***How to say it:***

- This Bardism can serve as a tribute to any great person, and not only a husband. It can also with a few changes memorialize a woman: substitute *women* for *men* in line 1, and *lady* for *lord* in line 5. Feel free to change *O see, my women* to *O see, my friends*, or *my colleagues*, or *my family*, or *my people*.

- Cleopatra begins by speaking to Antony, draped in her arms like a secular *Pietà*. She asks him three questions, which he of course does not answer, so midway through line 4 she turns her attention elsewhere: to her women, telling them that the world's crown has melted. The exclamation "My lord!" at the end of line 5 might also be addressed to the women, but I've seen it work more effectively as an intimacy that connects Cleopatra one last time to her love.

  All this is to say that a key to speaking this speech is to consider carefully just whom you are addressing. You must do as Cleopatra does and address first the late hero for whom you grieve—by speaking to his spirit in the air, perhaps—then address your listeners, then return briefly to your lord, and then speak again to those around you, telling them all the leveling depredations his absence imposes on the world.

- Cleopatra's three questions in the first section of the speech should build in intensity, as all three-part groupings in Shakespeare should. The next section of the speech, addressed to the women, is composed of a list. It has more than three parts, but it too must build in intensity: (1) the crown melts, (2) the garland withers, (3) the flagpole falls, (4) children are the same as men, (5) difference is erased, and (6) nothing remarkable remains. As you work through these six images, note that the first five are brief and rendered in quite simple language. Allow them their simplicity. The last image is longer and much more complex in vocabulary, syntax, and poetic texture. Allow it scope and space to express the grief and emotion of the moment.

- These are some of the key ideas whose richness and imagistic power can help you through this speech: *noblest*, *dull*, *sty*, *remarkable*, *moon*. And here are some verbs that will also lend a hand: *doth melt*, *withered*, *fall'n*, *are level*, *gone*, *is nothing left*.

## THE DEATH OF A WIFE

While fewer in number than widows, widowers also populate Shakespeare's *Complete Works*. Their pain is captured vividly in a quiet corner near the close of a muted and minor-key play, *All's Well That Ends Well*. It's a Bardism suffused with sympathy and condolence.

> He lost a wife
> Whose beauty did astonish the survey
> Of richest eyes, whose words all ears took captive,
> Whose dear perfection hearts that scorned to serve
> Humbly called mistress.
>
> —Lafeu, *All's Well That Ends Well*, 5.3.15–19

***In other words:***

His wife is gone. Her beauty dazzled the sight of even the most sophisticated eyes. Her speech beguiled every listener. Her utter perfection made worshippers out of people who resolutely refused to bow down to anything.

***How to use it:***

- This Bardism is a powerful third-person observation on the passing of anyone's beloved wife, but it can be a moving first-person expression of loss with the simple substitution of *I* for its first word, *He*.

## THE DEATH OF A CHILD

Death's icy touch always devastates, but when his cold hand snatches away a child, a special and profound sorrow plunges everything into a terrible bleakness. Perhaps because he knew personally the awful woe of losing a child, Shakespeare writes about it with surpassing power. In *Macbeth*, *Richard III*, and *King John*, children's deaths shatter not only their loved ones but the very plays in which they once lived: the plots of these works swerve into unremitting darkness with, respectively, the murders of Macduff's children, the princes in the tower, and young Arthur. In *King John*, the missing Arthur's mother, Constance, goes mad with grief, and declaims an eloquent Bardism on the loss of a little one.

> Grief fills the room up of my absent child,
> Lies in his bed, walks up and down with me,
> Puts on his pretty looks, repeats his words,
> Remembers me of all his gracious parts,
> Stuffs out his vacant garments with his form;
> Then, have I reason to be fond of grief.
>
> —Constance, *King John*, 3.4.93–98

***In other words:***

Grief, personified, has literally replaced my missing child. Grief sleeps in his bed. It goes on walks with me. It's cute in the same way he was; it says the things he said. It reminds me of all his wonderful features. It wears his clothes in an image of him. For bringing my child back to me in this strange manner, I've actually grown to like grief.

***How to say it:***

- I wish no one would ever experience what Constance does in *King John*, but I have seen her words bring solace to mourners in her sad situation. I've also heard at least one person—it was a speaker at a funeral—substitute another noun (*brother*, in this case) for *child* at the end of line 1, a rewrite that transformed Constance's lament for her young son into words of comfort for a grieving sibling.

## SHAKESPEARE ON MEMORIALS AND ELEGIES

*This was the noblest Roman of them all.*
—Mark Antony, *Julius Caesar*, 5.5.67

If you're scanning through this section of *Bardisms*, it's probably because you've been asked to deliver a eulogy at a funeral. That the request came to you means that you had some special connection to the deceased, and this connection ensures that every word of your memorial will perforce be suffused with the very pain and loss on which your remarks hope to shed comfort. Private grief is hard enough to bear, but grieving in public is of another order of magnitude altogether. Public grief taxes our every emotional resource, challenges our ability to control our own faculties, and demands dignity and composure in measures well beyond those required of us on any other occasion. Put another way, every funeral we attend is one too many, but funerals at which we are called upon to speak are particularly difficult.

From my own experiences ordering my thoughts at times of mourning, I can report that recourse to wisdom beyond my own has made the difference between paralyzed murmuring unworthy of the occasion and a momentary eloquence not my own that somehow served up a modicum of solace for myself and others. The wisdom to which I had recourse was of course Shakespeare's. After all, for every Bardism appropriate to happy life occasions, there is an equal and opposite Bardism appropriate to life's more challenging moments. For every Sonnet 116 paying tribute to the marriage of true minds, for example, there is a Sonnet 65 pointing out that there are no forces in the world strong enough to resist when "sad mortality o'ersways their power." Chapter Three showed how nuptials are the serial Shakespeare quoter's finest hour; below is ample proof that funerals are the equal and opposite occasions on which the Bard so magnificently articulates all that we feel in our hearts.

## MAY YOU REST IN PEACE

I've read this immensely moving text across a casket, heard it read at memorial services both grand and intimate, included it in notes of condolence, even sent it to a dear friend sitting vigil at a parent's deathbed. It is the greatest Shakespeare on Occasions Funereal.

GUIDERIUS Fear no more the heat o' the sun,
Nor the furious winter's rages;
Thou thy worldly task hast done,
Home art gone, and ta'en thy wages:
Golden lads and girls all must,
As chimney-sweepers, come to dust.
ARVIRAGUS Fear no more the frown o' the great;
Thou art past the tyrant's stroke;
Care no more to clothe and eat;
To thee the reed is as the oak:
The sceptre, learning, physic, must
All follow this, and come to dust.
GUIDERIUS Fear no more the lightning flash,
ARVIRAGUS Nor the all-dreaded thunder-stone;
GUIDERIUS Fear not slander, censure rash;
ARVIRAGUS Thou hast finish'd joy and moan:
BOTH All lovers young, all lovers must
Consign to thee, and come to dust.
GUIDERIUS No exorciser harm thee!
ARVIRAGUS Nor no witchcraft charm thee!

GUIDERIUS Ghost unlaid forbear thee!
ARVIRAGUS Nothing ill come near thee!
BOTH Quiet consummation have;
And renownèd be thy grave

—*Cymbeline*, 4.2.259–82

***In other words:***

GUIDERIUS Don't worry about the sun's heat anymore. Don't worry about angry winter storms. You've done your work on this earth. You've gone home now, and you've been paid for your efforts. Gorgeous boys and girls all return to dust, covered in it like chimney sweeps.

ARVIRAGUS Don't worry anymore about the disapproval of your superiors. No tyrant can hurt you now. Don't worry about food and clothes. As far as you're concerned, material things have no sway: a tiny blade of grass is no different from a mighty tree. People with political power, educated people, even doctors whose job is to defy death—no one can avoid the process of decay; everything and everyone comes to naught in the end.

GUIDERIUS Don't let lightning scare you,

ARVIRAGUS Thunder either, which frightens everyone;

GUIDERIUS Don't worry over people saying nasty stuff about you, or harshly judging you;

ARVIRAGUS You're done with both happiness and misery.

BOTH All young lovers—in fact, all lovers—have no choice but to sign the same contract you have, and return to dust.

GUIDERIUS May no mystic try to raise you from the grave!

ARVIRAGUS May no one try to cast a spell on your soul!

GUIDERIUS May no unsettled spirits trouble you!

ARVIRAGUS May nothing bad come near you!

BOTH May you finish your life in peace, and may your burial place be marked with due respect.

***How to say it:***

- Don't feel obliged to read the entire passage. The first stanza is quite beautiful and stands on its own, as does the third (shared) stanza and the five short lines that follow it. Should you wish to refer to the characters who speak this passage (actually, they sing it in the context of the play), they're two Welsh brothers whose names are pronounced *gwih-DEER-ee-us* and *ahr-vih-RAH-gus*.
- Take special note of the rhyme scheme of each stanza, which is ABABCC. That is, the first and third lines rhyme, as do the second and fourth lines, and lines 5 and 6 make a rhymed couplet. Try as you read the passage to work toward those rhyming words, which fall, of course, at the ends of lines—the position in the line where Shakespeare likes to place important words. He sometimes places key ideas at the start of verse lines, too, as he does here with *Fear no more* and *Fear not.*
- *Simple* is the watchword with this rich and highly poetic passage. Just say the words evenly and easily, as a comfort and reassurance to your departed friend or loved one, as though he or she could hear you. Your view is that the afterlife is a better place than the temporal world, a place free of what Hamlet terms "the whips and scorns of time." The person you're eulogizing has returned home, where he or she can at long last rest after a lifetime of labor and struggle.

## HE WAS AN ASTONISHING PERSON

Their somber tone notwithstanding, eulogies are celebrations. They recall what was inspiring and lovable about the deceased, and they don't have much room for any mention of the flaws, imperfections, disappointments, and shortcomings that made the person only human when he or she lived. Rarely content with sanitizing simplifications, Shakespeare writes a famous eulogy that manages to be extraordinarily loving and respectful, yet at the same time refuses to gloss over some hard truths about the person being memorialized. That eulogy is Hamlet's for his late father, and its justly famous phrases combine the positive and the negative in the same thought—a Shakespearean trademark: "He was a man, take him for all in all / I shall not look upon his like again." In other words, he was human, and even reckoned in toto, good and bad together, he was still pretty memorable.

I've researched this Hamletian Bardism's appearance in countless memorials, funeral remarks, and posthumous tributes, and, interestingly, I've found that almost every time it's quoted, only the second line survives. *Take him for all in all*, Hamlet's admission of his father's frailties, is nowhere to be found. I fully understand what motivates this omission, yet I also lament the dilution it represents. After all, if it's unadulterated praise you're after, Shakespeare offers plenty, particularly in his Roman plays, chock-full of formal tributes to great ones who've left the world too soon. Here are two that make for stirring and reverential memorials, and that speak for themselves without any need for editing or watering down.

First, Mark Antony's tribute over the corpse of Brutus:

> His life was gentle, and the elements
> So mixed in him that Nature might stand up
> And say to all the world "This was a man."
>
> —Mark Antony, *Julius Caesar*, 5.5.72–74

***In other words:***

He lived a fine-mannered life. The things of which human beings are made were balanced so perfectly in him that Mother Nature, maker of all men, could point to him and proclaim that he was the perfect example of humanity.

***Some details:***

This Bardism provides some insight into Renaissance notions of psychology. It was believed that four elements composed all matter: earth, air, water, and fire, which, when mixed together in various proportions (the verb used in the period was *tempered*), gave every substance in nature its particular character. In the human body, the four elements took the form of fluids called *humors*: blood, phlegm, yellow bile, and black bile. In proper temper these fluids composed a happy person—a person with a good *temperament*. Too much of any of the four, or too little, or some defect with one of them, would cause problems and throw a person into *distemper*, like a stray animal in need of an inoculation. Too much yellow bile, also known as choler, made you *choleric*: snappish, short-tempered, quick to anger. Too much black bile, also called melancholy, made you a depressive. Too much phlegm made you *phlegmatic*, or emotionless and dull. One way to restore the balance was to eat or drink things that had properties opposite the overabundant humor. Another was that medieval cure-all, bloodletting, because the humors were thought to circulate with the blood. Antony notes of Brutus that the great Roman required no such treatments, because the humors flowing through him were mixed in such perfect proportion that he was a showpiece of nature's craftsmanship.

Another eulogy. Antony dies, too, in Cleopatra's arms, as we saw above. This is how she memorializes him a short time later:

His legs bestrid the ocean; his reared arm
Crested the world. His voice was propertied
As all the tunèd spheres, and that to friends;
But when he meant to quail and shake the orb,
He was as rattling thunder. For his bounty,
There was no winter in't; an autumn 'twas,
That grew the more by reaping. His delights
Were dolphin-like; they showed his back above
The element they lived in. In his livery
Walk'd crowns and crownets. Realms and islands were
As plates dropped from his pocket.

—CLEOPATRA, *Antony and Cleopatra*, 5.2.81–92

***In other words:***

His stance straddled the ocean, like the legendary Colossus of Rhodes. His raised arm was like a heraldic emblem on the world's coat of arms. When he spoke to friends, his voice had the same qualities as the celestial spheres, the makers of heavenly music. But when he felt like subduing and terrifying the earth, he sounded like claps of thunder. As for his generosity, it was everlasting; it was like a perpetual harvest season that yielded more produce as more was gathered from it. The pleasures that delighted him made him stand out from the masses as a dolphin arcs above the water with each leap. Kings and princes were as servants to him. Nations and territories were like loose change that fell from his pockets.

***How to say it:***

- This richly poetic excerpt appears at first glance to be a lot more complicated than it actually is. At its heart is a simple list in which Cleopatra talks about various of Antony's features, in this order: (1) his legs, (2) his reared arm, (3) his voice, (4) his bounty,

(5) his delights, and (6) his livery. Each aspect of Antony gets its own description. Some are brief (his legs spanned the ocean), some longer (his voice sounded like celestial music to his friends, but to his enemies it sounded like an earth-shaking thunderclap). Try to work your way through the speech according to its six parts, and you'll find it flows easily and naturally.

- Another helpful approach to this speech is to phrase it one line at a time: cover the speech with a piece of paper and reveal each verse line one by one. At the end of each line, ask yourself for the next thought, the next piece of language, the next detail, then say it. For example, at the end of line 1, *his reared arm*, ask something like *did what?* You could answer in a zillion ways: "was muscular," "flexed with stunning strength," "frightened his enemies into submission." But Cleopatra answers with the beginning of line 2, *Crested the world.* Or, at the end of line 7, *His delights*, ask something like *what about them?* You could answer, "transported me to heavenly bliss," or "numbered too many to count," or "stirred love in every heart that knew them." But Cleopatra answers, *Were dolphin-like.* She—you—think about the next right image. She—and simultaneously, you—conjure the poetry to describe a man blessed with copious and wondrous personal gifts. And she—and you—render that description in surprising and unforgettable marine mammal imagery.

- Feel free to lift out only those features that apply to the person you're eulogizing, and to substitute feminine pronouns for masculine if it's a woman who's passed away.

***Some details:***

Throughout *Bardisms* I've offered paraphrases—equivalents in modern English—for Shakespeare's knottier poetic utterances. This speech shows the limits of that technique, and in doing so, it demonstrates something essential about Shakespeare's writing. Consider my phrase "As for his generosity, it was everlasting." That's how I render

Cleopatra's *For his bounty, / There was no winter in't.* To say it loses something in translation is the understatement of the century. Yes, my version communicates the basic sense of Cleopatra's thought, but it misses completely the dimension of her speech that makes it more than just simple communication. We might label that dimension, that quality of language that delivers more than meaning, "poetry." Paraphrases are lousy at capturing that. "Regular" language, the stuff of my modern translations, just isn't up to expressing high-octane metaphor such as that Cleopatra summons while eulogizing the hero who was the great passion of her life. She needs special language: the charged, idiosyncratic, spellbinding language of a great poet.

Students and friends often ask me to describe what it is about Shakespeare's writing that makes it so unique. I like to answer with a rather abstract concept: "Shakespeare" is a measure of the distance between everyday language and poetry, between *For his bounty, / There was no winter in't* and "As for his generosity, it was everlasting." Shakespeare is the X factor that transforms a simple idea into a metaphor, and that X factor is the very thing that makes us turn to him when our own expressive capacity isn't enough to give voice to what we feel. We know how grateful we were that our late loved ones were kind to us; Shakespeare memorializes their kindness by imagining it as an autumn without winter, as an endless harvest that yielded more, the more we gleaned from it. We need Shakespeare's help at our most emotionally charged moments, and we're grateful to his artistic prowess for helping us to know not just what to say but also what we feel.

## GOODBYE

Here are two brief Bardisms that eloquently put a period on an exemplary life. Use them at the conclusion of your eulogy, or in the closing of your condolence note. The first is yet another Roman encomium to masculine excellence: Brutus' stoic tribute to his dear friend Cassius:

> The last of all the Romans, fare thee well.
> It is impossible that ever Rome
> Should breed thy fellow.
>
> —BRUTUS, *Julius Caesar*, 5.3.98–100

***In other words:***

Goodbye, the last true Roman. Rome will never again have anyone like you.

Second, Horatio's celebrated farewell to his dear friend Hamlet:

> Good night, sweet prince, / And flights of angels sing thee to thy rest.
>
> —HORATIO, *Hamlet*, 5.2.302–3

**LET'S FURTHER THINK ON THIS . . .**

The 1964 Democratic National Convention came to a teary standstill when RFK recited this Bardism in memory of JFK. It's superb Shakespeare on the Occasion of a Memorial to a Loved One.

> When he shall die,
> Take him and cut him out in little stars,
> And he will make the face of heaven so fine
> That all the world will be in love with night,
> And pay no worship to the garish sun.
>
> —JULIET, *Romeo and Juliet*, 3.2.21–25

(The lines sound sublime when spoken with that Kennedy Boston Brahmin accent.)

## SHAKESPEARE ON GOD, SPIRITUALITY, AND FAITH

*Angels and ministers of grace defend us!*
—HAMLET, *Hamlet*, 1.4.20

"Still remember what the Lord hath done," advises King Henry in *Henry VI, Part II*, and in giving this counsel, he articulates something central to Shakespeare's worldview that can escape detection in our secular, postmodern world. The Bard, and his Elizabethan and Jacobean contemporaries, were devoutly religious. Sacred concepts were real and omnipresent in English Renaissance lives, and mentions in literature of the devil, the soul, angels, good, and evil referred not to intellectual constructs or belletristic abstractions, but to concrete things. God's hand was discernible everywhere, and the supernatural—ineffable forces beyond human comprehension—not only existed but held sway in day-to-day life. Birth, love, loss, and death, all the chapters of the human story, resonated with mystical overtones. These proved irrefutably that the plane of human existence was but one point on a spiritual spectrum that reached into realms knowable only by the Divine . . . and by poets, such as Shakespeare, who were touched by a spark of it.

This chapter's Bardisms on death are moving and powerful. But without their necessary Renaissance context, Bardisms on matters spiritual, they illuminate only partially. Here, then, the rest of the tale: Shakespeare on Occasions That Bear Witness to a Higher Power.

## IN GOD WE TRUST

These are two Bardisms that state simply and clearly the bedrock principle of Shakespearean religiosity: God exists, and in His perfection He guides and protects human lives.

> **God shall be my hope, / My stay, my guide and lantern to my feet.**
>
> —King Henry, *Henry VI, Part II*, 2.3.24–25

> **Heaven is above all yet—there sits a judge**
> **That no king can corrupt.**
>
> —Queen Katherine, *Henry VIII*, 3.1.98–99

***Some details:***

These two Bardisms come from opposite ends of Shakespeare's career. *Henry VI, Part II* was one of his first plays, *Henry VIII* one of his last. Although twenty-two years separate the two works, they each include passages that praise God as an ever-present source of reassurance, guidance, and hope.* I've spoken elsewhere in this book

---

* Note that the latter play refers to "Heaven," not "God." Around the midpoint of Shakespeare's career, the ascendant Puritan forces in Parliament managed to pass a law aimed at cleaning up what they regarded as the unholy excesses of the playhouses on the south bank of the Thames. A key provision: strict adherence to the Third Commandment, "Thou shalt not take the Lord's name in vain." With the arrival of this regulation, mentions of "God" on the English stage were out, and euphemistic references to "Heaven" or "Jove" were in. The First Folio reflects the far-reaching effect of this law: mentions of God in plays published in quarto before the legislation passed are hastily replaced with often clumsy abstract synonyms in the 1623 volume.

of how attractive it is to view the body of Shakespeare's work as a single unit with a beginning, middle, and end, and the juxtaposition of these two passages testifies to the appeal of this idea. In them, we can see a constant in Shakespeare's thinking, a central principle that endured unchanged through all the vicissitudes of a long career, and turbulent life, in the hardscrabble environment of professional London theater.

## A HIGHER POWER IS IN CONTROL

Replete with unadorned and starkly simple statements of God's omnipotence and goodness, the canon also adduces some metaphorical testimonials to the divine presence. My favorite is a quiet stunner from *Hamlet* whose wisdom and calm earn it a permanent place on my Shakespeare Top Ten.

> There's a divinity that shapes our ends,
> Rough-hew them how we will.
>
> —HAMLET, *Hamlet*, 5.2.10–11

***In other words:***

God creates an orderly outcome for our lives regardless of the mess we make of them.

***Some details:***

I cherish this Bardism not only for what it says about God but also for what it says about Shakespeare. (See? I know there's a difference.) In it, Shakespeare does one of the characteristic things that make him the towering genius he is. The sentiment expressed in the passage is lushly poetic, but the language that expresses that sentiment is plain and straightforward. It's a kind of anti-poetry, a metaphor made from the decidedly non-metaphoric. Indeed, the imagery derives from one of the most banal features of everyday life in the English Renaissance: thatched roofs. *Ends* refers to the tidy eaves on a thatched roof line; end thatches are chopped roughly from their stalks, then shaped neatly by the roofer who installs them. Thatching as a metaphor for our destinies: only Shakespeare—and perhaps cable television junkies addicted to home makeover shows—would talk about divine providence in terms of roofing materials. The originality, the wit, the quality of surprise are what make this passage so arresting, and what make Shakespeare my go-to guy.

## SOMETIMES YOU'VE GOT TO TAKE A LEAP OF FAITH

Religious or secular, devout or agnostic, all of us can admit that there are certain mysteries in life that defy rational explanation. A full moon strikes us as heart-stoppingly beautiful; November's bare branches are somehow green by May; our baby daughter's giggle erases a day's worth of workplace stress. What accounts for such things? There's no way to answer. Yet such things happen. They just do, they just *are*. Finally there's less point in asking why they move us than in simply surrendering to how moving they are in the first place. We can believe in them without knowing entirely what they are; we don't need proof to know that they are real. Belief in the absence of proof—this is the very definition of a concept that underpins all of Shakespeare's spiritual musings, a concept called *faith*. There are powers at work in our lives that we don't understand, and on those occasions when they tap us on the shoulder, our best course is to allow them to work their magic. Here's a Bardism that tells us how:

**It is required / You do awake your faith.**

—PAULINA, *The Winter's Tale*, 5.3.94–95

This Bardism needs no other words, no advice on how to say or use it, and no further details. "Believe," it tells us. "You must only believe." A fitting conclusion to this survey of Shakespeare for All Occasions.

# "I Have a Kind Soul That Would Give You Thanks"

## ACKNOWLEDGMENTS

Although I could fill this page with Shakespearean expressions of gratitude like those in Chapter Five, I'm going to try for a few paragraphs to resist the temptation, and to acknowledge the debts I owe some important people with words all my own.

First, to all the friends and loved ones whose life occasions I've cited as exemplars of how Shakespeare's eloquence suits any situation, my thanks for letting me expose your private emotions to public light. And to everyone in my life who's asked me to recommend a Bardism over the years, I couldn't have put this together without you.

I wouldn't have put this together without the urging and confidence of my dear friend Ben Sherwood. By way of thanks, I can only tell him that I hope with all my might that what I've produced lives up to what he knew it could be.

The publishing professionals who've supported me through the writing of this book have been superb in every way. To the great people at ICM—Katharine Cluverius, who got it started; Kate Lee, who closed the deal; and Sam Cohn, who makes everything happen—thank you. To Anne Cole at Collins, whose refined sensibility, clear head, great gentleness, and infinite patience have been nothing short of a godsend—thank you.

I wrote this book during a peripatetic period in my life. As a result, I imposed on the hospitality of libraries on both coasts of this country, and all sorts of random places in between. My thanks to the librarians and staffs of nearly two dozen of our finest temples to knowledge, and about fifty of the New York metropolitan area's best cafés and greasy spoons.

The staff of the Shakespeare Initiative at the Public Theater took up a lot of the slack created by my writing schedule, and I'm grateful. Thanks also to Oskar Eustis, a great Shakespearean, and to all the artists and teachers in my theater life, from whom I've learned so much about why Bardisms are so special.

I'd be remiss if I didn't convey my deep gratitude to William Shakespeare, who's enriched my life in countless ways, and who's always there when I need him. If only he'd listen to me and shave that crazy moustache . . .

Finally, my infinite, endless, huge thanks to my two best girls, Hilit and Tillirose. They made real sacrifices so that these pages could make their way into the world, and I'll never forget it. What's least in them is more than all that's in any RosalindPortiaViolaHermioneKatherineCeliaBeatriceHeroVenusHermiaPerditaMarina DesdemonaCleopatraCressidaMirandaSilviaJuliaHelenaOlivia ConstanceAnneVirgiliaJulietCalphurniaOpheliaGertrudeImogenCordelia. I love you, Hilit. I love you, Tillirose. Up-up!

*BGE*

*Brooklyn, 2008*

# "... Index to the Story We Late Talked of"

## SUBJECT INDEX


adoption, 5–7
adversity in love, 116–20
advice, 53–56
aging, benefits of, 159–60
apologies, 175, 177
appreciation, 173–74

bad news, 212
baseball, 62
birthdays, 70–72
blessings, 14–19
  for daughters, 14–18
  for sons, 19
bores, 170–72
breaking news, 211
brothers, 34–35
buzzkills, at parties, 183–85

celebratory eulogies, 244–49
childbirth, 3–7
childhood, 35–43
children, 40–43
  death of, 239–40
  ill-behaved, 42–43
  well-behaved, 40–41
choosing a college major, 45–48
Christmas, 68–70
cold weather, 213
comedians, 167–70
commencement addresses, 51–57
  advice in, 53–56
  imagination in, 56–57
compassion, 164–66
crying, of newborns, 4–5

daughters, 12–18
  blessings for, 14–18
  future prospects for, 14–18
death, 221–50. *See also* eulogies
  of children, 239–40
  eulogies after, 241–50
  of husbands, 236–38
  as inevitable, 230–35
  of loved ones, 235–40
  as natural part of life, 227–30
  of wives, 239
declarations of love, 81–83
defeat, after war, 141–42
distinction in battle, 127

education. *See* schooling
employment. *See* work
endless love, 110–15
engagement rings, 98–99
eulogies, 241–50
  celebratory, 244–49
  conclusion for, 250
  at funerals, 242–44
exercise, 57–63
  running, 60–61
  swimming, 61
  walking, 59–60
  yoga, 62

faith, 254–55
families. *See also* children; daughters; fathers
  brothers, 34–35
  daughters, 12–18
  fathers, 26–30
  grandmothers, 196–97
  husbands, death of, 236–38
  mothers, 23–26
  resemblance within, 8–9
  siblings, 30–35
  sisters, 32–34
  sons, 18–22
  wives, death of, 239
family resemblance, 8–9
fathers, 26–30
  advice to sons, 53–56
  sons and, 19–22
female tributes, during old age, 201–2
fitness, in old age, 193–95
football, 62
forgiveness, 175–78
funerals, eulogies at, 242–44

giving thanks, 172–74
global warming, 216–17
God, 251–54
good news, 212
grandmothers, 196–97
grandparents, 195–97

Halloween, 67
health care, 202–5. *See also* fitness, in old age
  physician ineptitude and, 207–10
  toothaches, 203–4
holidays, 63–72
  birthdays, 70–72
  Christmas, 68–70
  Halloween, 67
  New Years Day, 64–67
  Thanksgiving, 67–68
honor, 131–33
hosts, 181–83
hot weather, 213
husbands, death of, 236–38

ill-behaved children, 42–43
illness, perseverance through, 205
imagination, 56–57

jealousy, 117–20
judges, 154–56
justice, 152–57, 160–66
  mercy in, 164–66
  poetic, 162–63

kindness, 172–74
kissing, 93–95

lawyers, 162
life experiences, education from, 49–51
love, 76–81. *See also* making love; weddings
  adversity in, 116–20
  for brothers, 34–35

declarations of, 81–83
as endless, 110–13
for fathers, 28–30
hopeful, 84–85
as infinitely powerful, 77–81
jealousy and, 117–20
kissing and, 93–95
lust and, 96
marriage proposals and, 98–99
for mothers, 24–25
poetry and, 85–91
for sisters, 32–34
lullaby, 9–12
lust, 96

making love, 92–93, 96–97
kissing and, 93–95
lust and, 96
male tributes, during old age, 198–201
marriage proposals, 98–99
engagement rings and, 98–99
medicine, 202–5
futility of, 207
natural cures, 206–7
physician ineptitude and, 207–10
memorials. *See* eulogies
mercy, 164–66
middle age, 157–60
mothers, 23–26
maternal protection of, 25–26
motivation, for soldiers, 143–47

natural cures, 206–7
newborns, 4–5, 7–12
news, 210–13
bad, 212
breaking, 211
good, 212
New Years Day, 64–67
nostalgia, 192–93

oceans, 113–15
old age, 191–95
fitness in, 193–95
health care in, 202–5
infirmity during, 205
nostalgia in, 192–93

parties, 179–85
buzzkills at, 183–85
calls for, 180–81
hosts' welcome to, 181–83
physicians, 207–10
poetic justice, 162–63
poetry and love, 85–91
prayers, for soldiers, 127–29
pride in work, 150

rain, 214
religious faith. *See* faith
reputation
honor and, 131–33
of soldiers, 129–31
rest, from work, 150–51
revenge, 134–36
running, 60–61

schooling, 43–51
choice of study in, 45–48
commencement addresses, 51–57
from life experiences, 49–51
seasons, change of, 216–20
seizing the moment, 145–47
siblings, 30–35
sisters, 32–34
soldiers, 121–29
defeat for, 141–42
distinction in battle for, 127
honor of, 131–33
motivation for, 143–47
prayers for safety for, 127–29

soldiers (*continued*)
  reputation of, 129–31
  seizing the moment for, 145–47
  victory for, 139–41
sons, 18–22
  fathers' advice to, 53–56
spirituality, 251–55
sports and exercise, 57–63
  baseball, 62
  football, 62
  running, 60–61
Springtime weather, 213–14
storms, 214–16
swimming, 61

taking a break, from work, 151
thanks. *See* giving thanks
Thanksgiving, 67–68
threats of violence, 136–37
  dismissal of, 138–39
toasts, for weddings, 100–107
toothaches, 203–4
tributes, during old age, 197–202
  for females, 201–2
  for males, 198–201

victory, in war, 139–41
violence, 134–39
  revenge and, 134–36
  threats of, 136–37

walking, 59–60
war. *See also* soldiers
  defeat after, 141–42
  victory in, 139–41
weather, 213–20
  change of seasons and, 216–20
  cold, 213
  global warming and, 216–17
  hot, 213
  rain, 214
  in Springtime, 213–14
  storms, 214–16
wedding rings, during vows, 110
weddings, 100–107
  celebration after, 107–9
wedding toasts, 100–107
wedding vows, 109–15
  endless love as part of, 110–15
  ring exchange and, 110
welcome greetings, 181–83
well-behaved children, 40–41
wit, 166–70
wives, death of, 239
work, 147–51
  breaks from, 150–51
  enjoyment of, 149
  pride in, 150
  respect for necessity of, 148–50

yoga, 62

# INDEX

Numerals in *italic typeface* refer to the author's commentary; numerals in roman typeface refer to Shakespearean excerpts.


Adams, John, *233*
Adams, John Quincy, *233*
adoption, *5–7*
advice
  in *Hamlet*, 53–56
  to soldiers, *143–47*
aging, in *Othello*, 159–60
Allen, Mel, *63*
*All's Well That Ends Well*, 5, 7, 57, *122–23*, *222*
  comic relief in, *123–24*
  death in, 239
  forgiveness in, 177–78
  jealousy in, *117*
  prayers for safety in, 128–29
  war in, 125
*The Anatomie of Abuses* (Stubbes), 155
antithesis, *xxv–xxvii*, *29*, *47*, *109*, *165–66*, *218*
*Antony and Cleopatra*, 34
  birthdays in, 71, *72*
  brotherhood in, *35*
  death in, 237–38
  eulogies in, 246–48
  lust in, 96
  news in, 211
  parties in, 179–81
  work in, 149–50
apologies, *175–77*
  in *Hamlet*, 177
  in *The Merry Wives of Windsor*, 175
Arden, Mary, *24*
Aristotle, *47–48*
*Ars Amatoria* (Ovid), *47*
Asimov, Isaac, *48*
*Asimov's Guide to Shakespeare* (Asimov), *48*
*As You Like It*, xii, *xvii*, xli–xlii, xx*n*, 30, 33, 63, 84, *92*, *122*, *156*, *221*, *222*
  adversity in love in, 116
  antithesis in, *109*
  childhood in, *39*
  death in, *226*
  endless love in, 110–11, 114–15
  fitness in old age in, 193–95

*As You Like It* (*continued*)
  hopeful love in, *84–85*
  imagination in, virtues of, 57
  parties in, *179*
  publication date of, *115*
  sisterhood in, *32–34*
  sisters in, *32–34*
  sports in, *58–59*
  staging for, *15*
  victory in war in, *140*
  weddings in, 100, 108–9
Autumn, Emilie, *96*

bad news, 212
Barker, Harley-Granville, *10*
baseball, *62–63*
Bay of Portugal, *114–15*
Becket, Andrew, *119–20*
Beckett, Samuel, *5*
Berra, Yogi, *52*
*The Bible*, *14–15*
birth, *1–5*
birthdays, *70–72*
  in *Antony and Cleopatra*, 71, *72*
  in *Julius Caesar*, 71
blessings, *14–18*
  for daughters, *14–18*, *20–22*
  for sons, *19–23*
  in *The Winter's Tale*, for daughters, *14–18*, *20–22*
*The Book of the Courtier* (Castiglione), *126*
bores, people as, 170–72
brothers, *34–35*
  in *Antony and Cleopatra*, *35*
  in *The Comedy of Errors*, *34–35*
"Brush up Your Shakespeare," 84–85
Buffett, Warren, *52*
Burbage, Richard, *222*

*Cardenio*, *175*
Carter, Jimmy, *234*
Castiglione, Baldassare, *126*
Cervantes, *175*
childbirth, *3–5*
childhood, *36–40*
  in *As You Like It*, *39*
children, *40–43*
  death of, *239–40*
  in *Macbeth*, *240*
  poorly-behaved, *42–43*
  as redemption for past acts, *40*
  in *Richard III*, *240*
  well-behaved, *40–41*
  in *The Winter's Tale*, *40–41*
  in *As You Like It*, *40–41*
chivalry, among soldiers, *125–26*
Christmas, 68–70
Churchill, Winston, *52*
Clinton, Bill, *66–67, 234–35*
cold weather, 213
comedians, 167–70
*The Comedy of Errors*, 3, 34, 67, *123*
  brothers in, *34–35*
  hosts' welcomes in, 183
  jealousy in, *117*
commedia dell'arte, *187–89*
commencement addresses, *51–57*
  *Hamlet* and, 53–56
  imagination and, *56–57*
  *King Lear* and, *52*
Commonplace Books, *xiv–xv*
compassion, in justice, *164–66*
*The Complete Works of Shakespeare*, *xi*, *xix*, *19*, *70*
*Coriolanus*, 25, *93*
  wit in, 166
Costello, Elvis, *95*
Couric, Katie, *211*
Craig, Larry, *130*
Cranmer, Thomas, *15*
Cruise, Tom, *121*

*Cymbeline*, xii, *93*
eulogies in, 242–44
jealousy in, *117*
losing in, 139
making love in, 97
perseverance past illness in, 205
as tragicomedic work, *215*
victory in war in, *141*
wedding toasts and, 107

daughters, *12–18*
blessings for, 14–18
death, 158, *221–50*. *See also* eulogies
in *Antony and Cleopatra*, 237–38
of children, *239–40*
grief and, *241–42*
in *Hamlet*, 226–27
in *Henry IV, Part I*, *227*
in *Henry IV, Part II*, *227*
in *Henry VIII*, 228–30
of husbands, *236–38*
as inevitable, *231–35*
in *King John*, 240
of loved ones, *235–40*
in *Macbeth*, 230–33
in *A Midsummer Night's Dream*, *235*
as natural part of life, *227–30*
in *Othello*, *227*
in *Pericles*, 235
in *The Tempest*, *224–25*
in *Twelfth Night*, *226*
in *The Two Noble Kinsmen*, 228
of wives, 239
in *As You Like It*, *226*
declarations of love, *81–85*
in *Othello*, 82–83
in *The Tempest*, 81
defeat, after war, *141–42*
in *Henry IV, Part II*, 142
de Sade, Marquis, *97*

Devereux, Robert (Earl of Essex), *123*
*Dictionary of the Proverbs in England in the Sixteenth and Seventeenth Centuries* (Tilley), *136*
distinction in war, for soldiers, 127
*Don Quixote* (Cervantes), *175*
Dylan, Bob, *52*

Edison, Thomas, *48*
education. *See* schooling
Edwards, John, *130*
Einstein, Albert, *52*
Elizabeth I (Queen), *123*
endless love
in *Romeo and Juliet*, 111–13
in *As You Like It*, 110–11, 114–15
engagement rings, 98–99
English Renaissance, *222–24*
role of religion during, *251*
enjambment, *xxiv*n
eulogies, *241–50*
in *Antony and Cleopatra*, 246–48
as celebration of life, *244–49*
conclusions for, *249–50*
in *Cymbeline*, 242–44
in *Hamlet*, *245*, 250
in *Julius Caesar*, 245–46, 250
in *Romeo and Juliet*, 250
*Euphues, or the Anatomy of Wit* (Lyly), *169*
exercise. *See* sports and exercise

faith, *254–55*
in *The Winter's Tale*, 255
fathers, *26–30*
advice from, in *Hamlet*, 53–56
in *King Lear*, love for, *28–29*
love for, *28–30*
Favre, Brett, *62*
*A Few Good Men*, *121*

Fields, W.C., *40–41*
fitness, during old age, 193–95
Fleetwood Mac, *181*
Fletcher, John, *175*, *227*
Flynt, Larry, *77*
football, *62*
forgiveness, *175–78*
  in *All's Well That Ends Well*, 177–78
Franklin, Benjamin, *52*
Furness, Horace Howard, *118*, *120*

Gale, Richard, *143*
Gandhi, Mahatma, *52*
Gibson, Charlie, *211*
Gigante, Vincent "the Chin," *225*
global warming, *217–18*
Globe Theatre, *15*
God, *251–55*
  in *Hamlet*, 253–54
  in *Henry IV, Part II*, *251*, 252–53
  in *Henry VIII*, 252–53, *252*n
good news, 212
Gore, Al, *216*
grandmothers, 196–97
grandparenthood, *195–97*
  grandmothers, 196–97
  in *King John*, 195
Greenblatt, Stephen, *xix*
grief, *241–42*
*Guinness Book of World Records*, *114*

Halloween, 67
Hall, William, *89*
*Hamlet*, 18, 23, 48, 62, 63, *123*
  antithesis in, *xxvi*
  apologies in, 177
  bad news in, 212
  Christmas in, 68–70
  cold weather in, 213
  death in, 226–27
  eulogies in, *245*, 250
  fatherly advice in, 53–56
  God in, 253–54
  heightened language in, xxvii–xxviii
  military preparedness in, 144
  paraphrasing for, *xxiv*
  phrasing in, xxxiii–xxxvi
  poetic justice in, 162–63
  revenge in, 134–35
  spirituality in, 251
  thanks in, *172*, 174
  Valentine's Day in, *66–67*
Hart, Gary, *130*
Hart, William, *89*
Hathaway, Anne, *13*
Haughton, William, *89*
health care, *202–5*
  futility of, 207
  in *Henry IV, Part II*, *203*
  in *Henry V*, 202
  medical professionals and, *203*, *207–10*
  natural cures and, 206–7
  in *Pericles*, 207
  for toothaches, 203–4
*Henry IV, Part I*, 42, *72*, *113*, *141*
  bores in, 170–72
  death in, *227*
  tribute to older males in, 198–99
*Henry IV, Part II*, 68, *92*
  death in, *227*
  defeat after war, 142
  God in, *251*, 252–53
  good news in, 212
  health in, *203*
  lawyers in, 162
  nostalgia in, in old age, 192–93
  old age in, 191
  rain in, 214
  Spring weather in, 214

victory in war in, 140–41
warm weather in, 213
wit in, 166–67
work in, 151
*Henry V*, 24, 30, *127*, *222*
antithesis in, *xxvi*
honor in, 132–33
military preparedness in, 144
motivation for soldiers in, *143–44*
soldiers in, *125*
*Henry VI, Part III*, 19, *38*
tributes to older females in, 201–2
*Henry VIII*
authorship issues for, *175*
children as redemption in, *40*
death in, 228–30
God in, 252–53, *252*n
hosts' welcome in, 181–82
parties in, 179
thanks in, 174
Henry VIII (King), *15*, 16
Herbert, William, *89*
Heston, Charlton, *205*
holidays, *63–72*
birthdays, *70–72*
Christmas, 68–70
Halloween, 67
in *King John*, 64
New Years Day, 64–66
Thanksgiving, *67–68*
Valentine's Day, *66–67*
honor, *131–33*
in *Henry V*, 132–33
hosts, welcome from, *181–83*
in *The Comedy of Errors*, 183
in *Henry VIII*, 181–82
hot weather, 213
Hughes, William, *89*
husbands, death of, *236–38*
in *Antony and Cleopatra*, 237–38

iambic pentameter, *xxx–xxxiii*
stresses in, *xxxi–xxxii*
illness, perseverance through, 205
in *Cymbeline*, 205
imagination, *56–57*
in *As You Like It*, 57
"Imagine," *57*
infancy, *1–12*
newborns, *4–5*

Jackson, Andrew, *119–20*
jealousy, *117–20*
in *Othello*, 117–18
in *The Winter's Tale*, *117*
Jefferson, Thomas, *233*
Jonson, Ben, *12*, *215*
judges, character of, 154–56
*Julius Caesar*, xiv, xxxii, *92*, *127*, 214
antithesis in, *xxvi*
birthdays in, 71
eulogies in, 245–46, 250
memorials in, 241
response to threats of violence in, 138–39
swimming in, *61*
taking advantage of the moment in, 145–47
victory in war in, 140
work in, *147*
justice, *151–57*, *160–66*
compassion in, *164–66*
judges' character and, *154–56*
poetic, *162–63*
from wisdom, *152–53*

Kennedy, John F., *233*, *250*
Kennedy, Robert, *250*
*King John*
death in, 240
grandparenthood in, 195
holidays in, 64
New Years Day and, 64–66

*King Lear*, 4, 28, 49, 51, 62
antithesis in, *29*
commencement addresses and, *52*
death in, *226*
jealousy in, *117*
learning from life experiences in, *49*
love for fathers in, *28–29*
middle age in, 158–59
newborns in, *4–5*
soldier preparedness in, 145
threats of violence in, 137
work in, *147*
kissing, *93–96*
in *Troilus and Cressida*, *93*
in *Twelfth Night*, 94–96
*Kiss Me Kate*, 84
Kline, Kevin, *177*
Koppel, Ted, *127*

Laine, Cleo, *95*
lawyers, 162
Le Carré, John, *89*
Lennon, John, *57*
Leonard, Robert Sean, *177*
Lewinsky, Monica, *66–67*
Lincoln, Abraham, *52*, *233–34*
*Lives of the Noble Greeks and Romans* (Plutarch), *141*
losing, in *Cymbeline*, 139
love, *73–81*. *See also* declarations of love; making love; weddings; wedding vows
adversity in, *116–20*
as endless, *111–15*
for fathers, *28–30*
hope for, *83–84*
jealousy v., *117–20*
in *Love's Labor's Lost*, 77–81
lust v., *96*
marriage proposals and, *98–99*
for mothers, *24–25*
in *Othello*, 82–83
through poetry, *85–91*
proposals for marriage and, *98–99*
in Sonnet 18, 85–87
as timeless, *102*
unrequited, *77*
in *Venus and Adonis*, 76–77
weddings and, *100–115*
*Love's Labour's Lost*, 68
comedians in, 167–70
love as theme in, 77–79
victory in war in, *141*
lullaby, *9–12*
in *A Midsummer Night's Dream*, 9–12
music composition for, *10–11*
lust, *96*
Lyly, John, *169*

*Macbeth*, xxii, 26, *40*, 49, *92*
antithesis in, *xxvi*
Clinton influenced by, *234–35*
death as inevitable in, 230–33
death of children in, *240*
Lincoln influenced by, *233–34*
maternal protection in, *26*
motivation in, 143
paraphrasing for, *xxiv*
Reagan influenced by, *234*
revenge in, 134
soldiers in, *125*
weather in, 213
making love, *92–97*
in *Cymbeline*, 97
kissing, *93–96*
in *Measure for Measure*, 97
in *Othello*, 97
Margaret (Queen), *201*
marriage, in *The Two Gentlemen of Verona*, 98

marriage proposals, *98–99*
engagement rings and, *98–99*
Martin, Ned, *63–64*
*Measure for Measure*, *85*
making love in, 97
thanks in, 174
tributes to older males in, 199–201
medical professionals, *203*
failures of, *207–10*
in *The Rape of Lucrece*, 208
memorials, *241–42*. *See also* eulogies
in *Julius Caesar*, 241
*The Merchant of Venice*, *85*
antithesis in, *165–66*
jealousy in, *119*
justice in, 160
mercy in, 164–66
news in, 210
wedding rings in, 110
wit in, 166
mercy. *See also* compassion, in justice
in *The Merchant of Venice*, 164–66
*The Merry Wives of Windsor*, 40
apologies in, 175
*Metamorphoses* (Ovid), *47*, *77*
meter, *xxix–xxxii*
iambic pentameter, *xxx–xxxiii*
Michaels, Al, *63*
middle age, 157–60
death and, 158
in *King Lear*, 158–59
in *Othello*, 157
*A Midsummer Night's Dream*, 9–12, 26
adversity in love in, 116–17
antithesis in, *218*
change of seasons in, 217–20
death in, *235*
varied interpretations of, *11–12*
wedding vows in, 109
work in, *147*, 150
*Miles Gloriosus (The Braggart Soldier)* (Plautus), *123*
military, in Shakespeare works, *122–25*
real-life inspirations for, *122–23*
Miller, Arthur, *210*
mothers, *23–26*
absence of, in Shakespeare works, *23*
love for, *24–25*
protection by, *25–26*
Mountjoy, Christopher, *161*
Mountjoy, Mary, *161*
Moussaoui, Zacarias, *163*
*Much Ado About Nothing*, xxxi, *122*, *169*, *222*
distinction in battle in, 127
jealousy in, *117*
toothaches in, 203–4
music composition, for lullabies, *10–11*

natural cures, 206–7
natural sciences, *6–7*, *48*
natural stresses, in iambic pentameter, *xxxiii*
newborns, *4–5*, *7–12*
in *King Lear*, *4–5*
in *Sonnet 3*, 8
news, *210–12*
in *Antony and Cleopatra*, 211
bad, 212
good, 212
in *The Merchant of Venice*, 210
New Years Day, 64–66
*New York Post*, *132*
*New York Times*, *xxii*
Nicholson, Jack, *121*
North, Thomas, *141*

*The Norton Shakespeare*, *xix*
nostalgia, in old age, *192–93*
in *Henry IV, Part II*, 192–93
in *Romeo and Juliet*, 192
in *The Taming of the Shrew*, 192

old age, *186–95. See also* tributes, during old age
fitness during, 193–95
grandparenthood in, *195–97*
in *Henry IV, Part II*, 191
with infirmity, *205*
nostalgia in, *192–93*
in *The Tempest*, *205*
"O Mistress Mine," *95*
O'Neal, Shaquille, *60*
*Othello*, xx–xxi
aging in, 159–60
death in, *227*
declarations of love in, 82–83
jealousy in, 117–18
making love in, 97
middle age in, 157
reputation in, 130–31
Ovid, *47–48*, *77*
*Oxford English Dictionary*, *218*
*The Oxford Shakespeare*, *xix*

Papp, Joseph, *37*
parties, *179–85. See also* hosts, welcome from
in *Antony and Cleopatra*, 179–81
buzzkills at, *183–85*
in *Henry VIII*, 179
hosts and, welcome from, *181–83*
in *Romeo and Juliet*, *179*
in *The Taming of the Shrew*, *179*
in *As You Like It*, *179*
*The Passionate Pilgrim*, *88*
*Pericles*, 24
death of loved ones in, 235
futility of health care in, 207
storms in, 214–16
Phelps, Michael, *61*
phrasing, *xxxiii–xxxvii*
enjambment and, *xxiv*n
with verse lines, *xxxiii–xxxvii*
*Physician's Desk Reference*, *206*
Plautus, *123*
Plutarch, *141*
poetic justice, in *Hamlet*, 162–63
poetic love, *85–91*
Porter, Cole, 84–85
prayers, for soldiers, *127–29*
in *All's Well That Ends Well*, 128–29
prose, verse v., *xxix*
prosody, *2–3*

rain, 214
*The Rape of Lucrece*, *89*, *209–10*
failure of medical professionals in, 208
Reagan, Ronald, *52*, *234*
reflection, in old age, *192–93*
through tributes, *197–202*
religion, during English Renaissance, *251*
religious faith. *See* faith
reputation, *129–33*
honor and, *131–33*
in *Othello*, 130–31
in *Richard III*, 129
of soldiers, *124–25*
revenge, *134–36*
in *Hamlet*, 134–35
in *Macbeth*, 134
*Richard III*, *40*, *222*
antithesis in, *xxvi*
death of children in, *240*
engagement rings in, 98–99

grandmothers in, 196–97
reputation in, 129
soldiers in, *125*
work in, *147*
Rizzuto, Phil, *63*
*Romeo and Juliet*, *93*
endless love in, 111–13
eulogies in, 250
lust in, *96*
natural health cures in, 206–7
nostalgia in, in old age, 192
parties in, *179*
publication date of, *115*
Roth, Philip, *12*
running, *60–61*
in *The Winter's Tale*, 60
Russell, Bertrand, *89*

Sanchez, Ricardo, *143*
"Say You Love Me," *181*
Scalia, Antonin, 157
scansion, *xxx–xxxiii*
schooling, *43–51*
choice of study in, *45–48*
from life experiences, *49–51*
in *The Taming of the Shrew*, 46–48
in *The Two Gentlemen of Verona*, 49–51
seasons, change of, *216–20*
in *A Midsummer Night's Dream*, 217–20
Seven Ages of Man, xli–xlii
*Shakespeare* (Van Doren), *143–44*
*Shakespeare and All That Jazz*, *95*
Shakespeare, Edmund, *31–32*
Shakespeare, Hamnet, *13*
Shakespeare, John, *30*
Shakespeare, Mary, *30*
Shakespeare, William
absence of mothers in works of, *23*
bible as reference for, *14–15*
collaboration with other writers, *215–16*, 227
death of son, *13*
legal experience of, *161–62*
natural sciences and, *6–7*, *48*
relationship with daughter as inspiration for, *13–14*
*She's Gotta Have It*, *xx*
siblings, *30–35*
brothers, *34–35*
sisters, *32–34*
*Sir Thomas More*, *219*
sisters, *32–34*
soldiers, *121–29*
advice to, *143–47*
as chivalrous figures, *125–26*
defeat for, *141–42*
distinction in battle, *127*
emotional volatility of, *124*
in *Henry V*, *125*
in *Macbeth*, *125*
motivations for, *143–45*
prayers for safety for, *127–29*
preparedness for, *124–25*, *129–33*, *144–45*
reputation of, *124–25*, *129–33*
in *Richard III*, *125*
*sprezzatura* and, *126*
taking advantage of the moment for, 145–47
victory in war for, *139–41*
Sonnet 3, 8
Sonnet 18, 85–87, *90*
Sonnet 23, xii
Sonnet 65, *241*
Sonnet 104, xii, 72
Sonnet 111, *148*
Sonnet 116, xii–xiv, *103*, *108*, *241*
rhyme scheme in, *103*
as wedding toast, 100–105
Sonnet 126, *90*
Sonnet 135, *91*

Sonnet 138, *88*
Sonnet 144, *88*
sonnets, *88–91*
  mystery of authorship of, *88–89*
sons, *18–22*
  blessings for, *19–23*
*The Sopranos*, *134*
spirituality, *251–55*
  in *Hamlet*, 251
Spitzer, Eliot, *130*
sports and exercise, *57–63*
  baseball, *62–63*
  football, *62*
  running, *60–61*
  swimming, *61*
  in *The Tempest*, 59–60
  yoga, *62*
  in *As You Like It*, *58–59*
*sprezzatura*, *126*
Spring weather, 213–14
Stewart, Patrick, *xxii*
storms, 214–16
stresses, in iambic pentameter, *xxxi–xxxii*
Stubbes, Philip, 155
swimming, *61*

*The Taming of the Shrew*, xx, 43, 44, *92*
  antithesis in, *47*
  choice of study in, 46–48
  nostalgia in, in old age, 192
  parties in, *179*
  thanks in, 173
  work in, *147*
*The Tempest*, xiv, 12, 62, *175–76*, 214
  age with infirmity in, *205*
  as autobiographical, *175–76*
  death in, *224–25*
  declarations of love in, 81
  fitness in, 59–60
  jealousy in, *117*
  refusal of formal schooling in, 45
  thanks in, 173
  as tragicomedic work, *215*
  wedding toasts and, 104–7
thanks, 172–74
Thanksgiving, *67–68*
Theobald, Lewis, *119*
theophanies, *15*
Thorpe, Thomas, *89*
threats of violence, *136–37*
  in *King Lear*, 137
  response to, 138–39
Tilley, Morris, *136*
*Titus Andronicus*, 197
toasts, for weddings, *100–107*
toothaches, 203–4
tributes, during old age, *197–202*
  for females, *201–2*
  in *Henry IV, Part I*, 198–99
  in *Henry VI, Part III*, 201–2
  for males, *198–201*
  in *Measure for Measure*, 199–201
  in *Titus Andronicus*, 197
*Troilus and Cressida*, *85*
  jealousy in, *117*
  kissing in, *93*
Twain, Mark, *52*
*Twelfth Night*, *60*, *92*, *113*
  death in, *226*
  kissing in, 94–96
  party buzzkills in, 183–85
  thanks in, 173
  work in, *148*
*The Two Gentlemen of Verona*, 49–51
  jealousy in, *117*
  marriage in, 98

*The Two Noble Kinsmen*, *175*
  death in, 228

unrequited love, *77*

Valentine's Day, *66–67*
Van Doren, Mark, *143–44*
*Variorum Shakespeare*, *118–19*, *136*
*Venus and Adonis*, 76–77, *89*, *209*
verse
  iambic pentameter in, *xxx–xxxiii*
  phrasing with, *xxxiii–xxxvii*
  prose v., *xxix*
victory, in war, *139–41*
  in *Cymbeline*, *141*
  in *Henry IV, Part II*, 140
  in *Julius Caesar*, 140
  in *Love's Labour's Lost*, *141*
  in *As You Like It*, *140*
violence, *134–39*. *See also* threats of violence
  revenge and, *134–36*
  as threat, *136–37*

*Waiting for Godot* (Becket), *5*
Walken, Christopher, *177*
war
  in *All's Well That Ends Well*, 125
  defeat after, *141–42*
  distinction in battle, *127*
  victory in, *139–41*
War of the Roses, *201*
*Washington Post*, *66*
weather, *213–20*
  changing seasons and, *216–20*
  cold, 213
  global warming and, *217–18*
  hot, 213
  in *Macbeth*, 213
  rain, 214
  in Springtime, 213–14
  storms, 214–16
wedding rings
  in *The Merchant of Venice*, 110
  during vows, 110
weddings, *100–115*
  celebrations of joy after, *107–9*
  vows, *109–15*
  in *As You Like It*, 100, 108–9
wedding toasts, *100–107*
  *Cymbeline* and, 107
  *Sonnet 116* as, 100–105
  in *The Tempest*, 104–7
wedding vows, *109–15*
  endless love as part of, *111–15*
  exchange of rings during, 110
  in *A Midsummer Night's Dream*, 109
Weinstein, Jack, *225*
well-behaved children, *40–41*
Wilde, Oscar, *89*
Wilkins, George, *215*
Williams, Brian, *211*
*The Winter's Tale*, 8, 14, 20–22, 41
  blessings for daughters in, *14–18*, *20–22*
  children in, *40–41*
  faith in, 255
  jealousy in, *117*
  running in, 60
  as tragicomedic work, *215*
wisdom, justice from, *152–53*
wit, *166–70*. *See also* comedians
  in *Coriolanus*, 166
  in *Henry IV, Part II*, 166–67
  in *The Merchant of Venice*, 166
wives, death of, 239
work, *147–51*
  in *Antony and Cleopatra*, 149–50
  in *Henry IV, Part II*, 151
  in *Julius Caesar*, *147*
  in *King Lear*, *147*

work (*continued*)
  in *A Midsummer Night's Dream*, *147*, 150
  respect for necessity of, *148–50*
  rest during, 150–51
  in *Richard III*, *147*
  in *Sonnet 111*, *148*
  in *The Taming of the Shrew*, *147*
  in *Twelfth Night*, *148*
Worth, Irene, *177–78*
Wriothesley, Henry, *89*

yoga, *62*

# "If We Do Meet Again, Why We Shall Smile"

## KEEP IN TOUCH

Have you a favorite Bardism of your own?

Have you heard someone quote the Bard for some occasion on which his lines seemed especially clever, apt, or moving?

Have you heard a public figure quote Shakespeare in a surprising context?

If so, then please point your Web browser to **www.bardismsbook.com**. There you'll find a link to e-mail your favorite Bardisms, as well as additional original material not in this book. The Bardisms Web site aims to keep Shakespeare's immortal lines an integral and enjoyable feature of everyday speech. "There's magic in the (World Wide) web of it."

Please visit often, and please send any questions, comments, or thoughts for Barry Edelstein to barry@bardismsbook.com.

"Thanks, thanks, and ever thanks."

# "Is It a World to Hide Virtues in?"

## ABOUT THE AUTHOR

Barry Edelstein is a theater director noted for his work on the plays of William Shakespeare. He has staged over half of the Bard's plays, as well as other classical and contemporary works, at theaters around New York City and the United States. Some highlights: at Classic Stage Company, *The Winter's Tale*, starring David Strathairn, which the *New York Times* called a "stirring production," and *Richard III* with John Turturro and Julianna Margulies; *As You Like It*, starring Gwyneth Paltrow, at the Williamstown Theatre Festival; *Julius Caesar* starring Jeffrey Wright for New York's "Shakespeare in the Park"; at the Public Theater, *The Merchant of Venice*, starring Ron Leibman in an OBIE Award–winning performance as Shylock; and, at various venues, Kevin Kline in three separate one-night-only Shakespeare "concerts." Edelstein directs the Shakespeare Initiative at New York's Public Theater and heads that institution's "Shakespeare Lab" conservatory program. He has taught Shakespearean acting at USC, the Juilliard School, and the Graduate Acting Program at NYU, and in lectures and master classes around the United States and abroad. Edelstein was artistic director of New York's award-winning Classic Stage Company from 1998 to 2003, where he directed a half dozen plays and produced a dozen more. He directed the film *My Lunch with Larry*. He has written about theater-related subjects in the *Washington Post*, *New York Times*, *New Republic*, and *American Theatre*. His book *Thinking Shakespeare* (Spark Publishing, 2007) has been called "a must-read for actors" (*New York* magazine) and "one of the most useful acting guides available" (*American Theatre*). A graduate of Tufts University, Edelstein holds an M.Phil. in English Renaissance drama from Oxford University, where he studied as a Rhodes Scholar. He lives in Brooklyn with his wife, Hilit, and their daughter, Tillirose.